CW01111349

'Oi, Key'

To Fleur, Aaliyah and Harrison

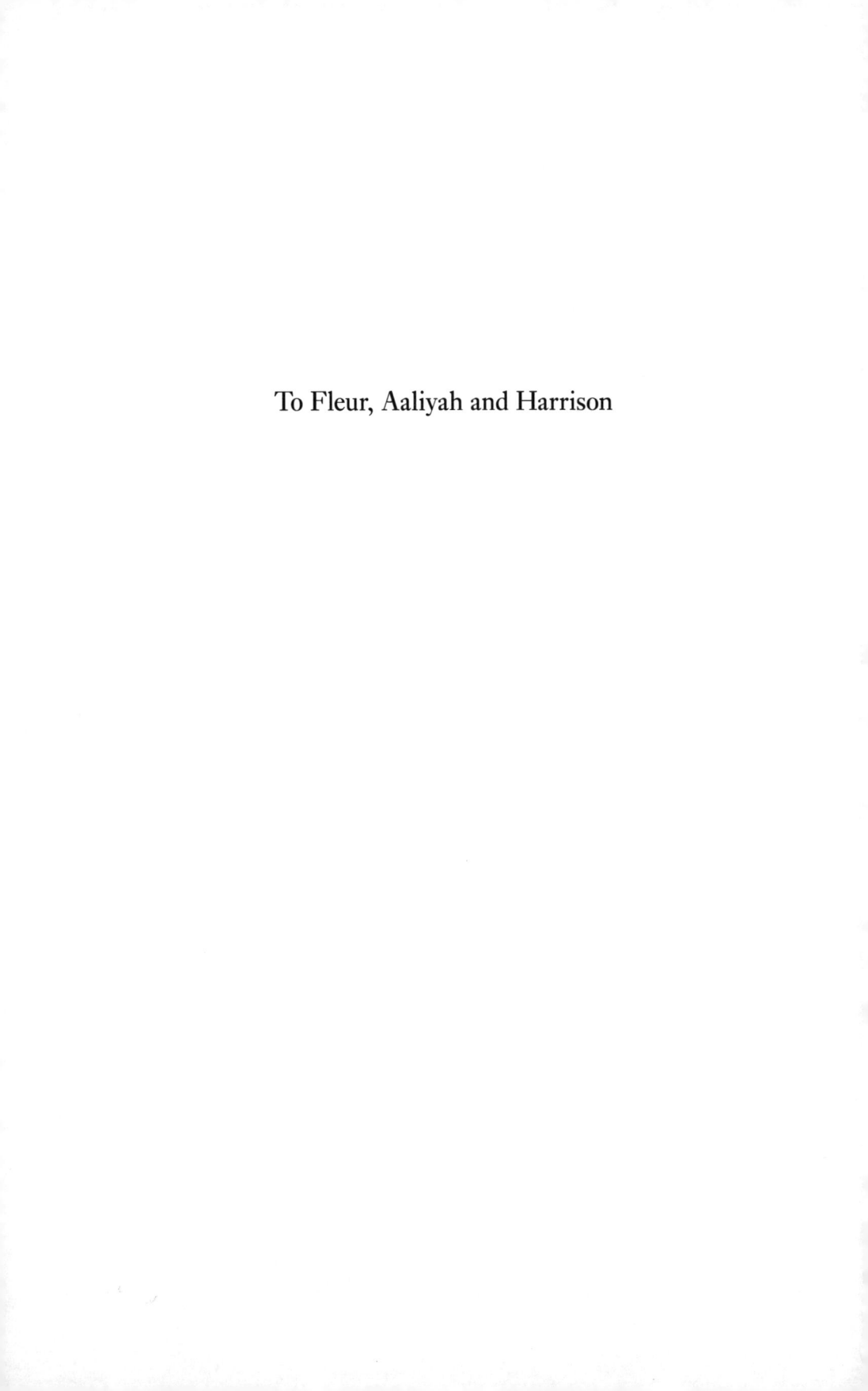

'Oi, Key'
Tales of a Journeyman Cricketer

Rob Key

with

John Woodhouse

WHITE OWL
AN IMPRINT OF PEN & SWORD BOOKS LTD.
YORKSHIRE – PHILADELPHIA

First published in Great Britain in 2020 by
White Owl Books
An imprint of
Pen & Sword Books Ltd
Yorkshire - Philadelphia

Copyright © Rob Key, 2020

ISBN 978 1 52676 821 6

The right of Rob Key to be identified as the Author of this work has been asserted by him in accordance with the Copyright, Designs and Patents Act 1988.

A CIP catalogue record for this book is available from the British Library.

All rights reserved. No part of this book may be reproduced or transmitted in any form or by any means, electronic or mechanical including photocopying, recording or by any information storage and retrieval system, without permission from the Publisher in writing.

Typeset in INDIA by IMPEC eSolutions
Printed and bound in England by TJ International Ltd.

Pen & Sword Books Ltd incorporates the Imprints of Pen & Sword Archaeology, Atlas, Aviation, Battleground, Discovery, Family History, History, Maritime, Military, Naval, Politics, Railways, Select, Transport, True Crime, Fiction, Frontline Books, Leo Cooper, Praetorian Press, Seaforth Publishing, Wharncliffe and White Owl.

For a complete list of Pen & Sword titles please contact

PEN & SWORD BOOKS LIMITED
47 Church Street, Barnsley, South Yorkshire, S70 2AS, England
E-mail: enquiries@pen-and-sword.co.uk
Website: www.pen-and-sword.co.uk

or

PEN AND SWORD BOOKS
1950 Lawrence Rd, Havertown, PA 19083, USA
E-mail: uspen-and-sword@casematepublishers.com
Website: www.penandswordbooks.com

Contents

Foreword by Andrew Flintoff		vii
Chapter 1	Cry Me a River	1
Chapter 2	Planks	16
Chapter 3	People from Australia	29
Chapter 4	No One Gives a F*** in China	39
Chapter 5	The Critical Mass	45
Chapter 6	Fred	53
Chapter 7	A Coach is What You Get to the Ground In	65
Chapter 8	Captain	77
Chapter 9	The Grind	97
Chapter 10	Perspective	105
Chapter 11	Nasser	122
Chapter 12	The Red Handkerchief	127
Chapter 13	Serve and Volley	132
Chapter 14	Warney	142
Chapter 15	The Speed Merchants	150
Chapter 16	Murali	155
Chapter 17	The Times They Have a Changed	160
Chapter 18	Blue Sky Thinking	165
Acknowledgements		181
Rob Key Career Statistics		182

Foreword

I have a picture at home. It's of me and Rob Key walking off the field together at Old Trafford having just shared a century stand in a successful run chase against West Indies.

So rarely did me and Keysy get a chance to bat together and here we were, two mates living out the dream of winning a Test match for England.

As we neared the target, so Keysy was approaching his hundred. He was on 90 with us almost over the line. I was still in the 40s.

'Keysy,' I said, 'I'm just going to drop anchor while you get your hundred.'

He looked at me. 'No,' he insisted. 'You can't do that. Finish the game. Me and you walking off together having won is far better than any hundred.'

Nothing says more about Keysy than that moment – the fact it was more important to him for us to get over the line together. And that, ultimately, is what you play for. Your county, your country, it doesn't matter – if you're not playing cricket, any sport, with people you have relationships with, then what's the point?

I hit a couple of sixes and that was that. I walked off with my mate. Amazing – I loved it – and yet somehow it felt bittersweet. When I look at that picture, I still think about it to this day – 'It could, and should, have been another Test hundred for Keysy.' I don't have many regrets in cricket, what's done is done, but that is one of them. He deserved that ton completely.

There's another reason I remember that game. I was getting some real pepper from West Indies quick Fidel Edwards. I couldn't get out the way, and every time I was hit I kept looking down the other end. And there, every time, was Keysy, the master of fast bowling, shoulders bouncing up and down, laughing. He'd play the same deliveries so easily. It was so frustrating!

But that was Keysy. If I were to pick someone to go and bat against the world's best bowlers – the likes of Wasim Akram, Allan Donald, Glenn McGrath, Shane Warne – I would pick Keysy above anyone else. He is, no doubt about it, the best player not to play 100 Test matches. He has never quite received the credit for how good he actually was, right up there with the very best, especially against fast bowling. His problem wasn't the speed merchants, it was the numpties. He'd do all the hard work against Brett Lee and then get out to Damien Martyn. He was that classic cricketer – a man who truly thrived off a challenge.

I did once manage to get him out. It was the worst wicket of my life. I was just coming back from injury and Lancashire were playing Kent down in Canterbury. Keysy was opening the batting. My first ball was a loosener, back of a length. It hit him in the midriff and trickled on to his off stump. He looked up at me. I won't say what he called me, but it began with a letter very early in the alphabet. He needn't have bothered – I was genuinely gutted that I got him out. I wanted Keysy to score runs, to play for England. I knew what a class act he was. When he got his double hundred against the West Indies at Lord's, it meant far more to me than the century I got in the same series. I was far happier seeing him raise his bat twice and be on the honours board than with any runs I scored.

That closeness had been there right from the first time I clapped eyes on Keysy. He was like no one me and Steve Harmison had ever met before. We had just one question: 'Who is this bloke?' He was a bit of a novelty, very funny in a miserable way, someone who could stop me dead in my tracks with a single comment.

Equally, I think he was intrigued by me and Harmy. He would never stop doing a northern accent – or what he thought was one. Even now, he picks me up on missing words – 'You're not speaking properly.' Same with Harmy. Always funny, though, never any malice. And to be fair, he got a bit back. Keysy is from the south-east and speaks with that 'Aw' right, Fred?' accent. Awful.

It was evident straight away that the three of us got on. We did everything together – played together, ate together, drank together. When we were on tour we would more or less live in each other's rooms. For me, that was what playing the game was all about. In any team you will have people you get on with, others you don't, and within that mix there'll be a couple who are almost like family.

We should have played more together for England and I sometimes feel guilty that I was maybe one of the reasons he didn't. I think the then coach, Duncan Fletcher, could handle two similar personalities in a team in me and Harmy, but I don't believe he wanted the three of us. That, I think, he considered would have been to the team's detriment.

Keysy also suffered from people thinking he was unfit. He was actually nothing of the sort. Keysy was actually incredibly fit, albeit because he used to play hockey … a grown man playing hockey, I still can't get my head round it. He used to take me to his hockey club and I'd be looking at him, thinking, 'Come on Keysy, get a grip.'

Keysy would have made the England team stronger every day of the week. If he had been there in the 2005 Ashes as well as me and Harmy, what was already an unbelievable summer would have been absolutely perfect. Similarly, if I'd had him in my team when I was England captain, it would have been a different kettle of fish. I would have drawn on him so much. He has an immense cricket brain. He knows the game inside out. The only comparison I can make is with Shane Warne. Both see cricket differently to anyone else.

If anything, Keysy is underused in cricket. He would be one of the greatest batting coaches ever. While some coaches talk in riddles and clichés, Keysy gets straight to the point. He sees things that I and so many others don't. He has played with so many different people, so many different characters. He is a mine of knowledge and that's what we see now with his punditry. No surprise to see how well Keysy has done with Sky. He's a different level. Listen to him analyse the most complex themes on TV and his words make perfect sense.

There is one thing that baffles me, however – his relationship with Nasser. He used to hammer Nasser and now look at him; he's all over him. I hear Nasser has even got his own chapter in this book. Disgraceful behaviour.

I still see Keysy all the time. A lot of people you play with and against, you never clap eyes on them once the cricket stops. No chance of that with Keysy. In all honesty, I can't spend enough time with the man. The only reason I did a bit of T20 commentary was to be in the pod alongside him. To be fair, he looked after me well. I don't have half his knowledge and he told me all about the players so I knew who to look out for. He was so good to me, only occasionally stuffing me, like telling me someone was a well-known player's son so I'd repeat it on commentary. In that partnership, Keysy was, for sure, the expert. I was like *Anchorman*.

These days, Keysy has swapped the cricket gear for the golf clubs, although he's never going to be as good as he thinks he is. He has his own way of trying to outdo other players, like the huge sniff he tends to take on your back swing.

He continues, as ever, to be a noted joke and song thief. Down the years he has taken credit for all my best work. When we went on an England A tour together, I wrote a song for the team and set it to the tune of *American Pie*. He took credit for all the good verses while mine, apparently, were all the hopeless ones. I have also got used to him calling me Trev. Work that one out for yourselves.

Keysy remains a man always in your corner. He will always back you, always be there for you. When, while dressed as Elvis, and singing *Sweet Caroline*, I fell over the speaker at the T20 finals, he was one of the first to get in touch. Although, admittedly, that was because he thought all his Christmases had come at once.

But the best thing about Keysy is that, when it comes to his cricketing life, he is happy with it. And so he should be. He was one of the great batsmen of his generation. Ridiculously talented. Ridiculously good.

He has now forged an incredible new career for himself and it's great to see him doing so well. He's got a fantastic family, brilliant kids, and, in Fleur, a lovely, if long-suffering, wife.

He deserves all those things and more. The game of cricket, and so many people in it, myself included, owe Rob Key a lot. He is, and continues to be, one of the great blokes.

Andrew Flintoff
March 2020

Chapter 1

Cry Me a River

On Wikipedia, I am down as having three nicknames: Keysy, Bobby and Pudding. The latter isn't the most flattering and reflects a period where me and Andrew Flintoff worked out how to change each other's entries. Some 'facts' stuck, some didn't. I put on Fred's that he was the heaviest baby born in Lancashire. He put on mine that I was the sweatiest man ever to score a double hundred.

I extended the idea to Kent. On Matt Walker's entry, bearing in mind he's not the tallest bloke, I wrote that he lost out for the title role of Willow to Warwick Davis in the Hollywood fantasy of the same name. I added that he was subsequently a stand-in for Dobby, the house-elf in *Harry Potter*.

Fred, while being a big lad at times, especially between the ages of zero and one, was always very strong. He had periods when his physique was criticised, but it wasn't career-long, like mine. In truth, Fred was an athlete and actually held a few records for fitness tests. I was slightly different – athleticism wasn't my forte. But I wasn't alone. Very few people treated their body like a temple. Smoking and drinking was just a part of the county game. Alcohol, in particular, I soon found out, was woven into its fabric. My first time as twelfth man, at Worcester, I turned up at the hotel the evening before the game and found our coach, John Wright, sitting in the bar. He told me to go and get him a lager and lime. I did, and came back with a Coke for myself.

'Put a Jack Daniels in it,' he told me, at which point it occurred to me that I probably wasn't going to be playing the next day. But if I thought I was in for an easy four days, coasting along as twelfth man, I was very much mistaken. Wrighty, for some reason, had got it into his head that I wasn't very fit. Alan Ealham, the seconds' coach, thought I had puppy fat and in the end it would go. When we did the bleep test (a fitness exam that entails running between cones ahead of a bleep that comes faster and faster), he'd tell me, 'Don't bust a gut, just get to level 12.'

Wrighty, though, was different. Every day on that trip to Worcester, he made me run down the river. I hated it with a vengeance. Wrighty would run down the river as well, but, always trying to get one up on people, would go on his own, arming himself with knowledge of various markers along the way.

2 'Oi, Key'

The first day he told me I had to run the riverside path and report back what a sign said in a field about 3 miles away. From the start, pretty much every sign I saw said 'Private! No fishing!', so I stopped after 200 yards, went into Worcester and had a coffee. I returned to the ground, saw Wrighty, and my punt on that being the notice further down the river was proved correct.

Wrighty was canny. Next day he sent me off to the same sign, but this time with a ticket to put on it. That way, he would be able to check. But I wasn't to be beaten that easily: I gave it to someone else who was running down the path, and he did it instead. Next time I saw Wrighty, he was boiling.

'Oi, Key!'

I thought I'd been rumbled and went over expecting to be hauled over the coals.

'You put it on the wrong sign, didn't you?'

I had to think quick.

'Sorry, Wrighty,' I blurted, 'I must have been confused,' and went off, wiping the beads of sweat from my forehead.

On the third day, I set out for the run again. I was sat lazily by the river when I spotted Wrighty in the distance on his way. Desperate to escape his wrath, I climbed into a tree. Later, when he asked how come he'd not seen me on the river, I told him I'd got bored doing the same run and gone a different way over the fields.

But there were few, if any, flies on Wrighty, and by the fourth day he was starting to suspect something wasn't quite right. This time, he started running down the river and said I had to catch him up. In my naïvety, I thought when I got alongside him that that would be it; we'd stop, and turn back.

I sprinted after him and quickly caught him, at which point he said, 'Come on, we'll go down to the sign and back.' It was a 6-mile run – way too far for me back then – and, as we turned, I was puffing and bluffing in equal measure. I needed a plan. I had a thought. I told him that him running ahead and me catching him up on the way to the sign had given me something to aim for.

The bait had been dangled. 'OK,' he bit, 'let's do that again.' Off he went, and off I let him go, several hundred yards before he turned and shouted for me to follow. I thought I'd never catch him, let alone beat him back to the ground, but that was before I'd spotted the kid on the path with a scrambler bike. I persuaded him to let me jump on the back and, via a nifty route, was back at New Road in no time.

Inevitably, it turned out he'd clocked me. To say he was absolutely fuming would be an understatement. It would have been a whole lot simpler to have just done the run, but, again, fitness wasn't the style it is today. To be a first-class cricketer didn't mean you had to have the build of a cover model from *Men's Fitness*. In fact, a decent measure of unhealthiness was woven into the fabric of the game. My first one-day competition was the Benson & Hedges Cup. The sponsors would come into the dressing room and put 400 packets of fags on the table, at which point there'd be a mad scrum among the players to grab as many as they could. I was on eight grand a year then. No way did I want to be spending money on fags if I didn't have to – because, yes, like pretty much everyone else, I was a professional cricketer who liked a fag every now and again. I hadn't always been like that. OK, when the Bunsen burners came out at school, we'd roll a splint in paper and smoke it because we thought it made us look good, but it rarely went further than that. I didn't smoke properly when I was a lad because I wanted to be a professional cricketer. Thing was, when I actually made it into first-class cricket, straight away it seemed to me that all the best players were smokers, so, Bingo!, I might as well do it too. By the end of my career, the situation had turned on its head. Hardly anyone was smoking then – you were an outlier if you liked a fag – whereas at the start, nearly everyone in the first team smoked. Most kit catalogues came with an ashtray.

But it wasn't like I thought of myself as unfit. When early on in my career we played Durham – a shock to me as I didn't even know they played cricket in Northumberland (I didn't even think it was in England!) – we'd had them in trouble at 127-9 in their first innings only for them to end up with 229. I spent most of that innings on the cover boundary, harbouring a theory that if I ran with rhythm, I'd be faster. That wasn't quite the case. While I thought I'd developed a truly lovely stride pattern, eating up the grass, I was actually simply jogging. Every time a shot went out to deep cover, I would do my finest rhythmical running, and as I did so, the ball would go past me for four. I couldn't help wonder why my teammates were getting annoyed at me.

I had to see out a session that night. As I put my pads on, our captain, Steve Marsh, was properly chewing us out with the kind of football-style bollocking that never really happens when a team is about to bat. Cricketers are so precious that no one says a word to them when they're about to head to the wicket, apart from Martin McCague, our fast bowler and number eleven, who had a tendency to state, 'I'll get my pads on,' as he saw me and my fellow opener David Fulton get padded up.

Marsh gave Matt Walker, one of my best mates, a real going over, and I was giggling to myself as I gleefully listened to this expletive-strewn rant. Unfortunately, he then turned to me.

4 'Oi, Key'

'You, you fat ****, you can start running after the f***ing ball, you lazy f***ker.'

I was 18. I didn't know what was coming at me. I did have a thought, though: 'I'd better get some runs.'

And thankfully, after being 60-odd not out overnight, I went on to get my maiden first-class hundred.

The bleep test was pretty much all that mattered as regards fitness, specifically reaching level 12, which I never failed – well, almost. I did stutter preseason when I came back from the England A tour to Zimbabwe, where I'd put on two stone. But that was a one-off. Even when the rest of the squad dubbed me Jimmy Fivebellies as I arrived late for the coach to go on a team-building exercise, I had still earlier passed the bleep test. Coaches and teammates may have thought I was going to muck it up, but I never did. Certainly, I took it more seriously than Graham Cowdrey. We did a fitness course at Kent, and England fitness coach Dean Riddell came down to oversee proceedings. At level 2 on the bleep test, Graham's phone went off in his pocket, a lovely little ringtone, at which point he stepped out of the test and took the call. Dean was becoming progressively more apoplectic as the conversation went on and on, with a good few levels of the test passing Graham by before he signed off with a breezy 'See you later!' and started running again. Dean had a right go at him, but it was Graham's benefit year, so it was understandable he felt he had to answer. And he never aspired to be the next Usain Bolt.

I had a low heart rate, which meant I was fitter than I looked. In the first year of the England Academy, an intake of young players at Loughborough, I came third on the fitness test. Even when I was 36, I would still beat half the Kent squad. Aerobically, I was good; I just never did anything that might tone me up. I couldn't think of anything worse than sitting in the gym lifting weights. Bicep curl and all that? No thanks. I'd give it three minutes and that would be it. I couldn't be bothered. It used to drive me mad. Nowadays, players work to specific strengthening routines every day with fitness trainers. The game is so much more professional. I don't think I ever lifted a single weight. As a senior player, I used to go running with the dog, and that was the end of it.

Nevertheless, issues with body shape followed me round. I tried all the various fad diets, didn't have chips for years, apart from nicking the kids', but was never really educated in how to lose weight. I had no clue how to address fitness any differently. I would constantly think, 'As long as I can pass the bleep test that will be it.' Once I'd reached level 12, the pressure was off, and I was straight into the season. At that point, there was no time for fitness.

I was there to score runs, and as long as I did that, I was OK. For me, it was always about feeling that I had earned the right to succeed. And I always did.

Occasionally, specialist trainers would appear, but they rarely, if ever, made a great deal of difference. We had a sprint coach come down to Kent, banging on about technique and seemingly determined to go through the full range from John Cleese's Ministry of Silly Walks. At one point, she got her best sprinter down to Canterbury and told him to race against Michael Carberry. Carbs was no slouch, and beat him hands down. That was the end of that.

But not all coaches were so easily dismissed. When it came to my international prospects, Duncan Fletcher's view of me was, to my mind, undoubtedly skewed to some degree by what he perceived as a lack of fitness. Had I been a great fielder like Paul Collingwood then I would have been more of an asset. But I never was that great fielder. I always had to score runs; otherwise I was going to miss out. In cricket, you have athletes and then you have batsmen. Virat Kohli is both, Ricky Ponting is both. Sachin Tendulkar, on the other hand, is a batsman. Rahul Dravid is a batsman. At Kent, I was offered captaincy; for England, I was a one-dimensional cricketer.

The all-rounder Samit Patel was another who was often chastised about fitness, especially at international level. When I captained the England A side to New Zealand in early 2009, Samit was in line to play in the one-day stuff. As ever, there'd been talk of him not being fit. And, as ever, in the months before the trip we knew we'd be fitness tested. Now the one thing I learned quickly about scheduled fitness tests is there's no point doing the first one well. The key is showing improvement. That's what the coaches are looking for. So don't kill yourself early on; just do enough. Put the effort in later down the line.

Early on, we had the 23-7 test. The aim was to run as far as possible in seven seconds. The further you reach, the more points you get. Then you turn and have twenty-three seconds to get back to the start, which is easy, before off you go again. It was like the bleep test and was the basis of the judgement made of a player's ongoing fitness. I couldn't help watching Samit. While the coaches weren't looking, he was gaining an extra 5 metres' distance on his seven seconds.

I had only one thought: 'What is he doing?' A month later, we were flying out, and the test would be repeated before we set off. Samit, like all of us, would be required to show an improvement on this first test. Unless he could find a way to add even more yards while no one was looking, he was never going to get as good a score as he did first time round. I knew he was in trouble before he'd even thought about it. The moral of the tale is simple: always concentrate your efforts, whatever they may be, on the second fitness test.

Others would try to find a different way around fitness issues. Darren Gough was always looking for answers to shed unwanted extra pounds. In Australia, in 2002 – a tour in which neither he nor Fred would actually take part because of injury – both were sitting out the traditional Lilac Hill warm-up game. They were sent to the gym with the fitness trainer instead. The trainer went off to see how the other players in his charge were getting on while Goughy and Fred climbed morosely on to an exercise bike to warm up. In front of them on the TV screen flashed an advert – magical pills that promised weight loss without the need to train. They couldn't get off the bikes quick enough, heading straight to the shop for the medication. When the fitness trainer returned, they were both sat relaxing with a smoothie. Fred and Goughy joined up with us later at Lilac Hill. With its festival atmosphere, there were tables full of cakes, biscuits, all sorts of treats, wherever you looked. The cogs in their heads were whirring. They could eat whatever they wanted. The pills would simply get rid of the lot. Goughy took a pill and immediately wolfed down a cake.

'My heart rate has gone up,' he exclaimed. 'The pill's doing its job already!' It was the very height of professionalism.

And they didn't work.

Different diets were always coming out and I wasn't alone in investigating what they entailed. The Atkins diet looked quite appealing. It seemed you could have as much meat as you wanted – sausages, bacon, burgers without the bread … all sorts of stuff. Me and Fred were raring to go when we heard that the guy who invented it had suffered from heart disease. Instead, going down the Goughy route, Fred found some pills – Xenical. The view was that these things would separate the fat from the rest of the food so you could eat what you wanted and, miraculously, all you would deposit in the toilet was fat (apologies if you're reading this over breakfast). We didn't look into it any more than that. At that point, we were in for any sort of quick fix we could get our hands on. All was going swimmingly until we realised the pills had a startling side effect: yes, it involved the toilet, but more in that you never knew when you might need to go. Fred would be waiting to bat, only to find himself ensconced on the toilet, even once having to do an emergency clean-up job in a sink in the dressing room at Lord's. The oil painting of the incident has yet to appear on the Long Room wall.

Booze, in particular, was one of my – and many other players' – downfalls. For the majority of my career, in the background of nearly every professional cricketer was alcohol. In the days when the Sunday League was still going, squeezed in between the third and fourth day of a Championship match, with a 1.30 pm start, it would have been positively rude not to go out on the Saturday night. Back then it was one out, all out, and if you weren't there, you might well be shunned. Whatever town we happened to be in, we'd get blind drunk, before a nice lie-in and then play the game. This was before fitness trainers had even been invented; a completely different world. Even on a normal day, we would pick something off the drinks menu to be ready and waiting for us at the end of play. Nowadays, it's the complete opposite. When stumps is called, players are refuelling on fitness drinks, jumping in ice baths and having specialist massages. T20 has made the need to be an athlete even greater. We were left to our own devices, which we very much enjoyed.

At the end of the nineties and into the noughties, cricketers played it pretty hard on and off the field, just as they had for decades. Matt Walker was an early hero of mine at Kent. When I came into the Kent set-up at 16, he was already playing Under-19s for England, as well as internationally at hockey. He was a gun sportsman, proper schoolboy legend – but one who also liked a night out. Playing alongside him in the seconds, we had a match up at Worcester.

'I'm rooming with Matt Walker,' I told the hotel receptionist.

Alan Ealham, the coach, was stood next to me.

'You are not!' he said. He knew Matt would all too happily lead me astray – and I would offer very little resistance. We both got put in with some other lads, but, inevitably, we still met up later. Worcester was always good for drinking – tight, compact, lots of pubs – and we went out and got drunk with some of the old pros, and then rounded it off with a curry. I spent the whole night puking up, which was unfortunate for James Baldock, the poor fellow I was rooming with. James took health and fitness very seriously. He had left the pub early and headed back to the hotel to do a whole gamut of exercises to get ready for the next day. It didn't do him much good. He didn't get much rest that night.

The next morning in the warm-up, Alan Ealham made me run more and more.

'It sounded like there was a whale in the hotel last night,' he was telling everyone. 'Someone was throwing up all night.' I thought I was going to be sick all over again.

I was one not out overnight. Poor old Baldock nicked off for next to nothing, and me and Matt went on to get hundreds. The game never seemed to teach you the lesson it should have done. Then again, when you are young you think you are invincible, and sometimes you get away with it. Also, you don't get the truly debilitating hangovers that afflict you later in life. Nowadays, if I went out drinking until 7.00 am, you wouldn't see me for three days, let alone find me running around playing cricket. But twenty years ago, it was all part of the game.

We had one of the biggest nights ever when we were playing Yorkshire. I was 23, playing well, and had got a hundred in the game. Later, we met up with Andrew Symonds in a nightclub. He was clearly smashed. Simmo could drink beer but not spirits, which hadn't gone unnoticed – I would always stuff him with a few vodkas, given half a chance. We were in a student club in Canterbury, so already standing out like sore thumbs, when I saw Simmo fall over at the bar. I rushed him into the disabled cubicle, where he slumped clumsily on the toilet. The door was wide open – 'Here you are, everybody – meet Kent's overseas player!'

We finally got him to bed, but next morning he was still three sheets to the wind, as, to be fair, was I. Dave Fulton, the skipper, came up to me.

'Simmo's still pissed – how about you?'

'No, no. Not me. I was in bed early. Watched a bit of telly and lights out.'

For the whole of that first session, Simmo was sprinting up and down, giving it all the verbals.

'Come on, lads! Let's do this! Let's get stuck in!'

And then he hit the wall.

He didn't say another word … until the last ball of the day, when he took one of the most unbelievable catches anyone will ever see. We all just looked at each other – 'How the hell has he managed that?' Even in the grip of the harshest of hangovers, Simmo could still pull off miracles.

That was Simmo; he was prone, as we all were, to go out for a few beers, only to find, as Micky Flanagan might say, he'd 'got the taste'. That was what happened when he was dropped from the Australia team for the one-day game against Bangladesh at Cardiff in 2005. Before he knew it, it was 5.00 am. We've all done that. We've all gone out with the best intentions, had a couple of drinks, a few beers, and then somebody says, 'Let's have a tequila!' and before you know it, it's getting light and you're strolling into a hotel. It happened to me once when I was captain of Kent. We were playing at Surrey and a bit of a heavy night in London ensued. Graham Ford saw me at the ground the next morning.

'Are you all right?' he enquired of the ashen-faced and decidedly clammy spectacle afore him.

And I just thought, 'Jesus! No!'

I wandered off to find a toilet away from the dressing room. I was sick about twenty times. As I was doing so, I looked up and there were four Kent members stood at the urinal. I was in a terrible state.

Getting out for the night at Lancashire was a bigger challenge. John Wright banned me from going out when we played them. More precisely, he threatened me with the sack if I was caught with Freddie. Naturally, it made not a jot of difference – we would still end up in a Chinese at four o'clock in the morning with Freddie singing away, broadcasting our presence to the world, as if he actually wanted me to get into trouble. In the morning, I'd brush my teeth ten times, thinking I'd pulled the wool over Wrighty's eyes, only for him then to see Freddie was still drunk. At that point, he was in no doubt as to the identity of his partner in crime.

Thing is, cricket is no different to any other job – overdo it the night before and you know you are in for just the longest day. It felt like such a good idea at the time. Out there having a great night, telling everyone they're going to be your best man, a kebab, bed at 5.00 am – 'LIFE JUST DOESN'T GET ANY BETTER THAN THIS!' And then you wake up two hours later and all you can think is, 'Oh my god!'

Nevertheless, it was a great lifestyle. We would just train, play, and go out – such good fun.

One of the good things about drinking as a player is you are accruing plenty of experience for if and when your turn comes as captain. Because I'd done it myself, I knew only too well when players had been out.

At breakfast, I always looked for the bloke who was the most happy. Because he thinks that's the way to get you off the scent. He'll be there, sunglasses on (another giveaway), giving you a big smile – 'All right, Keysy?' – and all you're thinking is, 'Jesus, how much did you have last night?' The bloke who's sat there moaning and miserable, more than likely has nothing to hide – he's probably just had a bad night's sleep.

Young players in particular would stuff their mates without a second thought.

'Jesus, looks like Colesy's had a few,' I'd say to Sam Billings on the morning of a game.

'Oh yes,' he'd reply straight away, 'he's as pissed as a fart.'

'Oh. So were you with him then?'

'Yes – but it doesn't matter about me because I'm twelfth man.'

Matt Coles had a reputation for going out at Kent – always fun as captain because he just couldn't hide it. I pulled him over one morning. As ever, he'd been grassed up by one of his mates.

'How many beers did you have?'

'Three.'

'Right. I'll give you one chance to be honest. If you lie to me now, that's it, we're done.'

'OK, maybe five.'

'Last chance.'

'Well, maybe seven.'

Personally, I'd be dead if I had seven beers, but I knew with Matty it was unlikely to be the end of it.

'Right, I've only asked you about beers. How many shots did you have?'

'A few.'

'How many spirits?'

'Well, a few vodka Red Bulls.'

'So, basically, you've had seven beers, a shitload of shots and a load of vodka Red Bulls?'

'Well, yeah.'

It's hard to police that kind of behaviour. All you can really do as a captain is tell the player off and keep an eye on them. Matt Coles had two spells with us, and when we signed him the second time, I made sure he roomed with Sam Billings. Bilbo was ambitious and if Matt was going out living it up all night, I'd soon know about it. Also, Bilbo would have a go at him and keep him in check.

As a leader, though, it's important to recognise that everyone is different. At the England Academy in Adelaide, where we had access to some of the finest coaches in the world, Ian Chappell had given us a talk about captaincy. Ian thought he was a great captain, which he obviously was, and key to that was understanding of the individual mindset.

'If I hadn't let Doug Walters go out smoking, gambling and drinking til three in the morning,' he told us, 'he wouldn't have averaged 50 in Test cricket.'

As young men not averse to a late night and a drink, we thought that was the best line we'd ever heard. I thought to myself that was absolutely what leadership should be, working out what is best for people – not necessarily letting everybody go out, but accepting that everybody is different.

Ian had a case in point right there in the Academy. While we were in Adelaide, Freddie was called up by the full England team. It was like watching someone escape Alcatraz. To celebrate, we went out and got absolutely hammered, returning about 6.00 am, Steve Harmison with champagne bottle in hand. Bed, while vital, wasn't an option – Fred was leaving imminently, but typically hadn't packed any of his gear. As we desperately fought to keep him awake, Harmy was frantically getting all Fred's stuff together. The team manager, Nigel Laughton, was absolutely fuming because Fred was clearly going to be late for the airport. In the end, however, he was ready. He walked down to reception with his blazer on. Trouble was, he had nothing else on with it. Nothing whatsoever. He was greeted by a none-too-pleased Nigel.

'What are you going to wear?' he shouted.

Fred opened his blazer. 'A smile,' he said.

Head coach at the Academy, the Australian wicketkeeping legend Rod Marsh knew it was necessary for players to let their hair down. At Christmas he told us, 'Right, I'll take you to the best bar in Adelaide – Crazy Horse.'

He asked us if we'd heard of it. 'No, no,' we all replied.

As we walked in, the waitresses greeted me and Harmy by our first names. Not that it mattered too much. Rod was savvy enough to know what a group of young cricketers get up to. He had, after all, been one himself.

Crazy Horse had become our regular Tuesday night haunt. We had a trainer who thought fitness was the best thing ever, while we thought it was the worst. He used to tell us he couldn't understand why so-called elite athletes would want to go out and drink and abuse their bodies. It meant we never seemed to have a day off. Even on a Sunday, we'd be there reporting for duty at 7.00 am. That meant we couldn't go out on a Saturday and get mullered, so on a Tuesday, ahead of a slightly easier day on Wednesday, off we'd go to Crazy Horse.

Whatever a trainer might think, you can't just treat players like robots. The house we stayed at was called Del Monte … although when it came to some of the rules and regulations – no butter, for instance – we weren't all that willing to say yes. Rules like that, as far as we were concerned, were made to be ignored. Bread without butter? What a nonsense. We'd sneak down the shop to buy stuff like that. We were also meant to eat in, but truth was, while the original Australian intake used to receive the minimum wage, we were getting quite well paid, so instead of the terrible food, all very healthy, served up at the house, we used to go to the Italian restaurant down the road.

Sharing the place were some of Australia's finest elite cyclists. They were great athletic specimens who could pull off the Lycra look with aplomb. Then there was us, a load of drinking, smoking, young blokes, apparently the best England had to offer.

That's not to say there isn't a place for fitness. Putting on two stone in Zimbabwe that time, mainly through drink, was hardly ideal, but, well, it was the rainy season. What else was I supposed to do? Everybody thinks the best place to tour is Australia or the West Indies. But actually, it's the less obvious places – where you're forced to spend time together and come up with things to do – that are the places where the real bonding happens. Zimbabwe was a case in point. We had an Xbox 360, played cards with our coach, John Emburey, drank a lot, and went out to dinner. It was the rainy season, so I hardly played, and everything seemed to cost about 50p. It was where me, Freddie and Harmy got very close – basically, our Club 18-30 Ibiza trip.

On one occasion, we were taking an 8.00 am flight from Harare to Bulawayo. A few of us strolled back into the hotel at 7.00 am after a big night out only to be confronted by the sight of team manager Phil Neale. We were petrified of Phil, a man who didn't take any prisoners and expected standards to be upheld. Each of us held the same thought: 'We're in real shit here.'

Phil looked at us. 'Hi,' he said, 'have you been out for a walk?'

He had thrown us a lifeline.

'Yeah, yeah,' I spluttered, blind drunk. 'We just got up early and headed out.'

And off he went. Result.

Had Phil got wind of another incident on that tour, then we really would have been for the high jump. We were drinking upstairs in a bar in Cape Town when Harmy delicately lobbed a glass at Fred, only for it to sail over a balcony and straight through a young woman's windscreen below. It caused a bit of upset – the girl quite rightly wanted some money for a new windscreen – and the next thing we knew, there was Harmy being arrested. We had to get Embers over to sort it out. Thankfully, he didn't tell Phil, and in the end it was all settled without Harmy being hauled off by the authorities. Good job, really; he was playing in a game at Newlands at the time.

'Where's your number eleven, mate?'

'Oh, he's been arrested. He'll be along if he gets bail.'

There are two types of people in the dressing room: those who want to go out to meet women, and those who want to go out to have a bit of fun and get drunk. Rooming with the former could be an issue. You might not see them until they crashed in at four in the morning with a 'guest'. I'd be lying there thinking, 'I've got to bat all day tomorrow and here's this fella 6 feet away doing this.' Horrific. I was the latter. I wouldn't get drunk night after night. I always thought of myself as a binge drinker. Everything would build up and build up, and then there'd be a massive release. For me, it was always the journey to getting drunk, starting off sober and then gradually getting worse throughout the next few hours. Nowadays, a lot of young players go out drunk. They aren't interested in the journey; they just want to get there. In my later years, when we had nights out at Kent, some of the younger lads would turn up hammered, having skulled as much vodka as they could at home to save money. For me, they were totally missing the point of going out in the first place, to share a great time with your teammates. That's where the journey comes in – you don't want instant blotto. Victory, especially, should be savoured, treasured. As a player, you don't win games of cricket for money, you win them to feel success and for the craic. Success is a great feeling, and it should be celebrated together properly, otherwise what is the point? If you have done well at something in life, whatever it is, you've got to sit back and enjoy it. Cricket is the same as any job – you live to go out. Take the good times when they come – because chances are, they won't come too often.

Take beating Australia in Sydney in the last Test of the Ashes series in 2002/03. We celebrated like we'd won the World Cup. And, in fact, in doing so, we realised how, over the previous six weeks, we'd made a terrific mistake, one that could again have been remedied by remembering the social side of the game. All that time, the mythology of the Aussies had been building in our heads, not aided by us making a point of not socialising with the opposition. The idea was we would try to do to Australia what Aussie manager Bobby Simpson and captain Allan Border had done to England in the eighties – turn the cold shoulder and treat the opposition like the enemy. What's good for the goose and all that … So when we headed to Australia, we similarly wanted to let them know we weren't there to make friends but to play hard, uncompromising cricket.

What we should have done, of course, is actually demystify the Aussies, get properly to know Warne, McGrath, Hayden, Ponting, Langer, and have a drink with them after the game. Instead, after two or three losing Tests, not only did some of us think such players were streets ahead of us, holding them on a pedestal, but we began to believe they disliked and looked down on us. Actually, nothing could have been further from the truth. As we eventually found out after our victory, the Aussies were actually bloody good blokes. We went into the Australian dressing room to congratulate our hosts, only to end up getting absolutely smashed with these guys we'd barely spoken to for two months. Brett Lee was there, knocking out a few tunes on his guitar, while I soon found myself sat next to Steve Waugh, chatting about Test cricket. All I could think was, 'Jeez, we should have done this sooner!' We wouldn't have ended up best mates, but we would have found out they were capable of experiencing the same fears and doubts as everyone else – the difference being that they had overcome them.

It was similar to England's Ashes tour under Freddie in 2006/07. I was a member of the back-up squad and went round to Warney's flat for a game of poker with him, Adam Vosges and Andrew Symonds. We stayed there all night playing cards.

'Jesus, I've barely been out with the England team,' I thought, 'and here I am with some of the greats of Australia.' Again, as ever with the Aussies, I would ask them about cricket and they'd tell me whatever I wanted to know. Also, they would ask my opinion, which, coming from the greats, means something. Again, the social side is an upside, not a downside.

Not that everything we did that night back at Sydney in 2003 was too clever. By the time we spilled out of their dressing room, it was knocking midnight. The transport back to the hotel had long gone, and not fancying – nor being particularly capable of – walking, it was unfortunate that someone had left a small motorised buggy, with trailer, like a groundsman might use, right there outside the SCG. Butch took the controls while several more of us jumped in the back. We'd actually got half a mile or so when someone found a modicum of sense and suggested this might not be a great career move – the land-based version of David Gower and the Tiger Moth. Duly we dumped the buggy and were fortunate enough to be picked up by some England fans who took our bedraggled bunch back to the hotel.

Some remain bemused as to why we celebrated that last Test win so wildly. We had, after all, lost the series 4-1. It's been said it was a hollow victory anyway, as the Aussies had already tied the series up and weren't fussed what happened at Sydney. As anyone who has ever played in an Ashes Test match – any Test match – will know, that is absolute rubbish. The idea that the Australians wouldn't turn up for a dead rubber is nonsense. I don't think there's ever been a cricketer, even in a dead series, whoever it's against, who, when faced with a chance of a Test hundred, hasn't done their level best to get it. Even against a pretty ordinary West Indies team, he would take it. There's no better feeling than that in the world. Same for bowlers with a five-for. It doesn't matter when, where, or who against, the chance is there to put yourself down in history. Test cricket is the absolute pinnacle. What happened at Sydney was we won a good toss. Butch and Vaughan played brilliantly and that meant we were always ahead in the game. To beat the Australians, we needed to play at our very best, but we also needed a hell of a lot of luck. Without either, we were gone – and that's what happened in the rest of that series. When the tide finally turned at the SCG, no way weren't we going to enjoy it. Those calories from that beer were wholly deserved.

Nowadays, some people tell me I look slimmer on TV than I ever did as a player, which I'm never sure is that much of a compliment. Others would disagree. May I thank personally the England supporter who turned up at last winter's first Test against South Africa at Centurion with a massive George Cross featuring the legend 'Who is Blob Key?', and also Nasser Hussain, who so graciously walked halfway round the ground to highlight it on live TV.

In the end, I just can't win. I can tell people I was actually a fit bloke until I'm blue (not red) in the face, but they still won't believe me. I went running with a mate of mine for the first time not long ago and he was surprised at how far and how quick I was able to go.

'You've got to be the most unlucky bloke in the world,' he told me, 'because you're fit but you don't look it.'

Therein is the story of my life.

Chapter 2

Planks

I had been kidnapped, blindfolded, and was now stood on a plank over an old flooded quarry. It wasn't quite what I had in mind for an occasion originally billed as 'paintballing', but there you go.

As I balanced on the piece of wood, I couldn't help but feel this was the absolute embodiment of everything I hated about team building. The seeds of our misery had been sown the night before, when, believing our day was going to be nothing too strenuous, we'd had a few drinks around Canterbury. Sambuca had appeared at one point, which is rarely a good sign. When we turned up at the appointed venue the next day, what we actually found was an army boot camp. This wasn't great news as we were all hanging. Barely had we arrived when we had to carry people on stretchers across various obstacles, Matt Walker subsequently twisting his ankle so badly he was ruled out for the whole of the preseason. We then did paintballing for what seemed like all of ten minutes before it was back to more fitness and, finally, the kidnapping. We were told we would be blindfolded and driven one by one to the quarry, where we would have to decide whether we were brave enough to jump. As Ed Smith clambered into the vehicle, only me and Mark Ealham remained. When it returned, Ealy was having none of it. He refused point-blank to do it. He wouldn't even get in the car to go to the plank. Instead, they put the blindfold on me. I was more than a little perturbed to discover it was wet. All I could think was, 'Jesus, am I really going to do this?'

The car stopped. Gingerly, I got out. They walked me, still blindfolded, along the plank and left me at the end.

Behind me, I heard, 'One, two, three … '

It was decision time. Was I going to do it or not? I had nothing to go on – none of my teammates had come back to where we started from.

'Jump!'

In that moment, I stopped. It was time to put a halt to these ridiculous proceedings. I told the instructors I wasn't going to do it. Cagily, I walked back in off the plank.

Of course, when they removed the blindfold it turned out the plank was actually on the ground. There was no quarry. No drop. It transpired that me and Ealy were the only ones to have refused. Ed Smith had definitely gone for it, going barefoot so as not to spoil his brand-new shoes, only to end up stubbing his toe in the inch-long drop, rendering him unable to play for two weeks. I don't know about team building, but the day certainly built a queue to see the team doctor.

There was an epidemic of such 'forward-thinking' concepts around at the time. One preseason at Kent, we had Fame Academy. We were taken to a private school and billeted in dormitories, sleeping in beds made for 12-year-olds, so short our feet would stick out the end. There was a fellow from the real *Fame Academy* on TV acting as a fitness trainer and, wait for it, singing coach. The idea was we had to come up with a team song, something I have always despised, and still do to this day. To my mind, there's nothing ruder than this Australian invention, which has spread like a virus into cricket across the globe. What happens is, from club cricket upwards in Australia, the winning team will gracelessly belt out its chosen song in the dressing room. Over the years, this nonsense has gradually seeped into county cricket, the more unimaginative sides simply taking one of the Aussie ditties and inserting their county's name instead. The away dressing room at Kent was above us, which meant that if we lost a game, we would have to sit there and listen to one of these bloody songs to the accompaniment of the players banging their bats on the floorboards. For me, the mere thought of singing in front of my teammates was both embarrassing and excruciating. More than that, though, it was just poor manners, rubbing it in. If you don't like someone and you beat them, shake their hand and tell them 'Well tried'. There's nothing worse than being told 'Well tried' when you lose.

Thankfully, to this day, I have never ever sung a team song. But if I become a coach, maybe I will have to change my opinion because the team song is everywhere now. Perhaps the players will demand one. It has to be said, I couldn't help notice that even some of our old guard found Fame Academy to their liking. Dave Fulton sang so hard he lost his voice. Min Patel and I, however, didn't share his fervour. We found the whole thing horrendous. Every night we waited for everyone to go to bed.

'We can't be doing with this,' we'd say, and just drive home.

Ricky Gervais said everything that needed saying about team building in *The Office*. The sheer inanity of so much of it is no better revealed than in the litany of awfulness that ensues during a staff training day complete with role play and David Brent's classic performance of *Freelove Freeway* on the guitar.

Sadly, those in charge didn't appear to think the same, and such events dogged me at regular intervals throughout my career. Prior to going out to the

England Academy in Australia, we had been dispatched to the military training college at Sandhurst. There we were split into teams to compete against one another in a series of exercises. On our team there was me, Freddie, Andrew Strauss and Nicky Peng, and, as usual, carrying something big and heavy – in this case, a stretcher with a dummy on it that was the weight of a human, as well as several bags of equipment – over an unfeasibly long distance, featured large. Straussy was clearly the brightest of us four, so he automatically became the one in charge. Soon enough, we realised the course was on a loop and reasoned that if we stashed the bags it would save us a lot of work. Certain items we did keep with us. Prior to the exercise we'd gone out to Tesco and got a load of food (well, you have to make yourself a little bit comfortable). It occurred to us that everyone else was taking the challenge very seriously while there was our group wandering around doing the bare minimum, to the extent that Straussy got us lost and we ended up walking round with our dummy in Sandhurst village. Later, it would become clear that our view that leaving our bags en route showed that great initiative wasn't quite shared by those in charge. They issued a severe reprimand. Not that it mattered to me. I wasn't in the army. As ever, it just seemed a complete load of nonsense. I had shown the desire to make it as a professional cricketer without needing to carry a lead-weighted mannequin across the lowlands of Berkshire.

Sandhurst was mild compared to some of the things that happened once we actually reached the Academy in Adelaide. At one point, we were presented with a psychologist telling us to flush negative thoughts down the toilet – complete with mini toilet to emphasise his point.

We would be tasked with such character-building tasks as going to the supermarket with a list of ingredients and then making soup for the coaches – which backfired when me and Straussy burnt the broth and they couldn't eat it anyway. Fortunately for them, they fared a little better with the main course provided by Simon Jones.

There was the odd beasting, too, not unlike that scene in *An Officer and a Gentleman* where Louis Gossett Jnr is hammering Richard Gere, except in our case, we had this old boxer shouting at us all the time. Elsewhere, we were introduced to yoga; again, not a great success – Graeme Swann and Harmy were messing around so much that the instructor started crying. We had to do the Warrior 1 pose – right leg stretched out, arms high in the air – stood in a line, and Swanny, inevitably, took the opportunity to push us all over.

I knew what the coaches were trying to achieve, but all of those innovations were a complete farce. The bottom line was we came back better cricketers because we were playing with and against great players, not because we had mastered the lotus position. Facing Fred, Harmy, Chris Tremlett, Alex Tudor, Simon Jones, Steve Kirby and Swanny in the nets, as a batsman it was hard not to improve.

Boot camps were a constant menace. Before we went on the England A tour to Zimbabwe, we did one in the Lake District. We had to put one another through a giant spider's web and build a raft, and then review how we'd worked together. The idea was to test us under pressure. What sort of pressure is there sticking someone through a spider's web or trying to build a raft? As a batsman, pressure is someone bowling at 90 miles an hour at your head. Building a raft might work for some people, but not for many batsmen.

Another session saw players split into teams to stack as many crates as possible before someone had to climb the pile. The only way me and Fred could add a little interest was by having a spread bet on the number of crates a player would ascend. Then, if one of us looked like losing, we would knock them off. It made for some brief and welcome respite from other joys, such as swimming in freezing cold lakes.

Such experiences are supposed to take players out of their comfort zone. What they actually do is get them so annoyed they end up bonding over how bad the experience is. If that's what team-building exercises are really all about, then they are doing it well.

When, yet again, we had a team-building week, this time with the Special Boat Service, a few of us were arguing with these blokes, these elite members of the armed forces, about how it was all just a load of nonsense, which, when I look back on it, is probably one of the more arrogant things I've done. But at 20, I just wanted to do other things. I wanted to get on and play the game, not be constantly forced into areas that were, at best, in my opinion, peripheral.

Of course, amongst all the fitness tests, the press-ups, the sit-ups, the runs at ridiculous o'clock in the morning, there is an awful lot of sitting down and talking. Team-building exercises always entail working out a code of conduct and ethics. Not that any working out is necessary. The code is the same every time – honesty, communication and hard work. I would sit there and think, 'People pay a fortune for this – to be told the same thing over and over again.'

The worst example I ever encountered was in the early days at Kent, when Matthew Fleming was captain and John Wright coach. They came up with the Core Covenant, a written set of values that we couldn't laminate until everyone had signed up. The Core Covenant, a sort of Magna Carta for county cricketers, was a huge piece of paper with headings – Honesty, Communication, Work Ethic, Togetherness, etc. Going to Wales orienteering was, naturally, deemed an important part of the process. Go to Wales any day of the week and you will doubtless find dozens of organisations finding a way forward through the medium of falling in a ditch with a compass.

It took two weeks to come up with the Core Covenant. And then off it went to be ceremoniously laminated. The first game of the season was at Middlesex. If things weren't going right during play, the Covenant decreed, we would employ a call sign whereby we would gather together on the field. That call sign, it was stated, was 'Mayday'. It didn't matter what time the Mayday call was made – middle of an over, whatever – or where we were on the field – third man, long-on, wherever – we would run in and convene with our teammates. In practice, this meant that if we were going round the park, the captain would shout 'Mayday!' at the top of his voice, we'd all hare in, he'd tell us 'We need to switch on', and then we'd all hare off again. Genius. I don't know why more teams hadn't thought of it.

Middlesex, it turned out, was a rain-affected game. There was clearly going to be no result. On that basis, with us all staying in Hampstead, we decided to head out to a karaoke bar. I say 'we', but I was less than keen to make listening to a succession of semi-drunken *X Factor* wannabes warbling down a microphone part of the evening. I hate karaoke. It goes on my list (long and detailed – Valentine's Day, New Year's Eve, etc.) of overrated things. But, of course, as one of the newest recruits, I got roped in to sing. Thankfully, alcohol anaesthetises the fear of looking foolish in front of teammates. Naturally, the three people before me looked like they'd come straight off the West End stage. And then there was me, 19 years old, giving it the full *Lady in Red*. I thought I knew the lyrics, which I soon realised I didn't, and as I geared up for the second verse, I could see people leaving. After I had strangled all life out of Chris de Burgh's greatest song, we ended up back at the hotel having a massive party. The next morning, which had pretty much arrived before we found our beds, we were all pretending we hadn't been out. It was a nonsense, really – everyone knew apart from the captain and the coach. That day, Middlesex set about batting for bonus points. I dropped Justin Langer on 10 before Martin McCague dropped him again on 30. It was all the ones who'd been out the night before making the mistakes. Langer went on to get a double hundred, and funnily enough, while Matthew Fleming had made the Mayday shout, it just hadn't seemed to work. We had all signed up to the Covenant without realising we had to rate ourselves after every day's play on a variety of subheadings, one of which was 'Have you given yourself the best chance?' At the end of the day's play, those who hadn't been out put 'Yes' to themselves and then grassed the rest of us up. Forget togetherness; thanks to the Covenant, there was now a massive rift in the side.

Whatever a day had brought, the Covenant was always there nagging in the background. Even if we'd been out in the field all day, it declared, as part of the work ethic criteria, we had to go back out and do fifty catches. We soon became heartily sick of the situation, to the extent that after play we would walk out and stand 5 yards apart, like Under-10s, and throw fifty catches at each other. Not hard ones, just the easiest we could do. Sadly, it didn't end there – we also had to do laps of the ground.

The nonsense that was the Covenant seemed to invade every part of our existence. The creed even included a ban on saying 'Hard luck' to a teammate when they got out. Someone could be dismissed in a really unlucky way – run out while backing up, perhaps – and they'd come back in the dressing room and no one would say a word to them. Think about it: if you don't say 'Hard luck' to a batsman when they come in, you don't say anything. It's not like you can say 'Good shot!' is it? As a batsman, when you go back to the pavilion, the worst thing you can get is silence. In fact, that extends to life. If I've upset my wife, then I'm much happier if she tells me than gives me the silent treatment, and to be fair, it doesn't usually take her long to give me a volley.

The Covenant was just too overpowering. It had us in a permanent headlock, with bodies being thrown everywhere. There were people grassing on one another, putting teammates away left, right and centre. 'So and so didn't do his fifty catches.' It was like the worst part of school ever. The whole concept had cost thousands of pounds of army training and team building, and resulted in the biggest load of nonsense I've ever come across. After two weeks, that was it. We all said we'd had enough. Where that laminate is today, I'm unsure. Hopefully, in a landfill somewhere.

Again, the paucity of team-building success stories emphasises that the success of sides is down to good players. That is my core belief. After England lost to Australia in the round-robin stage of the 2019 World Cup, they had a team meeting. They were very honest and talked about how they felt. They then came out and beat India in the next game. Jason Roy smashed it everywhere, delivering a great start, which got them back to repeating their efforts of earlier in the tournament. The bottom line is, he did that not because of a team meeting, but because Roy is an excellent player. Yes, as a captain or coach you have to monitor the collective spirit of the players, but the key will always be how good they are. I've played in teams with a great work ethic who loved each other. But actually, when I analyse it, the best Kent sides in terms of getting on with one another were the worst teams I've played in. I would listen to people saying 'What a great team spirit you've got' and think, 'Yes, but we're crap. I've got no one to open the bowling.'

A lot of people outside professional sport think achievement comes from being a family and loving each other. Sadly not. The idea that everyone in a team will get on is simply unrealistic. In any occupation, people don't always enjoy being with the other people they work with. You are in a dressing room because you are good at something, not because you are friends with people. One of the biggest myths in sport is that you all have to get on. My view is that the better teams actually have the most friction. To be the best in the world, a player has to be driven, and they can't let anyone get in the way of that. Tiger Woods would have been one of the worst team players ever. His Ryder Cup record suggests just that. But he is one of the greatest sportsmen of all time.

Good players achieve. Get the right ones and they will drive the culture and ethos because they've got ambition. Look at the England team that won the 2005 Ashes. Marcus Trescothick is one of the best players England have ever had, Kevin Pietersen the same. Michael Vaughan was one of the best captains in history. So many of that side have ended up on the all-time runs list for England, and that streak of brilliance is what won us the urn in 2005.

None of us who had witnessed KP's staggering thirst for self-improvement could ever have been surprised that he reached such levels of brilliance. Early on, he was sitting with the other players in and around the England set-up when he suddenly announced he was off to watch that summer's visitors, Pakistan, play in a warm-up game.

'Does anyone want to come?' he enquired.

The rest of us were adamant: 'No thanks, Kev, we're going for frappuccinos.'

We asked why he was so keen on watching a low-key, warm-up game attended by one man and his dog.

'I'm not sure how I'm going to play their left-armer, Tanvir,' he explained.

And I looked at him, thinking, 'That's why you're the best, because you're starting to think about how you're going to play Pakistan two weeks from now and working out a plan.'

Make no mistake, KP worked bloody hard. The switch-hit he developed came from him spending hours just standing in a net and hitting left-handed, shot after shot. This, bear in mind, was just after he'd been binned as captain, a time when the head might have dipped, but KP's desire to make himself an even more devastating player never waned. For me, it was amazing to see how someone on a different plane from everyone else worked. Perhaps some of his apartness came from his frustration with others not being able to do the same; their inability to apply themselves in a manner comparable to him. Two days on an army assault course wasn't going to fix that.

Take the best players out of any team and it will struggle. Australia are a case in point. They can wax lyrical about their culture but in that series they had two bowlers who were among the best who ever lived. When one of them, Glenn McGrath, stood on the ball in the warm-up and injured himself ahead of the Edgbaston Test, they lost. The game before, at Lord's, he'd taken nine wickets and they'd won.

What most people want – and it's the same in many walks of life – is to reach the top of the tree, with the kudos and the money that comes from that position. Focusing on oneself doesn't have to entail getting in the way of the people around you; that's just common decency. And a captain or coach should try to shepherd everyone in the right way so there's no friction, but ultimately you have to understand that those people are there because they are the eleven best available individuals to do one thing, not because they're nice people. It's a matter of absolute fact that some of the best players are complete gits – but that's probably why they're the best players.

We have this view that in any sport, those at the top have to get on. Much better to accept that actually, it's more than likely they won't. Look at Alex Ferguson. You can't tell me that all the players in the Manchester United dressing room across his twenty-six years in charge were mates. Chances are, some of them never even spoke to each other. But the first thing he said at his testimonial game, which featured some of the greats from his all-conquering sides, was, 'Look at the talent I had around me to work with.' Steve Jobs said the same: 'You've got to be the best talent scout you can.' And yet, you still have these coaches carping on about culture and how all the players get on and they've done this and done that together. No. You get the best players you can and your skill is then making them all work, in their own way, for the same goal. Poor man managers are so blinkered that they treat everyone the same way. They want to believe that people want to win for each other. Wrong. Only by truthfully putting yourself in another person's shoes can you really start to understand how to motivate them.

Everyone works with people they don't like. It's important to step back sometimes and recognise the situation is about nothing more than that they see things differently, that they are removed from you as a character. It doesn't mean you need to engage in a medieval feud, lay siege to their corner of the dressing room, or give stories about them to the press.

In the same way, it's important to note there's a difference between piss-taking and malicious intent. If someone is being horrible to you, stand up for yourself. If somebody is having a few jokes at your expense and it is done in good humour, then that is different. Learn to take it, whoever you are, because a dressing room is a very hard place to be if you're going to take offence all the time.

Take Swanny, who was a very good mimic. So good, in fact, he could fool people into thinking he really was someone else. We were bored in an Under-19 game so got Swanny to ring Dave Fulton, who was having his best year yet at Kent, purporting to be David Lloyd, who was coach of England at the time.

'You're playing so well, David,' Swanny told him in Bumble's familiar Lancashire brogue. 'You're getting closer and closer to playing for England.'

So convincing was Swanny that we felt a bit bad about Dave maybe taking it seriously and rang him later to tell him it wasn't actually Bumble but the idiot spinner from Northants. At no point was that anything more than a joke, and it was seen as such by all sides.

People like Swanny, Fred and me never meant any offence. We wanted people to take the mick out of us back as much as anything else. Those who take offence, most people don't want to be around anyway. Who wants to be around someone who gets offended all the time? A lot of people seem to wake up offended, just waiting for the next thing to offend them – even more so nowadays when they can have a good moan about it on social media.

Those who are properly malicious aren't hard to identify. They don't direct their nonsense towards their mates, they pick on those who are easy targets, and at that point it is just bullying. Any player, at any level, can be guilty of that. You have to remember that people are at different stages of their careers. If, as an old cynical pro, Andrew Symonds, for example, told me to hustle up a bit in the field, I, as a mate, would turn round and tell him where to go. If he said that to an 18-year-old just making his way, then chances are they are going to take it slightly differently. Talk to people in a way that indicates you want the best for them, not as if you are just being superior or horrible.

Also, take a look round sometimes. In a cricket dressing room, you know people better than their wives, their mums, their dads. In that environment, with the pressure, the inescapability of the closeness, the sheer amount of time spent in one another's company, you see what people are really like. I had teammates I played with for years who I probably went out socially with twice. Others I'd see every night. You are thrown together because you are eleven skilled people, not because you are eleven mates. Remember that and recognise that everyone, not just you, is living that life, and the person who has become the object of your ire, that maverick in the corner, perhaps, or that bloke with the rancid feet, might not seem quite so bad.

When you think about what it takes to be a great sportsperson, an elite sportsperson, actually it's going to be very hard for everyone to mould together. The best players I've ever seen are generally the most selfish. They may be great people, but ultimately, they are selfish. And that's the great thing about cricket – if your personal ambition is to be as great as you possibly can be, that will only help the team. Put together eleven people with a selfish agenda and you've got a chance of being the best team on earth.

Again, it's the same in many other fields. The ones who are at the top are the ones who are ruthless. The rest of us who didn't get there, somewhere down the line that has to be because we didn't make that same level of sacrifice. We might have had a good level of talent but so do a lot of people. It's the ones who are prepared to be steely along the way who succeed. That doesn't mean they have to be horrible about it. A person can fit in and try not to get in the way of anyone else, but deep down, when it matters, they have always been the ones prepared to make the extra sacrifices.

Nowadays, most clubs, international or county, offer sports psychologists to help cricketers make the most of themselves, comprehend their strengths and weaknesses, and how to address them. They have been intrinsic in many players reaching an understanding about themselves and their surroundings. When I started out, psychologists weren't involved in cricket to the same extent. We did have psychologists at Kent, but it was a fairly casual arrangement and wasn't always my cup of tea. In those early days, I found them a bit like salesmen pushing a one-size-fits-all agenda. Now I think they are much better, woven into the fabric of clubs, and there to help the individual, but when I was around they would give a speech to twenty of us at a time. That can't possibly work. I would imagine the first rule of psychology is that everybody is different.

I always believed I needed something real, based on evidence, to make me think. I couldn't stand chat based entirely around emotion. When I went out to Perth to see the batting coach Noddy Holder, I was introduced to an expert on the brain. He told me about hemispheres, how the left hemisphere of the brain is the statistical and analytical side that we use for the everyday mechanics of life, while the right side harbours creativity. As the left side of the brain pieces together nose, eyes and mouth, and allows me to recognise, unfortunately, Steve Harmison, the right hemisphere allows me to bat, because it is the talent side, and can give me the speed of thought I need on the pitch. That, to me, was brilliant.

He asked me a question: 'Did you ever hum a tune when you were playing?'

'Yes,' I replied, 'when I was a kid I used to do that all the time.'

'Why don't you do that now?'

'Because I can't. I'm supposed to be a professional sportsman. Humming isn't concentrating.'

'No, no,' he explained, 'that is concentration. If you are humming you are operating on the right side of your brain. You have to practise being on that side more. You have to fight those statistical, analytical, technical thoughts. Use them when you're on a bowling machine when you want to groove technique, otherwise get rid of them from your mind. Humming is a way of doing so.'

To this day, it's the best advice I've ever had. I didn't need any more. I'd been told from a scientific point of view what I needed to do and why, whereas if someone had turned round and told me about positive thinking, put me in a workshop with fifteen others all day, or made me carry a brick for 20 miles through a wood, it would have meant nothing. I needed a core reason why I should act in a certain way. I needed proof. I'm not a religious person for that very reason. There was science behind what he was telling me.

I'm not saying there isn't a role for sports psychologists. I believe their true value comes from the ability to listen, a quality that I also found in physios. Players sometimes need to unburden themselves, to rid themselves of simple fears. What people generally want to know in a team is that they're not on their own. When Murali played his first four-day game for Kent, he didn't get a wicket in the first innings.

'Keysy,' he implored me, 'tell everyone I'm trying.'

He was genuinely concerned that the other players might think he wasn't bothered about the county game. If a bloke capable of taking 800 Test wickets can have doubts, then I'm sure the rest of us are allowed to have them too.

Swanny was different again. Even as a kid, he always had that little bit of arrogance, and I thought that was great, but I knew also that not everyone feels the same. People can have a very different perspective on the same thing. I would often see players from Pakistan, for instance, whose outlook on life was totally different to some middle-class kid from England. They behaved not like they wanted success, more that they needed it.

Alliances build naturally in teams, they cannot be forced. Look at those four spearhead bowlers – Simon Jones, Matthew Hoggard, Harmy and Fred – who took the attack to the Aussies in 2005. They were all big mates. And they all had one thing in common: they were very unassuming. Together they shared the same ethos – no bullshit. If a person wasn't real, they didn't want to be around them. They had so much respect for each other. Wasim Akram and Waqar Younis were always trying to outdo each other, but those four never were. They had a bond back then, and they always will, because together they went through so much. Don't get me wrong; it's not like they've been in a war, but they have done those hard yards that only a bowler knows about, staring down the barrel of a thirtieth over on a hot day, on a flat pitch, doing nothing, while a batsman like Matthew Hayden smashes them everywhere. They had been through all that hardship together.

Wasim hit me on the head twice before I got to ten in my second first-class game for Kent. He had a horrible bouncer. You could see in his action what he was going to do, but he had such a fast arm, it made no difference. He would trot in and spit the ball out right at you. None of us in the Kent side found this hugely easy to deal with – except one. While the rest of us struggled to get a bat on it, Carl Hooper would block, block, block, and then do something remarkable. On this occasion, as I watched dumbfounded at the other end, he lifted Wasim into the scoreboard at Canterbury. He did so with no real pick-up.

Hoops was a proper genius, trusting his talent in the starkest of ways, never wearing a full helmet, just earpieces. It was said that against the real quicks like Allan Donald, he'd contemplate putting the grill on, but never actually did. In fact, a lot of the time when he played Donald he'd do so in a floppy hat. Hoops had no extravagant head movement. If Donald gave him a bouncer, he'd just move inside with inimitable grace.

The man could do things that we mere mortals had no choice but to sit back and marvel at. Batting against Saqlain Mushtaq at The Oval, none of us could pick his doosra, but Hoops got 90-odd. I asked him how he picked him. It turned out he couldn't. He was so good at coming down the wicket to play spin, it just didn't matter. The Kent bowler Alan Igglesden once batted with him in the tail and rather than taking a single at the end of the over to keep the strike, Hoops would chip threes. It was as if he was playing at a different level to everyone else.

Playing in the same team as Hoops was the first time I'd encountered such a remarkably gifted player, and one who so acutely, so obviously, didn't need to don the cloak of togetherness. Hoops had been at Kent for a while at that point, in the days when overseas players didn't just play for a season but stayed a few years. Early on, I wasn't convinced he knew my name. If he wanted to move me in the field, he would just click his fingers. Against Glamorgan, John Wright sent me and Hoops on a run down the Taff River. By now, I knew for sure he had no idea who I was, but, as we were jogging along, then doing a few sit-ups, he began talking about how cricket mirrors life: how you are as a player reflects how you are as a person.

'If you're a fighter or a battler,' he reckoned, 'then you won't be an elegant batsman.' That was his view, and it fitted like a glove.

As with many sporting geniuses, there had to be some leeway made for Hoops. While he was as talented as they come, it always felt as if there was a piece missing in his make-up. The captain, Steve Marsh, allowed him to do his own thing to some degree. He wasn't, for instance, going to train with us all the time. He was quite elusive from that point of view. Also, if the motor racing was on TV, his concentration could be lacking – he loved his cars. That was all right so long as things were going OK, but it caused a bit of a ruckus in the dressing room with the senior players later on in the year when we weren't playing particularly well. Hoops was at the point where he was just starting to have had enough of county cricket. I batted with him at Worcester and he didn't look at all interested.

'Are you all right, Hoops?' I asked him (by now, he did actually know who I was).

'I swipe today,' he said in that West Indian accent. I got out for 10, by which point he'd got 70. He went on to get a hundred off fifty balls. When he wanted to, he could destroy anyone. By the end, I imagine Hoops got frustrated with the rest of us because, maybe like KP, we couldn't do what he could. He saw the game so clearly.

Point is, you have to understand where everyone comes from and what makes them tick. There are ways and means, on a human level, of doing so. Blindfolding people and putting them on a plank? What are we thinking? What were they thinking? I know what I was thinking: 'Sod this.'

Chapter 3

People from Australia

Early in my career, the athlete Roger Black came to Kent. He spoke about being the best you can and to illustrate the theme held up his 400m silver medal from the Atlanta Olympics. His point was that he ran his best race. No matter what he did, there was no way he could beat the absolute legend that was Michael Johnson, by some distance the finest 400m runner the world has ever seen.

'This,' he declared, 'is my gold medal.'

The room went quiet while we considered what he'd said. And then, shattering the silence, a voice.

'It's f***ing silver, mate.'

Ladies and gentlemen, Andrew Symonds. Competitive Australian.

There are certain things about Australians that can make them mildly annoying. An overwhelming self-confidence is one of them. An extremely high opinion of themselves is another. As a young player, on the advice of Alec Stewart – one of my absolute heroes, who had seen me aimlessly wandering round half-cut at the Professional Cricketers' Association Awards and, quite reasonably, enquired what I was thinking of doing to improve myself as a player – I had travelled out to play club cricket in Perth. From the minute I walked into the dressing room it was an education. Not only did the Aussies have a great Test team and strong Shield competition, but every club cricketer thought they were Shane Warne or Matthew Hayden. Early on, a medium pacer, who'd played a bit of first and second-grade cricket, asked me if my club back in England needed an overseas player.

'Yes, mate, maybe.' I said.

'Great! First-class cricket!'

I thought he'd meant my old club side, Beckenham. With a typical Aussie lack of self-effacement, he immediately thought I was talking about Kent.

'No, mate,' I countered. 'We've got Rahul Dravid next year. We're not having you!'

But that's the way Aussies think. Their default setting is that they are just better. I'd turn up for practice and, with no compunction at all, not even the slightest recognition that I'd played first-class cricket in England, they'd put me in the third-grade net. The flipside of that was that for me to go out there and fend for myself when their preconceived idea was I was crap was a massive learning curve, as it is for any player still doing the same now.

When it came to an actual game, even a bit of a knockabout, they took everything so seriously. Aussies don't entertain the thought of 'a bit of fun'. They have to do everything at 100 per cent. We had one game where the opposition had a big bloke batting at number eleven who kept smoking our opening bowler into the seats. The bowler, unimpressed, took it upon himself to try to hit him with a bouncer, which he did, prompting the tailender to throw down his gloves and lump him three times. This was middle-of-the-road league cricket. It didn't need an umpire; it needed a referee and a bell to mark the end of each round.

The English cricketing authorities, clearly sick of the national team being roundly trounced by the men from Down Under, thought it would be a good idea if England's emerging talent was schooled the Australian way. Hence England's new Academy in Adelaide.

Fred, who I already knew from the England Under-19s, was on the trip, as were, among other notable names, Harmy, Straussy and Swanny.

The aforementioned Andrew Symonds and his fellow Kent Aussie, Mike Hussey, had warned me about Rod Marsh, having both been through the Australian Academy under his charge.

'Don't take Rod Marsh on,' was the message, 'because he will really punish you. He's a hard man and doesn't take to people giving him lip.'

Arriving at the Academy, all seemed good. The staff and coaches were friendly, telling us about the logistics of the place, and generally helping us to settle in. At the end of the welcome, the physio, Kurt Russell, happened to mention that Robbie Williams was playing in town on Saturday and asked if anybody wanted to go.

'Who the f*** is Robbie Williams?' asked Rod, a man possibly better attuned to the stars of the 1970s.

Swanny provided the answer. 'He's a f***ing singer, you Aussie c***t' – an interesting way to introduce yourself to the man who's going to be your taskmaster for the next three months.

The look on Rod's face and the tone of purple he was turning told Swanny that perhaps he had slightly overstepped the mark. Realising the extent of his error, he backed down very quickly and tried to explain who Robbie was, how he used to be in Take That, referencing a couple of his songs. It was a clawback of epic proportions, but fair to say that from that moment on, Swanny had his card marked.

As I sniggered on the inside – no way were any of us going to let Rod see how hilarious this all was – I didn't realise my name would soon be firmly lodged inside Rod's head too. Rod was actually a big mate of the then Kent coach John Wright, their careers having overlapped at international level. Early on at the Academy, John sent me an email asking me how I was going.

'I'll be running the place soon,' I told him, tongue firmly in cheek. 'Rod's easy to manipulate. He's a piece of cake.' As soon as John read it, he forwarded it straight to Rod. I didn't know any of this until I made my debut for England. At which point Rod sent me that very email. He'd had it the whole time.

Rod was hard. And that was what he deemed necessary. He didn't bring with him technical knowledge, he wasn't there to tell players how to bat or bowl, but he knew what it took to get to the very top. His Australian Academy had been ultra-successful, on occasion even beating the full England touring side. Some phenomenal players, including Adam Gilchrist, had been through the system Rod had set up. No wonder he was seen as the perfect man to come in and toughen up English cricket. He wasn't going to shy away from confrontation, tell people what they wanted to hear. Swanny would experience that more than most. Following the Robbie Williams incident, Rod would jump straight down his throat at every opportunity. On one occasion after we had lost a game, Rod said he wanted everybody to practise slip catching.

'I don't think the bowlers should have to do that,' countered Swanny, fearful of finger injuries, at which point Rod erupted.

'Why the f*** not?'

We all jumped out of our skins. Not only didn't Rod take any prisoners, but he was also the first real coach most of us had come across who would swear.

You could always spot someone who was putting on an act to give you a bollocking – Rod Marsh was not one of them. He would absolutely do it as himself. You knew it was him because you knew who he was. He wasn't acting. He wasn't putting on a voice. It was just him. Who he was. When you get people screaming and shouting when you know it's not in their nature, it loses its impact.

Whereas some people might have thought Rod was difficult or hard work, he was actually just striving to make us better. He was a great motivator. Always, always, with Rod, you knew he cared deeply for improving players. Whenever we had a game he would walk around the ground while the play was on. We'd hear him chuntering away. If one of our bowlers went down the leg side and was clipped for four, that was it, off he'd go – 'For f***'s sake!'

He treated us in such a way that we desperately wanted his respect. For him to say 'Well done' meant he really thought you could play – not that

Rod ever really issued praise, and nor did I ever feel I needed to seek it. Players knew whether he liked and respected them from the way he behaved. 'Feedback' and 'praise' are buzzwords in coaching, but it's not always useful or necessary to be so overt. When I got 170 against the Australian Academy, Rod shook my hand.

'You should have got 200,' he told me.

That wasn't a criticism; it was his way of telling me I was a better player than I was giving out. Rod might have been tough, but he was also a good man, very fair, who knew his cricket, and did whatever he could to ensure others reached their full potential.

In Ian Chappell, he had brought another hard man of Australian cricket into the Academy. The batsmen did an indoor session with him where he had Harmy, Freddie and Simon Jones throwing balls at our heads from 18 yards. It was the most daunting session I've ever faced – as terrifying as it was exhilarating. Another time, we had to play spin without our pads on, forcing us to use the bat, to hone technique. Ian was ahead of his time. This was well before DRS, when everyone would use their legs to pad the ball away.

The Academy felt like a proper boot camp with us effectively having to do Rod's sessions and then the England Academy programme on top of that. We started at seven in the morning with anything from a run to a lecture, and finished at eight at night with a lesson on sports science. So full-on was it that I used to set my alarm at lunch, go to sleep for an hour, and wake up to face whatever was coming in the afternoon. But Rod's approach at the Academy mirrored that of the Australian team: absolutely no nonsense. One day he had a go at us because, unlike the lads in the Australian Academy, none of us had been sick in training – a sure-fire sign someone has pushed themselves to the absolute limit. In my head I turned that round: Well, if we haven't been sick that means we're fitter than the Aussies! The accuracy of my conclusion remains open to question, but again Rod's message hit home. That afternoon, me and Fred did some boxing training.

'He's got a point there,' noted Fred of Rod's vomit-related observation. That session he took his intensity to another level, to a point where he was almost in tears. From that moment on, as much as Fred played hard, he trained hard as well, the result being he got himself so fit – a level that he maintained through the peak years of his career.

I liked Rod's and Ian's attitude because there was no in-between. You're either good or you're bad. You're either doing the right thing or you're not. You're either toeing the line or you aren't. There is no middle ground where people dance around what they think, which only brings mixed messages and confusion.

I never really imagined that the next time a senior England team would visit Australia, for the Ashes in 2002/03, I would be on the plane. Originally, Graham Thorpe was set to play after time off for personal issues but then, at the last minute, he pulled out. My call-up was a sign of continuity of selection. England wanted to get away from the time where a player got two Test matches. They wanted to stick with seven or eight players and give them a good go. It was one of Nasser's and Fletcher's big things. So, after a decent performance against India in the summer Test series, there I was, aged 23, on an Ashes tour. I would need every bit of the resilience Rod had put in my head.

There were so many firsts on that trip it was almost like a running joke in my head. I sat out the first match in Brisbane but the second Test in Adelaide was the first time I'd faced Glenn McGrath.

'Jesus, here we go,' I thought, heading to the crease. 'Glenn McGrath, what's this going to be like?' I soon found out. Glenn bowled a ball outside off stump. I left it.

'Nothing to worry about here, that's fine.'

Then he bowled another one in exactly the same place. Again, great.

'What's the big deal about this bloke?' I thought. 'He isn't rapid, he doesn't really move the ball, he has an action I can see, doesn't particularly sledge. It's not like he's Wasim Akram.'

The next ball was in exactly the same spot.

And the next.

And the next.

And that, I realised, was his trick. He just never bowled a bad ball. And the fact he never missed his line or length meant Steve Waugh could set a field of five or six slips and wait for the edge. At the other end, meanwhile, was Shane Warne. Together they put one hand each round the batsman's neck and strangled him with their brilliance.

If it had stopped with McGrath and Warne, it might not have been so bad, but their system meant that truly exceptional ability was all through the side because, while the Australian board was edging towards central contracts, as utilised by England, getting picked for the national team was, quite literally, the only way to make a good living out of cricket. If you were at the top of the tree you got paid well; anywhere else, you got very little. In fact, a lot of very good Australian cricketers had other jobs – fitness trainers, firemen, policemen. Players such as Justin Langer knew that if they were going to make a career as a professional cricketer, they had to play for Australia.

Subsequently, he did everything he could to maintain his position. He was as fit as anyone. If there was a tour to India coming up he would practise in the nets in four jumpers. The Australians' desire to win and stay at the pinnacle of the game put them on a different level. Since central contracts, Australia have produced good players, but nothing like in that golden era.

In their own backyard, with Steve Waugh in their side, it was hard to see how you could possibly beat them. Waugh played for two people. He and Mark were the Waugh twins – they might as well have been triplets. And then you had Gilchrist coming in at number seven.

The players who couldn't get in the Australian side said as much about its strength as those who were in it. In a warm-up game we played against Martin Love, who got 200 not out in the first innings and a century in the second. I stood there in the field (for quite some time) and thought to myself, 'How on earth are we going to beat the best Australian Test team, with Hayden, Langer, Ponting, and the rest, when we can't even get a bloke out who can't get in the squad?'

I liked to relax in the field, get into the tempo of the game, but with the Australians there was no chance of that happening. When Hayden in particular was batting, it was like being in a one-day match every ball. With some batsmen, you know they will leave the ball or pat it back to the bowler. You can switch off a bit. With Hayden, you never felt like that, ever. He was such a bully that relaxation wasn't an option – it was going to come at you hard at some stage and you had to be on your guard. You were permanently on edge, so drained by the end of the game. The only way to avoid physical and mental devastation was to get him early, which is where you needed your plans to come to fruition. At Melbourne, Nasser's theory was that Hayden was going to take the bowling on – not a difficult assumption to make; he pretty much always took the bowling on – so when Matthew Hoggard was given the first over, Nasser was insistent that whoever was at fine leg should hug the boundary in case he offered a top edge. It was Harmy who trotted off down to that position and as I watched him, I just knew there was no way he'd remember to stay on the rope. The MCG is a massive ground and he would come in a little because he'd be worried about saving the two. Also, Harmy had the baying mob of Bay 13 immediately behind him. Liable to receive either a volley of abuse or something a little more solid, it would be understandable if he edged a little way in. I was almost tempted to shout to Harmy to stay back, but by then, Hoggy was already running in. No prizes for guessing what happened next. Hoggy bowled Hayden a short one, he swung at it, and a top edge sailed straight over Harmy's head and bounced before the boundary for four. I hardly dared look at Nasser but when I did, he was absolutely seething. As a fielder in club cricket, where there's nobody there to call you up for it, if you make the same mistake you always call it as six to make it look like there was nothing you could have done. Otherwise you look a complete tool for walking in too far – one of the cardinal sins of cricket. When you're playing for England, however, you can't get away with it so easy. As much as Harmy must have wanted to signal six, instead he had to soak up Nasser's glares for the rest of the day.

Hayden, naturally, never gave another chance, certainly not to where I was standing for some of that day, a ridiculous drive position, mid-off, but 11 yards from the bat, like in Under-10s. Whenever anyone asked who wanted to field in that spot I would always put my hand up because the ball was never going to go there. Also, with the MCG being so large, being close in was definitely better than being in the outfield. It was so big I knew I couldn't throw the ball in from the boundary. I would just stand there in this no man's land position and watch the likes of Hayden smash us everywhere.

No doubt about it, they were the greatest team of my lifetime. People talk about the West Indies sides of the 1970s and 80s, but I would be amazed if there's ever been a better side than that Australian one. They had everything – great bowlers, incredible batsmen, and a wicketkeeper who changed the position forever.

Before that Australian team, Test cricket was 200 in a day. How boring must that have been? And then, all of a sudden, the Aussies were scoring 400 in a day. They revolutionised the game.

I asked Steve Waugh once, 'Did you have a plan to do that?'

'No,' he replied, 'we just told people to express themselves.' Freedom to play unlocks the shackles of fear.

Steve's side was front and centre of a time of great evolution for batting. The difference was intent. That intent has now spread throughout the system. People say that's down to T20. I would say it's actually down to Australian cricket – Hayden, Langer, Matthew Slater … players like them. And that was what England worked out when they finally beat Australia in 2005. England beat Australia because of Australia. Before then, Test cricket was about batting time and then scoring runs. The equation then became, scoring runs equals time. The game has never been the same since. Draws in Test cricket have gone out the window.

I made scores of one and one in that first Test. Eager to get off the mark in the next match at Perth, I bolted up the other end, only to slip on the rock-hard square and land bang on my coccyx, and, believe me, that really hurts.

I was jumping up and down, desperately trying not to show any pain in the middle of an Ashes Test match. And it was then that Warney came up to me.

'Hey, you idiot,' he told me, 'run on the grass.' Which was good of him. Once he got to know me a bit better, I'm sure he'd have let me do it again and again.

Not that there was much generosity of spirit from anywhere else. The Australian public never let up. Get in a taxi and the driver would pipe up, 'Any chance of a competition? We just want to see a contest.'

It got to the point where it was patronising. I'd be sat in the back with a fixed grin thinking, 'Oh, just f*** off mate.' Batting practice was no better? Two feet away they'd be hammering you from the back of the net.

It's in situations like this where Darren Gough came into his own. Goughy was blessed with an innate confidence. When we got to Australia he was the one who stuck his chest out. He didn't hide in a corner. As the Aussie public did their usual thing of telling the England team they were going to beat us and that we were crap, he would just look them in the face and meet them head on. In his mind, if he was with an England team going out to Australia, he was the one who was going to get them all out. He was the one who turned up on the trip believing 'I'm going to win the Ashes', while the rest of us were thinking, 'Hmm, we're going to have to play well if we're going to get anything out of this.'

And then, of course, Goughy was gone. He and another massive heart, Freddie, had both travelled Down Under in hope rather than expectation. Both carrying significant injuries, neither made it across the line in the end. Goughy was always going to be a big miss. He was hilarious, the bloke who kept everyone else going, to the extent there was an argument for keeping him around even when he was injured.

Some have described him as the gift that just keeps giving, and they're not wrong. We did a charity bike ride together once. He was the perfect companion, the sort of bloke you could sit alongside all day and would keep you highly entertained. The ride was from Truro to London, so not without its challenges. Classic Goughy, before we set off he rang me up and told me how he'd got the best bike for the job.

'It's amazing, Keysy, electric gears, everything.' He wasn't wrong. When he turned up at the start, it looked like something off the Starship *Enterprise*.

Off we went, getting on OK until we got to the first steep hill. We were done for. None of us could get up it. Even Goughy had to get off and walk. Most of us were ready to admit that maybe we weren't quite as fit or adept on a bike as we might have been. Not Goughy.

'It's set up for a pro,' he told us, 'so that makes the gearing more difficult.'

In Australia, there was, however, only so much he could do. His one-man band didn't have the circulation of the Aussie newspapers. At the press conference when we landed, Nasser made a point of saying how we would have to field well and take our catches. Of course, at our first practice session, the *West Australian* newspaper then took pictures of our players dropping the one catch in fifty they spilled to try to make us look totally inept. On other occasions, we didn't help ourselves. The tour opener was, as tradition stated, at Lilac Hill – always a potential embarrassment as the opposition, a Western Australian XI, generally included a few long-retired Aussie legends who should have been well past offering a threat. I still remember Nasser's pre-match speech about playing every game hard, setting the tone of the tour early. As such, he told Hoggy to bowl a bouncer first ball.

'Try to hit the batsman,' he implored the Yorkshireman, 'no matter who it is. It could be Richie Benaud striding out to the crease, it doesn't matter. We want to show we're out here to win.'

'Bloody hell!' I thought. 'Here we go! We're going to set a marker down here.'

It was a fast, bouncy pitch, Hoggy had the new ball in his hand, and we all knew it was going to be a bouncer. It would hit the batsman and we would really have set out our stall.

In ran Hoggy, puffing, blowing, giving his all. There it was – the bouncer. And there was Mike Hussey, ducking, quite effortlessly, under the ball. And that was it. We hadn't really discussed what to do if the ball didn't hit the batsman.

Eventually, with a couple of wickets down, David Hookes came out. A cult hero of the seventies, Hookes had been retired for years. Stood at deep midwicket, I looked on as he promptly smashed Ashley Giles into a marquee.

'We're on an Ashes tour,' I thought to myself, 'and here's David Hookes, aged 46, smashing us round with impunity.'

If that wasn't bad enough, the crowd had been on the lash since half ten in the morning, right on top of us from the start, giving us dog's abuse. As we slid to inevitable defeat, I realised, 'Jesus, we're in for a hard tour,' a thought only emphasised when someone shook my hand and said, 'Hello, I'm Adam Gilchrist.'

'I know who you are!' I thought. 'I've been watching you destroy opposition attacks for years.' He was a player and person I deeply admired.

For Nasser and other players of his era this was their last and only real chance to do something against the Aussies. The previous winter, they had won against the odds in Pakistan and now this was their opportunity to do the same in Australia and win the Ashes, the Holy Grail of cricket. But Australia weren't Pakistan. They weren't prone to wobbles, they didn't have players who were brilliant but unpredictable. Australia were a perfect block of precious stone that refused to be chiselled. By the end of that tour, the scars of previous Ashes battles had not been healed but deepened.

Myself, I went back to Kent thinking I had the game worked out.

'All you need to do,' I told our captain, Dave Fulton, 'is bowl like Glenn McGrath. Just stick it outside off stump and put seven slips in.'

He pointed out a flaw in the plan.

We didn't have Glenn McGrath.

Chapter 4

No One Gives a F*** in China

'Here's another one to steal the food out of my baby's mouth.'
I walked into the Kent dressing room for the first time aged 16. Not everyone was pleased to see me, particularly the second team captain. His words were harsh, but probably to my benefit. Very quickly I understood this was a cut-throat environment. In fact, the second team was a harder schooling than the first. Everyone was so insecure, a load of young upstarts trying to make it, combined with a bunch of cynical senior players who had been dropped from the upper tier. The next step for them was the trapdoor.

The Kent coach, John Wright, had a saying: 'No one gives a f*** in China.' What he meant was, ultimately, no one cares. It's up to you. You have a decision to make: either you front up or you run away.

The more you are put in that position at a young age, the better. If you have been protected all the way to 18, it's probably too late. Sometimes with your kids you wonder if you are trying to give them so much they won't be ready for when people give them nothing. My parents did everything they possibly could for me when it came to cricket. They drove me everywhere and would come and watch me. I am of course hugely grateful for their amazing help, but there was also a part of me that knew I had to take responsibility for myself. Terrible as it sounds, it started to annoy me that they would watch me all the time, to the extent that sometimes I would tell them I was playing at Dover when actually I was playing a home game in Beckenham. I'm sure people will think that's awful, and I understand why, but actually I was entirely right in seeking that independence.

As a kid, all I wanted to do was play cricket, and I never doubted that was exactly what I was going to do for a living. Teachers would tell me, 'You can't concentrate on cricket,' and I would say, 'Why not?' It was that self-same arrogance that meant I was never any better than a C-grade student. Now I have more interest in other areas of life, but as a kid was single-minded and blinkered.

I might not have been academic, but I was lucky to have a relatively sharp wit that got me by, honed in the dressing room, where it can be a necessity to grow up quickly. At Beckenham, the motto was, 'When somebody is down, kick them in the bollocks' – and that was on your own team. It was a pretty ruthless environment. Even if a fellow player was a good mate, you couldn't wait for them to get out so you could give them some abuse. And that was all a hugely relevant experience – an A-level in sporting life.

In a dressing room, with all the piss-taking and to and fro, you have to develop a tough skin. With my own kids, whatever path they may choose, that's one thing I want them to have – resilience to what life throws at them and confidence in what they can do. A lot of young people are very protected, and that means that, first day of work, they're going to get chewed up. In any walk of life, and especially sport, a young person is quickly going to realise they are not the best, they are not a superstar, and they are not going to get what they want simply because their parents are kicking up a stink. Which happens. As captain at Kent I had players whose parents would get involved, unhappy that their son wasn't getting much cricket in the first team. Very quickly I made it clear to those players that they were adults now. Parents can't fight their battles out in the middle. They can't intervene, have a quick word with the bowler, ask him to go easy, when he's trying to knock their head off.

Occasionally, parents would complain to the committee, at which point I would tell the player concerned that if it happened again while I was captain they would never ever play for Kent again. That wasn't me being horrible. Players have to learn, very, very swiftly, that to be 18 at school and to be 18 in professional sport is not the same thing. In professional sport you need to stand on your own two feet and face up. Any young player whose parents haven't taught them that by the time they reach county cricket is going to have a few rude awakenings.

Playing adult sport from a young age, 13 or 14, was a massive advantage for me when it came to the toughening up process. Very quickly I learned the game, and about the dressing room that goes with it. That was a definite plus compared to those kids who played only at school until they left and then found the adult dressing room an alien environment. It's another reason why I'm a big believer in kids being thrown in at the deep end. I hated it when I started at 14 playing club cricket with men, not being able to hit it off the square, knowing full well I was costing the team. I didn't get a fifty for pretty much the whole season until I finally got one in the last two games. Up to that point, I genuinely thought, 'What am I doing here?' But what that experience gave me was the resilience to do it again in the future. It taught me that while a struggle wasn't a particularly nice place to be in, I could come through. I had to learn that lesson myself. My mum and dad weren't going to help me, much as I wanted them to. I may not have realised it, but actually I was lucky that I had a captain who kept throwing me in there, and who would talk to me afterwards as well, giving me the knowledge of how to improve and the ability to put that knowledge to the test.

There was another element to this: being in a dressing room makes you have to get to know people. You can only sit in a corner for so long. You have to chuck yourself into that environment. At Kent, card games were going on all the time, mainly seven-and-a-halves, a form of blackjack, and I was soon taught how to gamble alongside the more senior players at the table. It was something else that helped me fit in, but again, not without the odd lesson hard learnt. We were playing at Leicester once and in a rain break, Min Patel proceeded to clean me out at three-card brag. I lost £377. I had two sevens, he had three of a kind. I thought he was bluffing. I wrote him out a cheque for £370. He ripped it up.

'No, Keysy, £377.'

John Wright banned me from gambling after that, because £377 was a lot of money. But I knew as a person I was changing. I could feel it in myself and I could see it all around me. My mates were struggling to pay for a pint in the pub and there I was with a salary. When I wasn't learning for myself, others would help me out. Every now and again, a mentor would take me under their wing and teach me about various characters – who to be wary of, the ones to ignore, the ones who grass teammates up. The dressing room taught me about human life, human character.

Wrighty was a fantastic bloke and an excellent coach. He wanted me to challenge myself properly. Early on, he came down to talk to me in the nets. He wasn't particularly happy. He thought I had talent but was a bit lazy. He gave me a dressing down.

'Your mark isn't the guys at Kent,' he told me, 'it's the likes of Carl Hooper, Mike Hussey, Matt Hayden.'

At the same time, his way of batting was that your wicket was your life and that was what he put on to us as a batting group. A lot of good came out of that, but for some people it requires a change and at that point you can end up overthinking – the worst thing any player can do. Cricket is a career on fast forward. A player is young only until 24 or 25, at which point they very quickly become a senior player. The real trick is being stubborn enough not to back too far away from the principles of what you did while on the way up. So many players, however, including me, end up doing the opposite. That naïvety, that innocence of youth, I wish I'd never lost. I wish I could have kept that mindset from my early days, rather than keep analysing my game as I got older. The first few years of my career, I thought I was going to walk into Kent, walk into England, and everything was going to be easy. Some may think that's a bad attitude, but actually, I think it's the best one. As a sportsperson, you have to have self-belief or what's the point? Trouble is, the older someone gets – and I've seen this in so many other sports – players, or, more likely, coaches, tinker and change, be it with mindset, preparation or technique. The way I finished batting was so different to when I started. If someone saw me at 18, it would be incomprehensible to them how complicated my game had become by the end of my career. But all you have to do is nick off a few times and the coaches are straight in there telling you how you must change things. Sadly, it's something that seems to happen more and more these days, from a younger and younger age. Kids have a natural instinct to hit the ball, same as if you put a goal in front of them they want to kick a football into it. And yet, so often I watch kids play, kids who've been taught by their parents perhaps, or club cricketers who maybe don't know so much, and always they've been shown how to block. None of them pick their bat up. The one thing the best batsmen in the world have in common is a similar backlift. They might stand differently, but the backlift, when they prepare to hit the ball, be it to defend or attack, has the toe of the bat pointing to the sky. Whether that's Viv Richards, Gary Sobers, Brian Lara, Sachin Tendulkar, or whoever, when they move forward to the ball, or go back, their hands are up. Yet still I see kids in this country with their hands held low, this 'rocking the baby' motion that so many coaches talk about. It makes no sense to me at all, and I'm not the only one. Justin Langer once asked Ricky Ponting what he did against the quicks.

'I try to keep my hands as high as possible,' he told him.

'Don't you keep them low? Dig out the yorker?'

Ponting just looked at him. 'Get them as high as you can.'

Take a kid who is 12 and an alright batsman, not necessarily Lara, and put him in front of a bowling machine at 60mph with a low backlift and watch them make that ball look like it's 100mph. Tell them to pick their hands up like a golfer and hit the ball back over your head and they could quite easily face a ball that's 10–15mph quicker. They will go from looking like it's going to kill them to smashing it around, and then you will see how much they enjoy the game. There were kids I grew up with whose dads would put them under so much pressure, having a go at them for getting out, and I could see them just hating the game. Other kids who were given the freedom to just go out there and score runs acted in a totally different way.

Cricket's big problem when it comes to kids is that if you're good it's a great game and if you're not, it's crap – you stand in a field, you don't bowl, and you don't bat. You just watch the other players having the fun. If you're the best player, you bat for the longest and then chances are you will bowl as well. Cricket is not a great game for those who don't excel. In football, you can at least kick someone up in the air, run around, and feel like you've contributed. In golf or tennis, you are always hitting the ball, but cricket isn't like that. Time and again I see kids who go an entire session without batting or bowling and think, 'They're going to work it out soon.'

The trick with kids is to help them all enjoy it. Let them hit a six. Let them try to smack it and then they can take that away with them after the game. If they are going to fail then they may as well do so while having a crack. When I look back at my own and every single half-decent cricketer's upbringing, most of the other kids were simply there to facilitate our game. That sounds horrendous, I know, but it's true, and that's why clubs have to remember that kids' coaching and kids' teams aren't about producing the next first-class cricketer, they're about giving those youngsters a love for the game. When the vast majority of kids give the game up, they don't do so because they aren't going to play for England, they do so because they are bored. Coaches and team managers have a duty to make sure cricket is fun and not talk about it as if it's life or death.

The requirement for kids to do everything, to bat and bowl, in junior leagues, is also an issue. Actually, if you look at it, there are only three or four seriously good all-rounders in England at this moment. Everyone says players have to be multi-skilled but the reality is that there's not many batsmen who bowl, and if they do it's not much cop anyway. Instead of always making kids bat and bowl through their age groups, we'd be better off letting them go down the route they fancy. If they are a good batsman and a moderate bowler, why force them to go down both routes? Again, that's where club coaches get it wrong with kids. To me, being multi-skilled means being able to bat and field, or bowl and field. It helps if you can do all three, but ultimately, the game is about being as good at your main skill as you can and then trying your best at fielding.

I have spent pretty much my whole life in cricket. In school I assumed I would be a professional cricketer. Had I known how many youngsters are sold that dream, I might not have been so arrogant. Trouble is, it's a dream attached to a business model. A lot of counties dangle the fantasy of professional sport, possibly because they are charging far too much for the coaching service they offer. Cricket isn't alone in that. Whether it's tennis, football, rugby, or whatever, those who come through a club's academy into professional sport probably amount to around 1 per cent of those in the system. The sportsperson who forges a long-lasting professional career is likely less than half a per cent. I played with more than 300 county cricketers at Kent. There was a constant churning – trialists, those who played in the second team for a year, those who featured in a handful of one-day games. The turnover of people in professional sport, the number of players who play one or two games and then just disappear, is just extraordinary.

I see it now with my own children. They travel through academy age groups, their paths charted on a diagram leading to professional sport. But there is one thing missing on that diagram … the moat full of crocodiles, the people on either side armed with bows and arrows. To get past that moat is near impossible. But of course, if you do make it, what awaits you is the promised land, and it is that vision that is the one being sold.

If the reality was presented, there would be far fewer parents giving the coaches earache all the time, parents who have no clear idea how tough it is for their children to succeed. By the age of 14 or 15, you know full well as a professional cricketer who is any good and who is not. You can tell within two balls, and yet those kids' parents will still be pushing them because they haven't a clue about the reality. I was lucky. From Under-11s I had Alan Ealham, a Kent legend, who looked after me all the way. He didn't coach me as such; he wasn't overly technical, but he advised me, pushed me, allowing me to work out for myself what I needed to do to improve my game. That was a massive asset. Tell people how to do things all the time and their natural coping mechanism is replaced by a desire for instruction. In a less structured environment I had to decide how I was going to play the game. When I was struggling I had to work it out. I didn't have someone giving me the answers all the time. I didn't realise it, but I was building resilience for professional sport.

I would need every ounce.

Chapter 5

The Critical Mass

We needed 10 to win. As indicated by a very large electronic scoreboard, I was on 90. Fred came down the wicket.

'Right,' he said, 'we need to get your hundred. How many do you need?'

'Er, well I'm on 90,' I told him, 'so that would indicate I need 10.'

Getting England over the line batting alongside Fred against the West Indies at Old Trafford in 2004 is my favourite moment in cricket. It was a quick pitch and we were in a bit of trouble having to chase 231 to win on the last day. Michael Vaughan had again showed his skill as captain by reassuring us before West Indies batted in the third innings that whatever they made we would chase it down. All I could think at the time was how far away that seemed, but it was his way of taking the pressure off the bowlers, and also set out our stall as an attacking team.

'Well, what do you think?' Fred enquired.

'No, no, no,' I replied. 'Forget my hundred, let's just win it. Let's just get this done.'

I was slightly cynical because I thought I might get out, and the one thing I always wanted, after everything we'd been through, from age-group cricket to academies, and onwards, was for me and Fred to walk off the pitch together after helping England to win a Test match. That was the dream. The absolute dream. Winning a game for England with your best mate – how many people does that happen to? Also, I had already scored a hundred in a Test match and thought I was going to get a lot more at that stage. Best laid plans and all that ...

Fred hit a couple of fours to get us over the line and that was it.

'This just couldn't get any better,' I thought to myself. 'I've scored a double hundred in the series and now I've won a game alongside my best friend.' It is one of the moments that I'm most proud of.

For me, that summer was incredible – 2004 was my year, the one to remember – while for England it marked the start of a great era. I could see this was a special side with an excellent leader. The bowling attack of Flintoff, Harmison and Hoggard was totally unforgiving while the batting line-up had real talent and resilience. I knew this was going to be one of the best teams in the world, and that was before Kevin Pietersen came in. Whereas Australia, South Africa and India had been strong for a long time, here was a new and upcoming, ambitious England team, as strong as any of them.

It was a frustration for me that I wouldn't be part of it as it moved into the summer of 2005. Having performed OK in the winter Test series against South Africa and at that point appearing to be fairly well established in the England set-up, and with Mark Butcher – a natural competitor for the position – injured, I thought I was going to get the nod before the pre-Ashes home mini-series against Bangladesh. I was waiting for the call from head of selectors, David Graveney. I was in a pub in Beckenham when eventually it came.

'You're the man in possession,' he told me.

'Brilliant,' I thought. 'That's it. I'm in.'

'But you're not anymore.'

It was like being on *The Weakest Link*.

'OK,' I thought. 'Well, that's that done.'

And it was.

When it came to the effective functioning of a team, Fletcher referred to the 'critical mass' – the idea that the overwhelming majority of a side should be of a similar mindset, pulling in the same direction. In a perfect world, be you a coach or a player, you'd want eleven people like you in the team and you'd go on to win everything. It would make your life easy. But that isn't the case in life or in sport.

In the England set-up at that point was me, Fred and Harmy. We were different characters and yet similar in lots of ways. Harmy was an introvert. Freddie and I combined introvert and extrovert while veering more towards the extrovert side. You gravitate to people who are like you, and for me that was Harmy and Fred. Together, we used to argue a lot and enjoy each other's company. Two out of eleven who have a different outlook, while still obviously wanting the team to succeed, is tolerable. Three who are seen as being disruptive is too many, even if they themselves might disagree with that judgment. When it came to the trio of Harmison, Flintoff and Key, I was the weakest link. I had to score runs and I wasn't always doing so. I'd done all right in Australia without ever quite having that moment where I established myself. I then came home and had a great chance to do just that with two Tests against Zimbabwe. I had an innings in each. I was given out at Lord's when I didn't hit it and then missed out at Chester-le-Street. As a batsman, you live and die by your actions. If you're not one of the fittest or best fielders around then you'd better make sure you score more runs than the bloke who is. My runs always had to do the talking, and they never quite spoke loud enough.

More than anything, you have to give people time to bed in. Can anyone ever relax with the fear of the axe looming round every corner? It wasn't as bad as it had been, but even in my era you still had to hit the ground running.

My career is no different to anybody else's from that point of view. If you look at Mark Ramprakash, John Crawley, or other batsmen who dipped in and out of the England side, they all have places along the road where something could have happened differently, or somebody could have acted in a different manner. Certainly, Ramps, as a 20-year-old, would have been nailed by many to play 100 Tests and be England's greatest batsman ever, but international cricket isn't that easy to predict. It's an inexact science. Graham Gooch didn't peak till he was well into his thirties. Gary Sobers, the greatest cricketer ever, didn't fly from the word go. Neither did Michael Vaughan, one of the best batsmen and captains of the modern era.

I could perhaps argue I was a victim of the times. There were some bloody good players around. The current England team has just gone through a long phase where they were crying out for opening and top order batsmen. When I was playing, there were loads of us. If you didn't come into that England side and score runs straight away then there were other people who could. Sometimes you are just born in an unfortunate era. I was part of one of England's most successful generations. But ultimately, one thing remains unchangeable – you have to score runs.

Fact is also that the skills Harmy and Freddie had were much more valuable than mine. By the time I made my debut for England, Freddie was becoming the man who balanced the team. Harmy, meanwhile, was a special talent, a one-off, and was always destined to have a great career with the national side. While they might not have shared Fletcher's ethos off the pitch, on the pitch they couldn't be faulted. They were so good that he couldn't do without them.

It was all very surreal to find myself part of that England set-up. I knew on the Ashes tour it was far too early for me to be picked for England. I had no idea what I was doing. Three years and fifteen Tests later, I felt I had found my feet at international level – and then they ditched me. The selectors were looking towards a new breed. Ian Bell got the nod for the two-Test Bangladesh series at the start of the home 2005 summer, while for the Ashes, Kevin Pietersen, who had showcased his trademark fearless brilliance in the limited overs format, was, quite rightly, seen as too good an option to ignore. It was obvious they had the makings of something special and could deliver consistent high-class performances with accompanying runs and the chance to build a team, not just of good players, but of utterly brilliant players.

While Graham Thorpe had started against Bangladesh, he too was jettisoned when it came to the real business against the Aussies. My disappointment for Thorpey matched that for myself. I had initially come into the team for him and then later we were both in the side together. I used to love watching Thorpey bat – I thought he was the best of his generation – but from what I'd heard, he could be a bit stand-offish, not always an easy character, the one who would stand up for himself and walk out of meetings. Rumour and reality couldn't have been further removed. When me, Straussy and Geraint Jones were the youngsters in the side he would come and sit with us at team meals.

'What do you think about Test cricket?' he would ask, and then talk with us over a few beers.

While I was away on the South Africa tour, my grandmother died. I went out for a meal that night with Freddie, Thorpey and Harmy, and the subject came up. Thorpe asked what had happened, offered his commiserations, and we all carried on eating. Later that night there was a knock on my hotel door. There was Thorpey with four cans of beer.

'I'm really sorry to hear about your grandmother,' he said. 'You must be struggling.'

It was such a generous gesture, so empathetic. We talked about life and cricket and I asked Thorpey about his own career, how it was that by the end he had started scoring a good number of hundreds whereas in the past he'd got more seventies and eighties. It seemed to me that he must have wished he'd converted more of those scores to tons. That was indeed the case, but he reminded me that when he played there were more than a few bowlers capable of getting you out even when you were well set on 70 – Ambrose and Walsh, Pollock and Donald, Wasim and Waqar, for example.

Thorpey was the one who taught me there were more ways to get out than bad form and more ways to score runs than surviving. Sometimes, he told me, he would watch a bowler such as Allan Donald and think to himself, 'Well, if I hang around here, I'm going to get out.' He reasoned that the more courageous way was to say, 'Sod it, I'm going to take a risk and try to throw a few counter-punches.'

It's little lessons like this that you learn throughout your career – too late, a lot of them – and Thorpey had learnt them all. His gutsy attitude was totally in keeping with his character. It says everything about him – gritty player, good on the short ball, scored tough runs – that he was well respected by the Aussies. And that was the thing; all the runs scored by those players of the nineties – Atherton, Nasser, Thorpe, Butch – were tough. They rarely or never played Bangladesh or an emerging associate nation. They must have turned up for England every summer, thinking, 'Here we go. Who's it going to be this year?'

The gift those players bestowed on the next generation was great experience and insight, Butch being a particularly great source of both. As a player whose career bridged the Athers, Nasser and Vaughan eras, he had a foot in all camps. Butch could go out to dinner with the older guys or socialise with us newer players and make us feel at home. We felt we could turn to him for anything, and his influence even carried on to the guys following us. To this day, Joe Root credits a good deal of his technique to watching Butch a lot as a kid.

As it was, I departed the England Test set-up at the same time as Thorpey and Butch, the difference being I was still near the start of my career while they were nearing the end. It's not something I'd ever complain about, because it was incredible to have been given the chance, but, looking back, my inexperience when I came into the side did give rise to certain issues. Too often I'd do OK against the good bowlers and then get out to the medium dobbers of the likes of Steve Waugh and Damian Martyn. At Perth in 2002, despite my reservations about Brett Lee, heading to the wicket thinking, 'Jesus! Here we go!', I actually did all right against him. One thing I'd worked out was that if he bounced me it wasn't a threat. It was going over my head. I actually saw off the real thrust of the Australian attack, got myself to 47, only to get out to the slow-medium pace of Damien just before tea. At the time I was thinking, 'You know what? After tea I'm going to have to face McGrath, Gillespie and Warne. This might be my only chance to get us a bit of a score.' Especially since, inevitably, I was by now batting with the lower order. This internal conversation, with the alternative view of not taking risks being offered by the rather annoying imp sat chattering on my shoulder, meant that I actually ended up getting caught between two stools. I was bowled. And from that point on, people used to bowl dobbers at me all the time. It became the bane of my life. That all began from yet another piece of brilliance from Steve Waugh, who had guessed absolutely what was occurring in my head.

Damien, being Damien, made a point of showing me that picture at every opportunity from then on, because every batsman cherishes their handful of wickets more than their thousands of runs. For me, that meant a grand total of three. I will take the memory of getting David Willey out at Canterbury to my grave. The more he played for England, the better that wicket became.

I don't regret considering that more aggressive approach. Often players get blamed for losing their wicket by using an attacking mindset, as if they never get out while playing defensively. When England were bowled out by Nathan Lyon in the first Ashes Test of 2019, most of the batsmen got out by prodding. At the end of my Kent career we got bowled out at The Oval. As ever, the coaches blamed the batsmen for playing too expansively, but actually every single player, bar one, had nicked off or got out lbw without playing a big shot. It was the same when Jason Roy was opening in the Test team. Pundits were saying there are no good old-fashioned openers anymore. The fact is, we had already tried ten openers, most of whom were exactly that. The only markedly different one was Alex Hales.

We accuse people of playing too many shots but as a batsman your only currency in the game is runs. How you get them isn't important. Ugly, good, quickly, slowly, it doesn't matter. But for some reason we seem to be happier if people are out blocking. I admire Trevor Bayliss because he is a believer in positive cricket. His view is that it's possible to defend positively as well as attack. That means committing to the shot, having purpose. Is scoring 10 in a hundred balls all right? I don't know if it is.

What is harder now is recognising which batsmen might work in Test cricket, who has the mental and physical capacity to deal with the ultimate examination of determination, personality and technique. When I started out in county cricket, pitches were poor. No one was scoring huge runs. Marcus Trescothick was picked for England averaging around 30 in first-class cricket. There was then a period where pitches improved and batsmen found it easier to score runs, which itself led to a belief that surfaces had become too batsmen friendly, that bowlers needed a helping hand. The answer, it was deemed, was to leave more grass on the pitch. But it seems there is always a knock-on effect that no one is expecting. Actually, all that did was help the medium pacers who could nurdle a batsman out with a bit of movement. That is no good for developing Test batsmen who need to bat for long periods against a variety of attacks. More recently, the toss has been tinkered with in county cricket in the hope it might get spinners into the game after several years where they were barely getting a bowl. The visiting captain was offered the opportunity of bowling first. Clubs would therefore be encouraged to produce better four-day pitches, making spin a more likely option, prolonging the game in general and helping produce players better suited to the Test environment.

Allied to this is a constant desire to tweak the Championship to make it more entertaining. What we really should do is come to terms with the fact that the Championship is for a certain audience. Only they are going to like four-day cricket and truly understand and engage with the intricacies of that format. There's nothing you can do to it to make it more entertaining for anyone else.

Others talk about four-day Test matches. Why? There is nobody sitting around who doesn't like cricket, and Test cricket in particular, saying, 'You know what would make me like that Test cricket? If it was four days instead of five.' No one. Same as there's no one sitting around saying, 'Do you know what would make me watch four-day county cricket? A change in the law so that it's up to the home team whether or not to employ the heavy roller between innings.' And yet we are constantly fiddling with the game. People who like four-day cricket like watching batsmen get hundreds and bowlers get wickets. You can't do anything to the format to make it more entertaining for those people, so we should just leave it as it is while creating as good an environment for England players to develop as we possibly can.

The best and most valuable batsmen in the long run are those who have learnt the value of switching off. It was Kent coach John Wright who reinforced that in me.

'To score a hundred, you only have to concentrate for three or four minutes,' he told me. 'Don't be concentrating when the bowler starts running in. Only when he's halfway through his run-up do you start focusing. As soon as that ball has gone, switch off again.'

I thought that was absolutely right. No one can concentrate for three hours solid, but they can concentrate for four seconds every couple of minutes. I took that advice on board straight away. People may think that if a player isn't concentrating they aren't taking the game seriously, but that is actually very much not the case. It's where physical tics are misunderstood. People see them as a sign of a player who is too wired into the game. I never really shared any of the tics that some batsmen exhibit, most noticeably nowadays Steve Smith, whose between-balls routine is reminiscent of the mid-1970s New York disco scene: left pad, right pad, thigh pad, box. I did try to copy Rahul Dravid; he would put his back foot into the crease, then his front, and tap his bat. I was front foot and then back foot as I didn't want to be a complete copy, but then I just forgot and stopped doing it. Subconsciously, I also used to pull the visor on my helmet. Tics, odd as they may seem, can be beneficial. Anything you repeat that makes you feel at home at the crease, be that marking your guard, fiddling with pads, or whatever, can deliver mental calm when there's chaos all around.

It feeds into watching from the dressing room. 'We need balcony support!' – I used to hate it when that cry went up at Kent. For me, there's nothing worse. A player only has a limited number of resources. If they're on the balcony watching every ball then they're using them up before they've even got out to the middle. Every time Kent struggled there would always be chat in the dressing room about supporting on the balcony. I never cared one bit. I couldn't have given the slightest toss whether anyone was watching me or not. I was doing my job, trying to get a score for myself and the team, and that was it. Balcony support? Really? If I'm waiting to bat I need to switch off. As captain, however, I would respect other people's opinions.

'OK,' I'd say, 'it doesn't bother me, but if you think it's something we need to do, that's going to help us play Mitchell Johnson a bit better than we have been doing, then we'll do it.

'That's the end of it,' I'd tell them. 'No one mention it again. But if any of you who's backed this now doesn't act on their words, I will hammer you.'

It would take about four overs out on the balcony before people were desperately climbing up the wall trying to get away. After a while, watching your workmates just isn't that fascinating. You don't see a balcony in Tesco so staff can watch the shelf-stackers for an hour before they start. Is there a balcony at McDonald's? PC World? No.

Do what you need to do to excel as a player; let them on the shop floor get on with it.

Chapter 6

Fred

Andrew Flintoff and I have something in common. We are both scared of the dark. For Fred, the fear can be traced back to when someone showed him *The Exorcist* when he was 10 years old. He'd been one of a group of kids going round washing cars to earn some money. Rather than pay, someone invited them in to watch one of the most terrifying films of all time. I wouldn't sit through that now, let alone as a 10-year-old. The film gave Fred night terrors, which resurfaced quite vividly in Zimbabwe with England A when the former Northamptonshire and Lancashire opener Mal Loye began telling ghost stories. Mal was recalling his old home, in excruciatingly shadowy detail. Every Friday night, Mal's parents would go out and he'd be left behind in what, we discovered, hairs up on the back of our necks, was clearly a haunted house. He'd be watching *Cheers*, he told us, to the sound of people running around upstairs. On another occasion, he revealed, his mum was brushing her hair, only to look round and find a figure – a 'heavy smoker', as Mal described him, because he had decomposing yellowy skin – barely inches away from her face.

Well, that was enough for me and Fred. With his roommate, the Glamorgan paceman Darren Thomas, out on the lash, Fred was desperate not to be on his own, wasting no time in heading in to sleep in the same room as me and Vikram Solanki. Both more than a little disturbed by Mal's stories, our logic was that we would be safe from the forces of darkness because, while neither of us was religious, Vikram definitely was – therefore, we reasoned, his presence would protect us from anything untoward. There were two double beds. Fred jumped in with me, naked apart from his boxer shorts. Not that the presence of others cured his restless mind. He was tossing and turning all night, so scared was he of the dark. Neither Vikram nor I got a wink of sleep, only dozing off as the sun came up, which at least meant home time for any local vampires. The result was all three of us overslept and missed the bus to the ground – an automatic fine. Mortified that his fear had kept me awake half the night, Fred paid mine. He's done many things on TV since retirement. *Most Haunted* isn't one of them.

Fred wasn't alone in having occasional sleep issues.

'Here boy! Here boy!'

I was confused. For one thing, I was in a hotel room. For another, I didn't have a dog.

Then I remembered – I was rooming with Graeme Swann.

'Come here boy!'

I looked over. He was sat up in bed.

'Good dog!'

When it didn't come, he started whistling to it, like he was on *One Man and His Dog*.

I was with England Under-19s. Over the years, I'd get used to Swanny talking in his sleep, especially this particular scenario where he harboured a fervent belief there was a dog in the room. He'd sit bolt upright calling this mythical mutt. That was if you were lucky. Other times, he'd be out of bed, chasing round the room trying to catch it.

Swanny's dreams didn't end with dogs. Occasionally, I'd be woken by him shouting and banging on the door – the inside of the door – 'Keysy, let me in!'

Then there were the conversations he'd have with himself, backwards and forwards with another character in his head.

'Where have you been?'

'What do you mean, where have I been?'

'I was just wondering.'

'I've not been anywhere.'

'I thought you had.'

'No, what makes you think that?' On and on. And on.

Swanny was perfectly capable of arguing with anyone in the day. But he was the only person I knew who could argue with himself in his sleep.

'What are you on about? You're talking rubbish!'

'No, you're talking rubbish!'

Sometimes, Owais Shah would pop up from Swanny's bed. Owais had a distinctive high-pitched voice. Swanny would spend his days mimicking him – and then do it in his sleep as well. Backwards and forwards as Owais and then Swanny. Who knows what was going on in his head? I was always of the opinion that I'd rather not find out.

Fred was never anything other than himself. As much as he probably shudders seeing himself lurch out of 10 Downing Street after the Ashes victory in 2005, that unfettered reality of personality and character is what endears him to people. He winces now his kids are of an age where they can Google him and see some of the things that come up, but ultimately, that's what made everyone like him. Fred always had a healthy perspective on what he was doing. He was always aware that he was playing cricket, always aware that it was a game, that it was fun, part of a life that should be lived to the full. In wearing that attitude on his sleeve, he put it right out there who he really was. A lot of sportspeople put on a façade but, actually, what you see is what you get with Fred. Whenever I watched him being interviewed, he never said anything that wasn't exactly him.

But that trip to national hero hadn't been straightforward. Fred became a target early in his career, and that wasn't always easy or fair for him to have to deal with at times. For instance, there was the odd story in the papers about his weight and what he was eating.

Thing is, when you are young, sometimes you need failure to teach you a lesson. A phenomenon from a young age, Fred was the best at everything. He could hit the ball harder than anyone else, catch the ball better than anyone else, and bowl at 90 miles an hour. On that Zimbabwe trip, he was the best player by a country mile. We were winning, he was doing bloody well, and none of us really thought he or we needed to do anything different.

Eventually, though, things started to go awry. He was out of the England team after an early taste of international cricket didn't go to plan, and when he turned up at Canterbury with Lancashire, I thought he looked out of sorts. He was hit on the head by Ben Trott – Trott was a good bowler but he wasn't particularly quick. Fred just didn't look the player I had grown up with. It was at that point, famously, that his agents, Neil Fairbrother and Andrew 'Chubby' Chandler, sat him down and read the riot act. Afterwards, Freddie asked to go to the Academy with the rest of the England youngsters to get himself fit. Had he not gone through that negative period, he wouldn't have been the cricketer he was. Everyone needs those moments. Everyone makes mistakes. A coach, an agent, is there to speed up that process, trying to stop players going through ten years of mistakes, but sometimes people need to have their tough times. Without them, they can never realise their full potential.

It should be remembered that Fred made his international debut as a 20-year-old in 1998 – recognition of his talent, playing well before his peers and his friends. The nineties was such a volatile decade to be an England cricketer. Only the toughest survived. Players had to look after themselves whereas nowadays, the England team, with the security of central contracts, is an altogether more relaxed environment, far removed from the cut-throat place Fred walked into. After that experience, Fred always took it upon himself to look after the younger players when they came in because he didn't want them to go through the same experience.

It was four years after Fred when I walked into that England dressing room. I was 23, and while things had clearly changed for the better, it was still daunting to push open that door. I was walking into somewhere with players a decade longer in the tooth than myself. Me and Fred were a different generation. Almost as if they were men and we were kids. They were men having kids! On the Ashes tour we both went on, Nasser joined his wife in Perth for the birth of their second child.

People forget that the great all-rounders, just because they are bloody good – they can bat well, they can bowl well, they can do it all – aren't immune to the same nagging self-doubts that plague the rest of us. What they are often better at is silencing those inner voices. If Fred walked out to bat without his helmet on, he wasn't any less nervous than anybody else; he was just better at fronting up to it. You see it now in his TV stuff. He's got more courage than anybody I've ever met, as so much of what he does is literally sticking himself out there to be abused. Because he went through that relatively tough time early on in his career, it's given him the strength to go on and achieve a lot more.

I find it a fascinating study to look at the great all-rounders. So often they are all or nothing. They are 120 per cent all the time. That is who they are. The one constant such people have in their lives is sport. Look at Shane Warne. The more chaotic his life, the better he was, as illustrated by the 2005 Ashes, when we just saw the very best of an already unbelievable player. It was extraordinary. He got more wickets than anyone and scored a whole lot of runs. He must still wonder how he ended up on the losing side.

These are people who, in adversity, reveal their best. Since the nightclub incident in Bristol, Ben Stokes has put so much into his game. He trains so hard – harder than anyone around him by some distance. When I am away with Sky on an England trip, I will see him bat for longer than anyone else, field for longer than anyone else, bowl for longer than anyone else, all at maximum intensity. England played a day/night game in Sri Lanka and, back at the hotel, as everyone wandered wearily back to their rooms, I spotted a figure in the gym – Ben Stokes, running on the treadmill for fifteen minutes at speeds I would never dare go near on a normal day, let alone at 11.00 pm after a day of full-on international cricket. For many players, fitness can be a bit like a New Year's resolution – give it a month and if there's no results straight away, forget it. People like Stokes are different. It might not happen straight away, but they know that eventually it will. Great talent delivers a focus. It did so for Fred in 2005 and is doing the same now for Stokes. Without the hardship, neither would have reached those incredible high points.

Those highs took Fred across the world, introduced him to new and amazing scenarios, cultures and people. But the real Fred was never washed away in the flood of new experiences. He has always stuck up for what he felt was right. He can always spot a bullshitter, a fraud. Anyone who is false in any way is done when they meet Fred. He has an absolute bullshitometer. The TV world he now occupies must have its fair share of these people. I would love to see his face sometimes because that's not what he's about at all. He is an honest person and he wants other people to be the same.

Cricket is also full of those who talk a good game when they think the right ears are listening but don't live up to it in real life. Fred could see through such people by a mile. They would forever underestimate his judgment and character on that score. If he felt that something was not right with someone, that, for example, they were getting away with under-performing because they were playing up to the coach, then that person was lost to Fred. Whatever business you are in, you always have the bloke who's a bit of a kiss-arse. His opinion was that you do something because you want to and it's the right thing to do, not because it's going to impress someone. Fred always said he was going to get as far as he could on his own terms, and he has. His integrity is second to none. He's at the top of everyone I know.

On the pitch, Fred was seriously quick and bowled a horrible heavy ball. Whereas other bowlers might kiss the surface, like when you skim a stone in the sea, Fred hammered the ball hard into the wicket. In Fred's case, the stone would have smashed straight through the surface of the water and slammed into the bottom. He is a tall man and every bit of his energy went through the ball. Generally, shorter players don't bowl that heavy delivery. Simon Jones would lightly stroke the surface. It would still bloody hurt when it hit you, but Fred rammed the ball in harder than anybody. He was so accurate as well, angling the ball in, on a line and length that wouldn't always get you out, but was just very awkward. Facing Fred was horrible. There was nothing like it. Virender Sehwag, the Indian batsman, not far off a genius, was happy not to take singles off every other England bowler, but he'd try like anything to get away from Fred. The Aussie great, Ricky Ponting, has said outright that Fred was the best England bowler.

All this came from such a simple action, allied to skill, strength, fitness, competitiveness and determination. Ultimately, the latter led to his downfall. The only way he knew to play the game was to keep on going, to leave nothing out on the pitch. Every ounce of his being was going into every delivery. I'd be standing in the slips and the ball would be whizzing down at a ridiculous pace. Fred was so fast, quicker than Harmy or anybody, when he got going.

He hit Shaun Pollock at The Wanderers once and I genuinely thought the ball could have knocked him out.

Fred's batting and bowling was very different. For a period in the mid-2000s, he was England's best batsman, and would have walked into any format as the number four. Even as an Under-19, he hit the ball as hard as the likes of Viv Richards. He was blessed with a simple technique where he could stand and deliver, while at other times rein in his natural attacking, stroke-playing urges. His hundred against South Africa at Lord's remains one of the best I have seen.

Fred also carried a weight of expectancy when he walked out to bat. The crowd would erupt when he appeared from the pavilion. When we batted together against the West Indies at Old Trafford, they cheered him hitting a single more than they did me hitting a four. He was a man who cleared bars. Everyone wanted to see him bat.

He made brave decisions. In the Ashes of 2005, he reasoned he was going to try a few shots. In doing so, he risked failure, looking like an idiot. Coming in at number six, generally the game is on the line. Start trying to hit Shane Warne out the ground and get out, you are going to be vilified for it. Those were the calls he had to make for himself. In that case, he decided to step back from the shackles of an intense batting experience and not try too hard, by which I mean he gave himself mental freedom to play his shots.

Some might say where his game fell down was captaincy. But Fred was a better England captain than he – and many others – ever thought. The circumstances were tough. For a start, he had a team demolished by injury. Secondly, he got the Australians on the rebound. And you really don't want to get the Australians on the rebound. He simply couldn't have picked a worse time to be captain of England. The team had gone from the perfect balance of 2005 to Saj Mahmood batting at number eight. No offence to Saj; he was a good bowler, but he wasn't a number eight. Marcus Trescothick, one of England's best-ever batsmen, had left the tour and Michael Vaughan was laid up with a serious knee problem. Basically, it was the classic England trip to Australia: if anything can go wrong it will. You could have put Mike Brearley in charge of that team and it would have made no difference. It was always going to be 5-0. They were throwing stones at bazookas.

Thankfully, Fred went out at the top when England claimed back the Ashes in 2009. The image of Fred, by then barely mobile, body in ruins, down on one knee, arms in the air, having run out Ricky Ponting at The Oval, is seared on every England fan's brain. These people – the Stokes, the Bothams, the Flintoffs – always have the best scriptwriters. Fred seemed blessed with the finest of all, like when Brett Lee, one half of the last wicket Australian partnership that so nearly got over the line in the Edgbaston Test of 2005, slumped to the ground as England won by two runs. Harmy was actually the one who first went to commiserate with Brett, and yet it's Fred, second on the scene, who was captured on all the pictures shaking Brett's hand and subsequently held up as the greatest sportsman ever. Then there was the other time at Edgbaston when he hit the West Indian quick, Jermaine Lawson, for six. Nothing too unusual there, except the ball ended up going into (and straight out of) the hands of his dad, Colin, high up in the Ryder Stand.

Occasionally, he wrote his own script. It's not unusual for cricketers to come out with a good line in the middle of battle, but of course it just so happens that it's Fred's 'Mind the windows, Tino!' that was immortalised on the stump mic.

West Indies fast bowler Tino Best was always chirpy. There had been some ongoing needle between him and Fred, going back to the Caribbean series the previous winter, and continuing through the domestic one-day games and into the Test series. Fred enjoyed a chirp too. He had a habit of laughing at his own jokes. In fact, often when he's got you in his sights and he's taking the mick, he doesn't hear your reply because he's laughing at his own words so much. He's got this ridiculous high-pitched laugh where he's giggling at himself all the time. When, at Lord's, Tino came to the crease, eyeing up Ashley Giles for some quick runs, it was no surprise when Fred, from slip, issued his warning about the windows. It was one of his stock phrases. He said it all the time. Tino, though, was the perfect recipient. First, he wasn't great with the bat. Second, he was prone to allowing himself to be wound up by fielders. It was a beautiful moment when it all came together and has become, justifiably, a popular YouTube clip, same as Fred's minor contretemps with Tino's teammate Dwayne Bravo the same year. Dwayne was really geeing up Fidel Edwards to go in hard at Fred: 'Get the big man out, Fidy! Come on!'

Fred was singularly unimpressed. 'Let's see if you're around in three years,' he told Dwayne. 'This game's got a funny way of biting you on the arse. I bet you won't be here.'

That was Fred's way, to come back at people, and few had the last word.

People sometimes think an ability to have a laugh and joke on the field compromises effort. It's simply not true. No one left less on the field than Andrew Flintoff. Against India in 2002, Fred was carrying a double hernia. He turned up at Headingley for the third Test thinking he wasn't going to play – understandably, since he could hardly move – but was convinced to take part. We lost the game by an innings. Fred got a pair. In the slips, meanwhile, he dropped the opener, Sanjay Bangar. Not that I can comment; stood next to him I dropped Sachin as well as Sourav Ganguly and Rahul Dravid, who all cruised serenely on to centuries. There's no worse feeling in cricket than dropping a catch. It's worse than getting nought. At that point, everyone goes silent. I never liked that. I always thought it was better to break the ice and take the piss. When Freddie dropped his chance, I enquired as to his favourite film, suggesting it might be *Drop Zone*, and conjectured that his favourite comedy would be *Drop the Dead Donkey*. I was just thinking of as many things with 'drop' in the title as I could. Even among friends, there's a limit though. When my own dropped catch tally reached three, Fred felt so bad for me he stopped pulling my leg back.

Throughout that match, Fred was overwhelmingly feeling he had let the side down. I looked on as, with the ball, he desperately tried to claw it back. From the slips, I watched him bowl over after over at the speed of light. His pace had gone up by 5 miles an hour, which is massive. It's a Test that's never talked about, but that's how much playing for England meant to Andrew Flintoff. He suffered, but he did so in silence.

He was exactly the same with training. At the Academy, Steve Kirby would scream his way through fitness training on the VersaClimber, a bit of kit that basically replicates a climbing motion, putting arms and legs through the mill. Kirbs was almost in tears whereas Fred would just get on with it and go about his business. Some people would make such a fuss in training, making out they were trying really hard when in fact they weren't at all. Cricket is like any other walk of life. You can always tell the ones who are doing it for real and the ones who are doing it for show. When it came to training, Fred was doing things that none of the rest of us were prepared to do. We would have to be told, whereas Fred would just get on and do it. Forget going down to Loughborough to train in front of the fitness coaches, he'd be off with Rooster, his physio, otherwise known as Dave Roberts, running up some of the most vomit-inducing hills in Lancashire.

In the end, when someone as competitive and determined as Fred is putting so much strain on their body, something has to give. Injury robbed him of a lot. He still had a lot more he wanted to do, especially playing a bigger role for Lancashire, the club he loved. Harmy and I were with him when he found out he had reached the end of the road. His knee could take no more. He was done. He was always going to be all right – he already had options outside of cricket – but he was gutted that his career was cut short. The flipside was he would always know he had given his all. Stomach-wrenchingly disappointing as it was for him to finish so early, any great cricketer would much rather have Fred's career, do it the way he did, than last longer. They would rather know they did absolutely everything, went through all the operations, all the heartache, all the crap, than play until the age of 37 half-cocked. If Fred hadn't gone through that, he wouldn't be the person that we all love. He was never destined to get to 35 as a cricketer. He was never going to be able to live out his dream of winning the Championship for Lancashire alongside his mates at Old Trafford. He put far too much into his England career to do that. A lot of cricketers, especially bowlers, have to sacrifice longevity for effort. Dean Headley was another. His knee blew up at a young age when he should have had so much more to offer. But he could always say he played for England – he played as hard as he could and a Test career was his reward.

For Fred, the reward was also the career that came afterwards. That's not to say I haven't occasionally looked at some of the stuff Fred has done since cricket and wondered, 'What? Why?' When he said he was going to box, all me and Harmy could think was, 'Jesus, what's he doing? OK, he's a big fella, but he's going to get into a boxing ring? Really?'

But the feeling of uncertainty is a drug for people like Fred. That's what drives so much of what he does.

Me and Harmy met up for Fred's fight with Richard Dawson at the Manchester Arena. We had a few pints of Guinness and strolled across to see him in his hotel just before he went over to the venue. I'd been reading about Dawson, about how he'd been locked up for assault and had been shot when embroiled in the drugs trade. He sounded like a villain from an old black and white movie – classic boxing material. And then there was Fred, from Preston, who'd bowled a few cricket balls and held a few catches in the slips.

Fred looked gaunt. He'd been on the caveman diet, so called because it consists of food that cavemen could hunt or gather – fish, lean meats, fruits, vegetables, nuts and seeds. Kebabs weren't a thing back then.

'I spent my whole life trying to get a six-pack,' he sighed, 'and now I've got one I don't want it.'

I couldn't get what I'd read about Dawson out of my mind.

'Jesus, have you seen this fella you're fighting?' I asked Fred.

'I don't want to know, Keysy.'

'Mate, he's done time.'

'Keysy, shut up.'

'I've never met a convict before.'

'Keysy!'

Fred was clearly nervous about what was going to happen. He was going into a boxing match with a lot of people saying he shouldn't be doing it, that it was disrespectful to the sport, and it would serve him right if he was put on his arse. Also, he was making his boxing debut on TV, whereas with most boxers, nobody would ever see their first fight.

Fred's wife Rachel was there. God knows how she must have been feeling, although she was probably used to these things by then as Fred would matter-of-factly say that taking on any testing situation was just mind over matter. In fact, Fred is the most mind-over-matter person I have ever met. He will think his way through anything, no matter how hard it is. In that way he is practically invincible. He reflects what we'd all like to be. The difference is he has the courage to do it.

Top Gear is another case in point. Again, he was putting himself out there to fail. People were waiting for it to go wrong, for it to slump in the viewing figures. Again, it has been a success. Why? Because Fred, like his co-stars Paddy McGuinness and Chris Harris, is such a down to earth bloke – what you see is the real them. And that then comes across in the show. The same goes for Jamie Redknapp and the others on *A League of Their Own*. These are such normal people that you know straight away that Fred is going to like them. Meet them yourself and you see exactly how that works. They're not fancy, they're not putting on a façade, they are who they are, and that ends up with a friendship like we all have with our mates down the pub. And then they transfer that to TV. Chris Harris takes the mick out of Fred about his wonky teeth. I never even realised he had wonky teeth. But that's the same kind of silliness we've all grown up doing with Fred, who, by the way, is the most merciless of all when it comes to picking up on other people's faults. Take Fred into your circle of friends and he will treat everybody the same. As much as he's going to hammer you, he's going to hammer your mates. He met a good friend of mine who had just started to put on a little bit of weight, to the extent the chain he was wearing was almost choking him. Fred's first line to him was, 'Did that chain used to fit you?' It's always done with a laugh, a smile, and if someone doesn't like that then they are better off leaving. Not that anyone does, because most people are exactly the same.

When Fred went into singing, appearing in the stage musical *Fat Friends*, it might not have appeared quite the same high-risk, adrenalin-rush, mission that was *Top Gear* or boxing, but I think that took the most bottle of all. It transported him somewhere completely different to where he'd been before. The appeal was the live rush, the element of unpredictability, the audience. He wanted that uncertainty, that sense of achievement when it went right. I went to see *Fat Friends* and, disappointingly, he was actually pretty good.

I was desperate for him to mess up and sing out of tune, ready to hoard a few opportunities to rib him, and yet he did it so well.

Again and again, he puts himself out there to the extent I can get really nervous because he's the only one of my friends really doing that. *Top Gear* is one of the biggest shows in the world. No one's been able to do it well since Jeremy Clarkson. I look at him every week on that programme and think, 'This could go horribly wrong' … bungee jumping in a car off a dam in Switzerland being a case in point.

I sit through Fred's shows with more butterflies in my stomach than any other thing I do. It's like watching your kids play sport. I watch my son playing football and all I can think is, 'Please don't score an own goal. I don't care if you do well, but just don't be shit, don't have a shocker and everyone be annoyed at you. I really, really don't want you to feel bad.' And it's exactly the same with Fred. He will always bounce back but I don't want him to have to go through any kind of pain. He's the only one who constantly puts himself in that position.

Forget batting and bowling, his seamless transfer to TV; Fred's super-strength was actually his ability to sleep, specifically an unbelievable ability not to wake up. While many people can slumber through an alarm, or with the telly on, Fred, especially after a few drinks, wouldn't have woken up if a nuclear bomb went off. The beauty of Fred was that he was astute enough to know he wouldn't wake up. As a result, he would often sleep with the hotel phone at the side of his head to give himself a better chance of responding to the alarm call. It rarely worked. Even when he stopped drinking, it didn't work. A load of us were staying in a country pub playing golf, arranging to meet at half-eight the next morning. Sure enough, when 8.30 came, there was no sign of Fred. It was just like when he played cricket. In his room there he was, still with the phone next to his head. Still not waking up.

As players, Harmy and Fred would always room together. I never roomed with Fred for one reason – we are both very grubby people, although Fred took it to a whole different level. When we played together for England at Old Trafford once, all of us had lockers, but Fred, whose home ground it was, just had a mountain of clothes on the floor. At home it would have been the equivalent of taking off every item of clothing for a month and just throwing it down in one area. As I was looking through it I even pulled out a dinner suit he'd worn a year before at the PCA dinner.

It kills me when people say Fred must have been hard work. He was the greatest team man there has ever been. His attitude to the game, and life, is probably the best of anyone I have ever met. He enjoyed his cricket. He had no agenda. He played as hard as he could, to the point where he broke himself doing it. What a career he had, and that is why he's gone on to have success. If he hadn't been like that, shown that determination, and done it with such great character, would TV shows have been falling over themselves to have him on board? There is no better person in cricket than Andrew Flintoff. There is no one who stuck up for people better, stood in their corner, than Andrew Flintoff. He was, and is, the best.

For all the big external stuff, though, the most important thing in Fred's life by far is his family. He is a family man first before anything else. He loves spending time with his kids and Rachel, and again that is all part of his integrity. Forget the showmanship, on the pitch or on TV; he would say that is a different person to the one he is at home, which is true. I'm not surprised to see him living back up north, which he has done for quite some time now. At the end of the day, he is a northern lad. Down south, people can be a bit more superficial. That was never going to sit well with him so he was always going to return to his roots.

Makes no difference. I can still hear him from Kent.

Chapter 7

A Coach is What You Get to the Ground In

Clint Eastwood was doing his thing, eyeing up several ne'er-do-wells in a small Spanish town dressed up as the Wild West. I was more than happy watching this as I love those old Spaghetti Westerns and *For A Few Dollars More* is perhaps my favourite.

And then, snapping me out of my suspended disbelief, a finger appeared. It pressed the pause button and its owner turned to me.

'What is Clint Eastwood doing here?'

I should point out that I wasn't on my own in this scenario. There were several other up-and-coming young England players. And the finger belonged to Dave Alred, who had made his name in rugby union as Jonny Wilkinson's kicking coach and was now exporting his expertise to other sports.

Dave asked again, 'What is Clint Eastwood doing here?'

To which my immediate thought was, 'Acting'.

'He's assessing the situation,' said Dave. I was slightly lost. Nevertheless, Dave pressed the play button, at which point Clint went 'Bang! Bang! Bang!' at several unfortunate individuals.

Clint, explained Dave, had been visualising what he was going to do and then followed through and done it. Dave was using that as a mirror for an effective way of playing Test cricket. Whether Clint Eastwood is aware of his part in the education of a new generation of English cricketers I'm unsure, but as I looked at him, in his poncho, trademark cheroot hanging out the side of his mouth, I had one thought and one thought only: 'This is absolutely bloody ludicrous.'

I have a problem with 'innovative' coaching methods, the main one being that, in my opinion, so many of them are just so much bollocks. Endless theories being spoken by multitudes of coaches, each thinking theirs is the one that's going to turn the sport upside down. Dave Alred was actually a lovely bloke, who had developed a form of coaching, top pocket, which elsewhere had paid dividends. Top pocket meant a skill being the absolute best it could possibly be, so, in Jonny's case, that would not just be kicking the ball between the posts but bisecting them perfectly. The cricketing version would be hitting the absolute middle of the bat. Now I'm sure top pocket works in rugby but cricket is an entirely different entity. In cricket, the main emphasis is on not getting out. Similarly, not all balls will hit the middle of the bat. There are too many variables of pace, length, line and shot.

We'd been on a coaching camp at Loughborough where we'd barely picked up a bat, and then, when we finally did get in the net, we had to do this top pocket business. If you didn't hit the ball in the middle of the bat, you were deemed to be out. If the bowlers didn't hit their length, they were gone too. In this exercise, whoever did the least to exhibit the wider skills of their discipline, was the winner.

I was facing Saj Mahmood, a good pace bowler but not the most consistent. First ball, he hit his length and I middled it.

'Was that top pocket, Keysy?' asked the coach.

'Yes,' I replied. He was satisfied. I had done the right thing.

Next ball, Saj missed his length by 5 yards. I had to play a backward defensive to a short delivery, which hit the stickers on my bat. The ball couldn't hit the middle for the simple reason it was impossible to get the bat that high. None of that mattered, of course. Under the rules of top pocket, I was out.

The coaches loved their clipboards and walked around as if they were in an exam. Jonathan Trott, for one, was getting more and more worked up in the net.

'Stop writing on your clipboard!' he shouted at one point. They didn't. If anything, it seemed like they were making extra notes of what he did.

Adil Rashid, meanwhile, delivered a beautiful googly, which bowled Joe Denly all ends up. Because Dilly had missed his appointed length, though, he had to do a fitness session at some ungodly hour the next morning.

I'm not stupid. I could see what was going on there – emphasising the idea that everything a player does has a consequence – but to me, a good coach lifts the pressure. Here were people putting us under pressure all the time. It led to a horribly mixed message.

'Yes, we want you to perform to your very best, but if you mess up you will have to come back and do a fitness session at six o'clock in the morning.'

So let me get this right: you want cricketers to show their ability, but don't factor in any element of the way the game is played, and then when it doesn't come off, because the parameters you have set are wholly unrealistic, you nail them? Really?

It didn't end there. At that time Loughborough had a new buzzword – super-strength. Rather than practising their weaknesses, the coaches said players should practise their super-strength. Firstly, though, we all had to decide what exactly our super-strength was. If I had to be part of this inane exercise, I considered, then my super-strength was playing fast bowling. So, from that point on, super-strength practice for me meant kind individuals firing balls at my head at 90 miles an hour plus. In effect, I was practising getting hit. Eoin Morgan was a little cleverer. He had identified his super-strength as slogging at the death in a T20. So there was me, the idiot getting peppered by missiles from the bowling machine, while Morgs was having a great time swiping balls out of the net. Things like that used to annoy me because I wasn't ahead of the game. It was certainly 1-0 to Morgs on that occasion.

Loughborough didn't hold many delights. We used to stay in halls at the university and get so bored. Me and Ravi Bopara used to go down to Tesco, buy clear wire, stick twenty quid on the end, and then sit in the student union with the cash in the middle of the floor. Every few minutes a student would come along, think they'd got lucky, and then as they reached down we'd yank the note out the way. It was one way to get through those times. Everyone had their own survival methods. Dilly, for instance, didn't like sleeping on his own so used to sleep on the floor in Saj's room.

The flipside of those Loughborough gatherings was you could, despite the craziness of some of the sessions, see the talent. Dilly was still in his teens and just so promising, his brilliance combined with an overwhelming naïvety. Once we asked him if he had ever been to a posh London nightclub.

'Oh yes,' he answered, 'the Spanish bar.'

'What's that?' we wondered.

'Café de Paris.'

On another occasion, Ravi rang him ahead of an evening meal. 'Do you fancy sushi?' he asked.

'I don't know,' pondered Dilly, 'is she fit?'

But that was Dilly. He had a childlike innocence. He just wanted to enjoy himself, driving the coaches mad because he wasn't taking the game too seriously, which personally I thought was so refreshing to see. Here was a young bloke who could bowl beautiful leg spinners and didn't have a care in the world. I would put him in front of a bowling machine, hooping 85 mile-an-hour outswingers, and he would be walking around the net trying to hit them.

'What are you doing?' I asked him.

'I was just trying to see how much I could get my wrists into the shot.'

'Well, if you just take one step and hit it, rather than walking around, it might be a bit easier.'

And yet, at the same time, he would ping the ball all over the place, hit it so well.

I could see straight away he was going to go on and be something special and yet coaches would try to burden him with consequences all the time. They couldn't comprehend that his lack of awareness of failure was one of his greatest strengths. Thankfully, he was largely oblivious to their methods. Why lay failure on him? A crazy lack of human understanding.

Players who can do it at a young age need to be given space, not smothered with other people's opinions. That's how Fred and Harmy found the best in themselves. Stuart Broad was another – he had talent, and confidence, in spades. I threw the ball to a then 19-year-old Broady as captain of England A against Sri Lanka on a bad Worcester pitch.

'Any thoughts?' I asked.

Not many bowlers that age would set their own field, but Broady was all over it.

'I want an extra cover because I'm going to bowl slightly fuller. I'm going to try to get him to drive.'

That was it. He changed the field round himself. Alastair Cook was the same with the way he played the short ball. Ian Bell another – I watched his cover drive on an England Academy trip and could just see his talent straight away: 'Wow, this lad is special!'

There's no escape from 'advice'. Even when you're playing at your absolute best, there is always someone putting something in your head. In 2004, I was absolutely flying, capped with a double hundred against the West Indies. I was batting in the nets when Fletcher came up to me. He had identified a shot through the leg side he felt I shouldn't be playing.

'Don't play across the line and hit it to square leg, play a bit straighter.'

I was in the form of my life so I'd never even contemplated what he was saying. Fletcher was a bloody good coach. Technically he was outstanding, but the consequence of his action was that I'd gone from not having any clue about this perceived weakness to suddenly being very aware of it. Next match, predictably enough, I got out to that very shot. Corey Collymore wasn't an outswing bowler. If anything, his deliveries angled in and remained that way. On this occasion, however, a delivery I felt was going down the leg side moved away and hit off.

'Shit,' I thought as a I walked back to the pavilion, 'not only have I got out, I've got out the way the coach told me not to.'

I walked into the dressing room not so much bothered about getting out as the way I had done it. Thankfully, it didn't take me long to realise that kind of thinking is ridiculous. 'You know what,' I thought, 'sod this. Stop caring so much.'

Next innings, I went out and got 90-odd.

Essentially, there are three types of coaches. Those who have a positive influence, those who have a negative influence, and those who are neutral. While many coaches would like to see themselves as a positive influence, the truth is, such people are actually few and far between. Cricket mirrors real life in that respect. We may remember one great teacher, boss, or business mentor from when we were younger because that's when we're a bit more impressionable, when we meet the most inspiring people in our lives, and are happy to do so, because we want someone who proactively advises and supports. The older we get, the less apparent such people become because at that point we think we know it all. The point is, that is fine. A lack of influence is not something a coach should be worried about. Actually, to have no influence is great. Give me a coach who has no influence or just doesn't get in the way, just allows you to do what you want, a facilitator, any day of the week. Most players would take that all day long. In international cricket, all the smart coaches pitch themselves as neutral, and that's where Peter Moores went wrong. When he stepped from coaching Sussex to coaching England, he tried to present himself as a real positive, someone who would make a massive impact, as he had done at the lower level, at which point he actually became a negative. Peter is a big work ethic man. His attitude is you do everything you can as hard as you can to get the best out of yourself. He has been proven at county level to be a fantastic coach. When he then stepped up to Test level, he made the mistake of not taking into account he was dealing with elite players. He should have realised that at the higher level a coach needs to take a step back, not forward. Better players don't require hands-on coaching, and as a coach you'd be foolish to try. Just let them go. Pull them into line when you think they are straying, but telling them how to play? No. In that way, an international coach is more of a manager. They don't actually have to do much. In fact, they are better off doing nothing.

Steve Smith is the ultimate antidote to over-coaching. As he says himself, 'Who would coach anybody to bat like me?' The greatest thing Steve has done is stay true to how he believes he should play. That takes mental strength, especially as a young player when so many different people are telling you what you should do. That mental strength has to extend to coaches – the mental strength to leave well alone. If they do feel the need to intervene, then it certainly should never be to place an awareness of a weakness in a player's mind. Much better to offer advice on how to improve a shot. That way a coach isn't highlighting an issue as a negative, they are simply improving the player, solving the matter without the player ever being aware there was a problem.

Every coach acts for what they think is the right reason, the betterment of the players, the side. They are always coming from a good place; trouble is, very few get it absolutely right. There was a definite period where it seemed a coach had to be doing something all the time - talking to players, advising them, making them watch videos of themselves, to the point where it was actually to their detriment, because it stopped them thinking.

Look at Steven Finn. Coaches pulled apart his action because he hit the stumps with his arm in delivery. Why interfere? Finn was a beautiful bowler. He should have been told, 'Don't worry about that, just bowl as well as you can.' Before Finn it was Jimmy Anderson. Coaches tried to prevent him getting injured by changing his action. He didn't bowl nearly as well – and got injured doing so.

Other coaches are paranoid about no-balls. But better a bowler deliver a few no-balls than bowl at 70 per cent because they are so concerned about it.

Thankfully, that tide of advice, or interference, whichever way you look at it, has now receded a little. A coach like Trevor Bayliss sees that the way to get the best out of players is to let them make their own decisions. From the outside it looks like that coach is doing nothing, but actually they are doing exactly the opposite. They are freeing up players as opposed to telling them 'You need to do this, do that, and this is how you're going to do it.' John Emburey, one of the great men of cricket, was before his time on that point. He would have fitted in now better than twenty years ago. When I was playing for England A, we had one coach who was forever setting out cones, shouting, making us do drills, whereas Embers preferred to talk about cricket, be approachable, playing cards with us, bowling in the nets (better than anyone else we had, even then), as involved or otherwise as a player liked. Embers might free you of your mental muddle by simply telling you to run down the pitch and hit the ball – which is actually a popular method among coaches nowadays. With an excellent captain in Michael Vaughan and a coach like Embers, who just *got* the dressing room, England A was one of the best set-ups I ever played in – a proper team. We won nearly every game. We were a bloody good side.

However, great relationships between players and coaches don't ultimately equate to team achievement. They don't hurt, but there is a desperation, because, I think, it makes a better story, to believe that good coaching equals great success equals excellent culture, as if close relationships are a massive part of the formula. I will put this simply: that's a load of rubbish. As I have emphasised already, if you have a bunch of players with no ability and good culture, there's only one outcome – you don't win anything. It's talent that takes teams places. Duncan Fletcher is a case in point. He understood the equation entirely. He never pursued a harmonious culture between the group, himself included. He was not a warm coach, not a coach who was going to sit round and have a few drinks with his players, a bit of fun. He never wanted to be that bloke, the nice guy liked by everyone. He was a hard man who gave nothing away. Man management wasn't necessarily high on his agenda. He knew that if he surrounded himself with good players it didn't matter – and Fletcher really could spot a special cricketer. He saw Harmy's potential straight away, as he did with Fred, and also Tres, the latter from one innings he saw him play for Somerset when he was coach of Glamorgan. Fletcher had an instinct for character combined with ability. He backed his hunches, and England are at that point again now. Players are getting picked for England who average less than 40 in first-class cricket. Coaches have removed themselves from stats. They see something in a player's game and then mix it with their character to make a judgment. For all the analytics coming into the game, it's ability plus character that matters most, and stats to measure character just aren't there. Fletcher understood that, so while he and Fred might not have been singing lullabies beneath each other's balconies, that was of no issue to the coach. Fletcher knew exactly what he had in Fred and that he needed him. If their relationship never moved beyond merely tolerating one another, then that was fine by him. Fred was in and that was that. Any questions over inclusion ended right there. With a player like me it was different. Fletcher never really rated me that highly. Had I performed better, I maybe would have had a closer relationship with Fletcher. As it was, I fell into the category of 'doesn't really matter'. Fletcher wasn't going to lose any sleep about dropping me from a side. He was pragmatic. If I wasn't giving him what he wanted he could cast his net wide for a replacement, bring in a Pietersen or a Bell. In that way, being the coach of the England cricket team is actually a slightly easier job than being the coach of a county team. OK, the pressure is ramped up a million times, but if someone isn't good enough, you bring someone else in. End of. In county cricket that option isn't there. A coach might have eleven players they know are crap but there's nothing they can do about it. They have to make the best of it.

While Fletcher was generally reasoned with his ability to see past personality clashes and pick the best players available, he appeared to have a blind spot with one in particular. Graeme Swann was a standout presence in any dressing room. By the age of 20, he was also the best spinner in the country. The problem he had was that for others, the two didn't always meld together. Swanny needed coaches to understand the way he was. Some didn't and took him the wrong way. Duncan Fletcher was one of them. He ignored Swanny to the extent that after a single one-day international against South Africa in 2000, he had to wait seven years for a regime change to get back in the side.

Swanny was always one to dive in head first. I'd played both with and against him from the age of 10, when he taught me my first-ever swear word. Kent Under-10s were playing Northants Under-11s at the Dartford Festival when Swanny came out to bat. I was fielding as Swanny – always a decent batsman as well as a tricky off-spin bowler – headed towards a half-century. In kids' cricket, batsmen rarely know their score because no one bothers with the scoreboard. However, when a wicket went down the new batsman told Swanny he was on 49. The very next ball, Swanny chipped it to me at extra cover. All I heard as he walked off was, 'I didn't want to know I was on 49 you ****ing wanker.' We all thought that was hilarious and it was an early indicator that Swanny was a bit different.

Swanny was undoubtedly an unusual character. But in so being he was no different than a good few other cricketers with a special talent. It somehow seemed that to be gifted in cricket meant the addition of a larger-than-life personality. But then again, cricket matches any other creative field. The greats of music, art, acting, whatever you care to mention, so many of them had – how shall I put this? – personality quirks. Maybe it's no coincidence that the likes of Mick Jagger and Stephen Fry love cricket.

Personally, I always liked players like Swanny. I always thought it showed gumption that they were prepared to speak their mind. Other coaches could see the same. As much as Swanny got off to an incredibly bad start with Rod Marsh at the England Academy, the Aussie coach, no wallflower himself during his playing career, appreciated those with the courage to be themselves. He saw it as character. It showed spirit. And he was certainly right to have identified it in Swanny.

Rod once pulled Swanny up. He'd hit a six over mid-off and then tried it again next ball, despite the fact the opposition had put a man on the rope. Naturally, it went straight down his throat. On his way back into the pavilion, Rod took Swanny to one side.

'You've got to start believing in yourself,' he told him. 'You've got to start thinking you're a better batsman than you're giving yourself credit for, then you won't do things like that.'

'Rod,' replied Swanny, 'I think I'm the best batsman in the world. That's why I keep doing shit like that.' And that's how Swanny was.

For my part, while Duncan isn't massively high on my Christmas card list, I could wholly appreciate he had a wonderful cricket brain. Close up,

I witnessed a man who was tactically and technically brilliant. His reading of the game was right up there with the best. Take Jacques Rudolph, who had got runs in the first Test of the South African tour. We had a team meeting about how to bowl to him. Everyone thought we should bowl outside off stump and try to get him to nick off playing outside his body. Fletcher saw the situation differently. He'd spotted something about Jacques' grip.

'Bowl straight at him,' he said. And he was absolutely right. Rudolph barely got another run in that series. Not one person had worked that out but Fletcher.

Ultimately, in all honesty, I was more worried about letting friends down than coaches. As much as I was Kent through and through, when I was batting I wasn't doing it for Kent, I was doing it for my mates in the side. When Dave Fulton was captain, if I nicked off mucking around, and it cost the side and cost him as captain, I would feel like I'd failed him. That was more of an issue for me than anything else. When you know you've let your team down, you don't need a bollocking. Players aren't stupid. They know when they've messed up.

Coaches need also to understand that respect is a two-way street. Sport is no different to anything else. If you've got a boss you don't care about, then chances are your performance will be affected. If you have someone you genuinely like and want to do well for, you will feel bad if you let them down.

Niceties between player and coach shouldn't matter. This is professional sport, not school. As a sportsperson, you shouldn't need people telling you how great you are all the time. If you need someone to be nice to you, you are in the wrong job. If you are out there playing for your country, you should be doing everything you can to move yourself forward, regardless. And that is the same for the coach. Both Fletcher and, in the early days, Nasser were there to do a job and they were going to do it the best they could. Nasser was the one who drove the change and Fletcher was the one behind the scenes who would add his input and ensure it happened. As a pair, they worked well – and that's where the captain/coach relationship is important in a way that player/coach doesn't have to be.

Not everyone realises that Nasser could not only do the man management stuff, but was much better at it than he's been given credit for. More of an emotional character, Nasser would speak to players all the time. Fletcher wouldn't say anything. He was just blank. The only time I ever saw Fletcher get emotional was when he reacted to a pundit in the media or on TV, at which point he would have them. Likewise, if someone spoke highly of him, he would be delighted. He used to read his press a lot so was clearly aware he was seen as cold and aloof, but it didn't change anything. With his players he remained detached and inscrutable, to the point where his emotion wouldn't change whether he won or lost. As far as Fletcher was concerned, the captain was the point of communication, plus he liked the idea of a senior management group – players such as Nasser, Michael Vaughan and Alec Stewart – who would work with him and then present the results to the team for debate. I actually never agreed with this idea. To me, a debate was pointless. They'd already done the work and made the decision, so what was the point?

The failure of the Moores/Pietersen relationship and success of Fletcher/Hussain reveals one absolute truth about the captaincy/coach dynamic: it's imperative they're on the same page. That's where the Fred/Fletcher dynamic proved problematic in Australia in 2006. On an Ashes tour, with its peculiar demands and pressures, the relationship between captain and coach has to be solid. If Fred trusts someone and likes them, he will fight for them and stick up for them no matter what. But Duncan Fletcher proved a challenge. Fred's way was to give absolutely everything. He would bowl as hard as he could, slamming that left leg down with such an impact you could hear the thud of his foot at the non-striker's end. If he then went back to the pavilion and didn't have a relationship with the coach, that would make life incredibly hard. As a captain, you can comprehend losing if you have lost to a better team but when you've also got to play a political game behind the scenes, it becomes so much tougher.

Fred was always going to say what he thought. He wasn't just going to say yes to everything. That's where Vaughan was so good as captain. He could deal with that kind of scenario and never let it bother him. He was an excellent man manager, loved that side of captaincy, and that's why he got the best out of Fred. Fletcher was the opposite. Chances are, Fletcher had made up his mind about Fred as a person long before that Ashes series. Even so, Fred, once he was in a working relationship, even with Fletcher, whom he didn't get on with, would still end up trying his very best to make sure that that partnership worked. The question is whether he had any give or take coming back to him. I know how important co-operative thinking is. As Kent captain, I found Graham Ford a great coach to work with because we just spoke about good batting, good bowling and good fielding, and tried to find people who could do that for us. We had a joint focus on taking the team forward. Lacking the resources and players that England could choose from, Fordy would do everything he could to make a player be the best they could, me included. If you were out of nick, he'd throw at you in the nets until it got dark to try to get you back into form. Because of our shared attitude to betterment, we never really had a clash.

A Coach is What You Get to the Ground In   75

I enjoy coaching and it may be something I do more of in later life, but I am aware that it's a minefield. It's no different from raising kids. Do you keep pointing out problems, areas of concern, or do you let your charges find out and make mistakes for themselves? No one gives you the definitive book on how to be a parent and the definitive approach to coaching doesn't exist either. How can it? Everyone is different. And that was something that struck me during my time at the England Academy in Adelaide – we used to do everything as a group, which I subconsciously questioned straight away. I always thought of the approach as being slightly redundant as surely everyone has their own way of doing things. What works for one person might not work for somebody else.

The disparate make-up of the Academy lads meant there was a real mix of characters. For every Harmy, a working-class lad from the North East, there'd be someone like Mark Wagh, who went to Oxford University – a real blend of people, with different psychological make-ups, different approaches, and recognising that difference has to be a part of any attempt at coaching.

Aussie coaches, with their 'can do' attitude, certainly offer a refreshing and powerful input. They have the ability to set off little explosions in your head. When the fog clears, you see everything with absolute clarity. This attitude can be best summed up in John Inverarity, the former left-arm spinner, an intelligent bloke, an academic, who went on to be one of the great coaches, coming to Kent and later recruited as an Australian selector. Me and Ed Smith were batting at Cambridge University against their off-spinner, the first game of the year, and were 60-odd not out at lunch. It felt like everything had gone OK. In fact, we were pretty proud of ourselves. We strolled into the pavilion and John was stood there.

'That was f***ing shit,' he said.

Now John wasn't a man who ever really swore much, and we were a little taken aback.

'That bloke cannot bowl,' he continued, 'and you are making him look like Muralitharan.'

I'd never been on the end of that type of attitude before. Most coaches up to that point took the view that your wicket was your life. All of a sudden we were being given a licence to have a go.

John took me down to the nets to prove his point.

'Place the ball where you think a spinner's perfect delivery is,' he told me. I spent a few minutes trying to work out exactly where it was, not quite getting the point of what I was doing. Eventually, I made my choice.

'Right,' ordered John, 'take your stance.'

I did as he said.

'Now use your feet. Get to that ball.'
I moved down the wicket.
'What's that?' he asked.
'It's a half-volley.'
'I don't know about you,' he said, 'but I would want to be facing half-volleys all the time. Use your feet!'

From that moment on, I became an OK player of spin. Purely because of the Australian mentality. John was right. Every spinner is trying to land the ball in one spot and if you use your feet and go late enough, you can turn it into a half-volley. It was a simple way to bat, and that was the mentality that Australians had.

It was another Aussie, Neil 'Noddy' Holder, who truly changed my career. Noddy, best known for coaching Justin Langer, emphasised the need to find ways to score, encouraging the high backlift.

'If people bowl in the channel,' he'd say, 'get in the channel and hit it.'

Noddy would make me feel better every single time I saw him. I wasn't alone. I've never seen a player go to Noddy and not come back improved. Ian Bell saw him, as did Michael Vaughan. He is the best batting coach in the world, bar none, based on a very simple method – go out there and be brave. Except courage isn't about not worrying about getting hit, it's about throwing counter-punches. It was so liberating to be told to play with freedom. I loved John Wright, when he coached Kent, but he was old school: your wicket was your life. Noddy made the game fun.

Maybe it's something inherent in their DNA that makes Aussies so free of mental shackles, so ready to be brave – possibly even beyond the reach of any meaningful coaching. Andrew Symonds was a case in point. At Kent, he was straightforward and none the worse for it. He might have been abrupt but a lot of what he said made sense. When it came to practice on Monday morning, for instance, his attitude was simple: 'If it's not done by then it's too late.' No one could honestly argue against that.

In a batters' meeting, meanwhile, the coach and captain were asking how we could improve. The conversation moved round the room, everyone analysing their approach. The spotlight fell on Simmo.

'I just see the ball and hit it.'

Coach that.

Chapter 8

Captain

'A day to get on the honours board, Keysy.'

I was waiting to bat at Lord's in the first Test against the West Indies in 2004 when Michael Vaughan passed me and offered this typically casual remark. Vaughan was clever. He knew how to plant a seed in someone's head. And that seed then took root. By the end of that day it had blossomed – I was indeed up on the honours board, as a double centurion.

Vaughan had the knack. Not *a* knack, *the* knack. He could make a player feel alive, at the heart of the team, without even trying. In the field, he would run over to a player and ask, 'What do you reckon? What should I do now?' He did it to me later in the same series, during the Old Trafford Test when Dwayne Bravo was batting.

'He's looking like he wants to play his shots,' I offered. 'I reckon you should go with a 7-2 offside field. Get outside off stump and I think he'll go chasing the ball.'

Vaughan did just that and we got him out. He ran over – 'Well done.' But in all honesty, he hadn't done it because he desperately wanted my opinion. He just understood that it was important to make people feel involved and be a part of what he was trying to do. Not everyone is equipped with those skills, and that is why he was a great leader.

Vaughan also understood that people struggle. He knew what it was like to fail, knew what it was like to nick off, not get many runs, feel under pressure. He also knew how to take that pressure off others by playing down his own brilliance. He wasn't one of those leaders who spent his time telling the dressing room how good he was. If he was doing well at lunch, I'd say to him, 'You're going all right here,' and straight away he'd come back with, 'Yes, but look at the bowlers.'

As a captain, you have to understand that you're not some kind of wizard controlling everything. It's the people you've got around you who will bring success. Meet someone in life who can't stop telling you how good they are at what they do and you're just waiting for them to mess up. At that point, you can say, 'There you go. That wasn't so good, was it?' Never a chance of that with Vaughan. He was so very good at playing his strengths down – and that, conversely, was his great strength. He believed not in dominating his team but in encouraging positive individuality. In the 2005 Ashes, he knew he had to take down Warne, Gillespie, Lee, McGrath, and by giving his players freedom of thought as well as ability, he did exactly that. The last thing you want as a player is to be thinking, 'I'd better not do that, in case'. Vaughan took all that off his teams. If a player got out doing something positive, he wouldn't hammer them for it, he'd tell them to do it better next time. Players like Flintoff and Pietersen, and now Stokes, respond to that kind of approach. What they don't want are restrictions, to be told 'DON'T!' Vaughan also knew that people like Fred need a release. They don't need treating like school kids. Sometimes as a captain you just have to get out of your players' way, especially serious talents. Vaughan's knowledge of people as well as cricket was what made him a great, great captain.

I had been fortunate enough to witness Vaughan's rare skill at captaincy six years before his moment of ultimate triumph. He'd been in charge of the England A team I was part of that toured Zimbabwe, hammering them in the process. Here was a young man who just got people. He had such a good understanding of each individual and always came at the game from an upbeat point of view, forever pushing a positive brand of cricket. Vaughan always made you feel you were a better player than you actually were. He understood the upside to people, understood what a Flintoff could be, what a Harmison could be, so, rather than beating them down for what they didn't do, he'd focus on what they could. His job was to get the best out of players and in doing so he was very shrewd, a characteristic that remained with him into the main job.

That shrewdness was apparent in Vaughan's own game. His dream winter Down Under, when he scored three centuries against an Australian side at the top of their game, displayed his cleverness. While the accepted position was one of survive and accrue, he worked out that playing this team was actually about scoring. Vaughan had spent hour after hour practising the pull and cut shot, in particular pulling off length deliveries. That was the difference. And that was why he flew on that trip while everyone else struggled. While some of the older generation would go on the bowling machine, programming it to mimic Glenn McGrath's length, and practise just leaving the ball, not getting out, Vaughan practised hitting it. It was a real eye-opener into the difference in mentality that can exist between generations. Vaughan had gone away and worked out how to deal with the best team in the world. Later, as captain, that gave him the confidence to push England's fast-scoring game plan that delivered the 2005 Ashes. In 2002, he was already three years ahead of everyone else.

Nasser, the actual skipper on that trip, was making his own contribution to the victory of 2005 by shaking up the England set-up to make it fit for purpose in the modern game. Without his determination to push through reform at the turn of the Millennium, England would have been in no position to be spraying the bubbly around at The Oval. However, as captain of the 2002/03 Ashes tour, there was only so much he could say or do. Cricket is an individual game – you need people to step up. Truth is, despite Vaughan's brilliance, as a team we didn't put enough runs on the board. Then, with the ball in our hand, we couldn't get them out. We had a sniff at Melbourne where they needed to chase a low score and we got a few wickets, but until Sydney, that was about as near as we came. What can you say as a captain when you keep getting beat all the time? Nasser would rally everyone, and was an intelligent captain, but if you haven't got the tools at your disposal there's nothing you can do. You can come up with the greatest tactics in the world, set a mind-blowingly inventive field, but when all's said and done, you need your bowlers to execute plans and your batsmen to score runs.

To emphasise the value of the individual, my standard line as a captain to players always used to be, 'Don't worry about what *we* need to do, just think about what *I* have to do.' The only one on that tour who could really say they'd done that was Vaughan. He was soaring while the rest of us were averaging under 30. You are never going to win anything like that. In fact, the idea that we could beat the Australians at Sydney in the last Test never really occurred to me. My only thought ahead of that game was, 'We're never going to beat this lot in a million years.' They were so good it was embarrassing and, while every team starts off with the best intentions, it never takes much for the old 'here we go again' attitude to seep in. In any sport, at any level, when you are down in confidence it is bound to affect you personally as well as the outlook of the team. At that point, it's very hard to swing momentum around. But in this case there was a key moment when, ahead of the one-dayers, which, unusually, were positioned between the Test matches, the former England one-day captain Adam Hollioake came in to speak to us. He had us all in his grasp, one of those moments when you realise everybody is hanging off someone's every word. Adam had knowledge. He had grown up with a lot of the Australians.

'You think they are invincible,' he said. 'You think they are too good. But I promise you that somewhere along the line you will have an opportunity. And you will beat them.'

And at Sydney we actually did. Adam may have passed on the captaincy baton of the one-day side at that point, but he could still identify what needed to be said, what those players, myself included, needed to hear. Those words resonated around the dressing room. They didn't win us the Test match – only a great performance on the pitch could do that – but great performances need a foundation of belief, and Adam gave us that.

At that point, I was still in the ranks at Kent. My long stint captaining the side was four years off. But captaincy wasn't alien to me. As a kid, I had to captain a lot. It comes with the territory of being a better player in a team. When it came to leading, I used to pick up a lot simply from watching others. I was always interested in what captains did tactically. At the same time, I would think about how I wanted to be treated as a player.

I would learn just as much from what people didn't do as what they did. At Kent, I watched Matthew Fleming and then Steve Marsh, very different characters who I felt had good and bad points. Ultimately, the trick as an aspiring captain is to pick the best out of everybody's positives and allow them to become the best version of them you can be.

For me, when I became captain of Kent, I was welded to the idea that to be a good manager you have to have an understanding of what a player is thinking. That was no problem for me; I've always enjoyed trying to work people out. I like to think it means you see things for what they are rather than adding a rose-tinted glow. That does tend to mean, though, that your wife thinks you're a miserable git. With cricketers, you have somehow to put yourself in their shoes and work out what matters to them. There is a truth to be faced here: in cricket, what generally matters to people is not the team, it is them. Deep down, with the best will in the world, they want to do their best for themselves, whether that's to earn money, play for England, or whatever. We play the game for our main skill. Bowlers want to take wickets and batsmen want to score runs. Rory Burns scored a century in his first Ashes Test and England lost. I defy anyone to say they wouldn't take that hundred and lose rather than make 15 and win. Any captain has to understand that in cricket it's a selfish agenda. Take that as a starting point and you can deal with it and come to terms with it. More than that, use it for your team goal. If I had a decent player at Kent, I would talk to him about how I wanted to help him play for England. His drive to improve for that personal target would help my side. Accept personal ambition in players and it will help you work with them much easier. There is nothing wrong with that mindset. It was fine with me, and something I always recognised. The same goes for an international player who dips in and out of a county side. We had the England wicketkeeper Geraint Jones at Kent. When he was dropped and came back to Canterbury he was going to be in a different place than a player who was heading in the opposite direction. Earlier, Mark Ealham's focus was clearly going to be on playing for England, too. There's nothing wrong with that. The point is to understand that point of view and use it to get the best out of the player concerned.

I knew also from my time in the ranks that players like a captain to be in their corner. Steve Marsh was a case in point. If an opposition player had a go at you, he was straight in there to back you up. Marshy was hard as nails. He took no prisoners, which, even on his own team, was worth bearing in mind. One preseason, we had a touch rugby tournament and had a bet on who was going to win. There were a few teams and mine knocked Marshy's out in the semi-final.

'Cheque or cash?' I enquired as I walked past him. That bollocking is still ringing in my ears.

I respected Marshy. He wasn't like most wicketkeepers of that era. What's the word? Mad. Instead of all the superstitions and inane routines, Marshy had one pair of gloves, went out, and used them. He was a normal bloke and, as a captain, that's not a bad starting point.

When I became captain, I followed Marshy's ethos of keeping a close eye on everyone and everything. I used to wear sunglasses all the time, which allowed me to do exactly that. I always worked on the theory that whatever I did it should be for someone's benefit. That justified my methods, gave them an absolute core. Even if I gave someone an absolute volley, I was only doing so to stop them from being an idiot or harming themselves professionally in the long run. I had learned from Rod Marsh at the England Academy that whenever you have a go at someone you should always do it from a point of view that you think they are better than they are putting out. It was one of the greatest lessons about captaincy I ever had. At Kent, I would say to players, 'I think you are capable of performing – the problem at the moment is you are not doing it.' No one can argue with that. The time a player really needs to get worried is when they have made a scratchy 20 and their teammates are genuinely saying 'Well done'. That's a pretty solid indication that those around you are thinking, 'That's as good as it gets.'

I would make every attempt to treat everyone differently. I knew that with intense introverts, if I can create that category, I needed to speak to them one on one. That could be about anything, be it the news, boxing, or the weather. The important thing was to start a conversation. There's no better way to do that than to make someone feel like you've got the same insecurities they have. If someone was struggling for runs, I might say to them, 'Jesus Christ, I don't know what end of the bat I'm holding at the moment.' That would get them talking and hopefully they'd come out of their shell a little.

The terminology used as a coach or captain is massive. If you want someone to bat the whole day, don't tell them to be there at the end because the message you are sending out is, 'Don't take any risks'. Best to approach the situation in a different way. Talk about trying to be positive early on, attacking the new ball, a message that allows personal freedom within the context of the game.

At its heart, captaincy is about trying to work out a way to communicate with people. It is also about accepting that, while obviously the best thing you can do as captain is win, it's not necessarily always in your control. You are at the mercy of your team, which is why the first thing has to be to try to get the best out of people around you. It is also about ascertaining how valuable they are. Take note: a captain never has an argument with the least valuable player. It just doesn't happen. Why? Because they are got rid of. Great players, by definition, are very hard to replace. They know that, and that's why it's always the best player who is hard to deal with. It is always a person the club needs.

I always thought if people knew I was there for them they would ultimately toe the line. Matt Coles, who could be a bit of a loose cannon, was a case in point. I'd be very blunt with him but he always knew I had his back. Also, as captain, I would see young players and actually prefer the ones who were arrogant and over-confident. That cocky brash youngster with a bit of character, I quite liked. I was of the opinion that if you didn't have that when you were young, when were you going to have it? Because life is going to beat the crap out of you along the way. For me, the lad who did everything right, was the great team man, did what he should, wasn't generally as good as the rest. The players who aren't quite good enough and lacking in confidence are never a problem because they are trying to do everything they can to keep everyone happy. The bigger a player is, the harder they are to manage.

Kevin Pietersen has become the go-to player when it comes to being a reference for someone who is 'hard work', and yes, at times, some people are pretty desperate to be around, but players are like that for a reason and a captain and coach has to make a decision whether they are prepared to go through that hardship for the return they deliver. I would always say take the hardship, understand that your time and effort is going to be worth it.

Some say Kevin Pietersen was virtually uncaptainable, but personally, I would have loved to have skippered him because there was so much upside. Of course, I say that as someone who never did actually captain KP. Andrew Strauss probably thinks differently about him. He was the one who really did work hard to get the best of him, and I can understand where he's coming from, but these are the players who, as a captain, make you want to get out of bed in the morning.

The main issues with KP stemmed from the fact he was someone who said things before he thought about the consequences. His personality, which made him the player he was, meant he would then dig in rather than backtrack. While many have held it against him, I actually enjoyed KP's forthright attitude, his self-confidence, and bluntness. He had that typically South African abruptness where there is a right way, a wrong way, and no in between. I always felt for him. I'm sure he was seriously hard work, and others who would say so spent a lot more time around him than I did, but I had sympathy for the position he was in, certainly when it came to friction with the ECB. Here was a man being offered the riches of the IPL and not being allowed to take them. No one else was in that position. It's all very well people saying, 'No, you're an England player, you've got to do this,' but he had other options, and within a couple of years he became a trailblazer for other England players wanting to go down that route. I always thought about how he must have felt when, as it became clear their players simply didn't have the required short-form skills to compete, England began encouraging players to go to the IPL. While KP was ditched, the IPL actually became a big part of England's success. Still people complain, though – 'Jos Buttler's been away at the IPL, he hasn't played any red ball cricket, and now he's in the Test team.' They need to recognise that these days we have to judge people in an entirely different way to as recently as five or six years ago. Put yourself in the shoes of someone who can earn a million dollars for six weeks' work and you will begin to understand why they think the way they do. When I was captain at Kent, if one of my players had come to me and said, 'I've been offered a fortune to play in the IPL,' no way would I have said no. We are talking life-changing amounts of money and the chance for immense personal betterment.

Realise the central driving force in a person and you can stop beating your head against a brick wall and start to understand that's just the way it is. The trouble is always worth it with exceptional players because there is such a return. The problem comes to a head when the return is deemed not worth the trouble anymore. For a player also, they must understand they are living a fine balance and that once their value is diminished, they will be gone. The problem with some cricketers is they don't work the equation out for themselves. When they are younger and providing for the team, then the people above will go that extra mile for them. Inevitably, however, when performance drops, the end is swift. When the opportunity presents itself, those they have crossed take it because they don't forget. It should also be worth noting that those with extreme talent are often loath to be told they are no longer needed. Their end is always spectacular by the very nature of their character.

England would argue that they got 100 tests out of KP before he became too much, but I still think there was more he could have done for the side. He was a great player for a good while after England jettisoned him. A team should play the best available players, and the undeniable truth was he was still one of them. His return wasn't yet diminished to a point where he had to go. Say what you like about Kevin Pietersen, but that England Test team was never the same once he was left out.

'Maverick', in cricketing terms, certainly captaining and coaching, is shorthand for difficult. It's a nice way of saying 'pain in the arse'. We all know people who are so in love with their reflection they would marry themselves if possible. Some people just don't realise they are a pain in the arse. Same in any business; if you don't think there are any arseholes in the room then chances are that arsehole is yourself.

As a batsman, captain, whatever, my basic mindset was that if there was a problem, I needed to sort it out myself. But I also had an understanding that it wasn't a good idea to be isolationist. Within the side, I felt it was important to have trusted voices. Joe Denly, my opening partner, became a very good mate, useful as he was a lot younger than me, and therefore saw matters through different eyes. Sam Northeast was the same, 21 when he came into the team, which meant I could go to him to find out what was happening with the younger players. Min Patel, meanwhile, was a quiet bloke but incredibly shrewd. Some may have thought he was uninterested in the team but actually he had more of a read on it than anyone else. Min would see everything and have a view to go with it. Travelling a lot with him, hearing his angle on the side, was another great help. Those voices were massive for me. As a captain, you crave someone to give you another view outside your own. When making a decision I always looked at things on the downside, always wanting to know the worst case scenario. That may sound negative in the extreme, but if you can come to terms with the downside then you can actually start moving forward. Having trusted people onside offered another view on what might happen if I took a course of action. Off the pitch, it would help with man management, for example when establishing why someone was acting differently in the dressing room. I was always, always, on a mission for information. The more you have, the more you can make an informed decision, which makes life a hell of a lot easier. Our physio, Nimmo Reid, was great from that point of view. Physios are always a great ally for a captain as players open up to them. I also had a good friend outside the club with whom I had played a bit of second team cricket in my early days. At that point, he looked after me as a newcomer. We'd play cards together and he'd explain what life was like as a cricketer. Afterwards, even though he was no longer part of the set-up, he retained a great eye for the game. Again, like Nimmo, he was prepared to be honest with me, and that is significant. When you are captain, most players tell you only what they think you want to hear. They don't want to upset you. When you become skipper, all of a sudden people nod their heads and laugh at you more. But I always thought those who went out of their way to make me happy were generally doing so because they didn't back their own ability and thought they needed to massage my ego to stay in the side.

Early on in my career I could be a bit of a handful. Aged 20, I wouldn't hide my unhappiness at decisions made in the dressing room or on the field. If I thought something wasn't great, I would struggle to stifle my opinion. If we hadn't enforced the follow-on, for example, and I thought we should have done, I would quibble about it without compunction. If somebody set the field without a backward point, I would be in the slips griping about it. I was constantly making people justify their decisions. Then when you become captain yourself, you realise that actually that's a bit of a pain in the arse. Thing is, when you're 20 you think you know everything. You just want to be heard. A lot of the time I was a jumped-up little t*** who thought he knew more than he did. I was probably a nightmare for people to have to deal with. It was only when I became captain and encountered people moaning and sulking about the fact I'd enforced the follow-on, I'd not done what they wanted, that I thought to myself how difficult I might have made it. As usual, it's not until you do a job that you realise how hard it is.

The fact I was like that at 20 at Kent didn't help me when it came to getting the captaincy. If anything, it went against me. There was a split vote on the committee because there was a school of thought that I was anti-establishment. Generally, though, I think such people end up better leaders because they challenge the status quo. They confront issues head-on rather than let others do it for them.

My mate on the outside further helped me challenge any degree of misplaced complacency. He was of a completely different mindset, sometimes brutally so. I rang him once.

'What do you make of our T20 side?'

'You don't get in it.'

That wasn't an insult, it was refreshing. I would have to up my game to justify my own place.

Captaincy, ultimately, is manipulation. I don't care how anyone else describes it, that is what it is – the simple act of trying to manipulate people to achieve a common goal. That can be great fun. If a player in your charge does well because of your input, it's a good feeling. But, in all honesty, that's not because they've done well. It's because you, as a captain, achieved something yourself. Emotions, essentially, are heightened.

Dave Fulton had the job before me. When I took over he told me an essential truth about the difference between captaincy and playing, which I immediately found to be true.

'The wins as a captain feel better,' he explained, 'but the losses feel worse. While as player you can lose but score runs and be happy, as captain, that release valve isn't there.'

He was right, of course. As a player, there is much less to be concerned about. You do your job, and try to contribute to a win. Score some runs along the way and, win or lose, you can be pretty happy. As captain, I noticed straight away that I could score runs, lose the game, and feel overwhelmingly crap.

There is something else to factor in as captain. In my time, counties were very much like an old boys' network – a private club, a place to socialise with friends, with the added bonus of a cricket field outside. They tended to be run by people who had retired and, understandably, wanted to get involved with the club they loved. Outwardly, they all wanted to help their club, but what they really wanted to do was get involved in the cricket. As long-time fans of a club, that's all well and good, and 99 per cent are wonderful, but what can all too easily happen is a few may end up playing a real-life version of Xbox's *Championship Manager*. Whereas with an Xbox you pick your fantasy team, here it happens with real people. Again, fine, until it starts going wrong, at which point some may suddenly find an opinion that somehow is seen as more worthwhile than that of the person who has been in the game all their life. At times, I would listen to people, some of whom hadn't even played the game before, and would think, 'How about I go into your business and start telling you how to run it?' Talking about players, as can happen in cricket clubs, as if they're numbers on a balance sheet never sat well with me. I would only make a decision on what was right for the team – staff, players and coaches. A committee member's motivation could well be something wholly different.

That's not to say all committees and their members are bad – far from it. The majority are perfectly fine, especially the members who have been players. They can, with authority, question the decisions you make as a captain, and equally, as captain, you should be able to answer the points that are put to you. Problems can come if you get one or more people on the general committee

First bat, the Prince Newbury, with what looks like a shocking grip.

Taken after an 11-ball 50. Will never get close to beating that.

On drive up the hill at Canterbury.

My Test debut with one of my best mates, Steve Harmison, and Nasser Hussain. Trent Bridge, 8 August 2002.
(Getty images)

(Getty images)

Walking off after my double century at Lord's, 23 July 2004. (Getty images)

The best feeling I had on a cricket field: winning a game for your country with your best mate. Old Trafford, 16 August 2004. (Getty images)

Winning the County Championship Division Two with Kent in 2009. (Getty images)

I hate fielding. (Getty images)

Just some of the many people Murali's foundation helps.

The IPL crew in Hyderabad.

Golf with Warne, Ponting and Crawley (the game drain). The Aussies have never beaten Crawley and I.

The day we all felt very old: Harmy's daughter Emily's wedding, 2019.

The next chapter. (Getty images)

with less insight into the game asking questions and making decisions. Just because they love the game doesn't necessarily mean they are qualified to do so. What is needed is those with imagination and leadership off the pitch to match what is hopefully going on out on the green stuff. The same theory applies as putting together a cricket team – you want the very best you can.

I captained Kent in two eras. The first was the good time when we had money, winning the T20 and putting together a decent, competitive side across all formats of cricket. The second was after the global financial crisis in 2008, when unrealistic expectations met with a massive downturn in available finances. Talk about when worlds collide.

At Kent, there were people whose view of the club was rose-tinted by the great era they had witnessed in the 1970s, when the county had incredible batsmen like Colin Cowdrey and Mike Denness, both of whom had captained England. Then there was Derek Underwood, one of the best spinners, if not the best, that England ever had, and Alan Knott, a brilliant keeper of global renown.

Kent is also a big county by surface area and is near London, which again can imbue a sense of grandiosity in some (I think, in general, that people in the south overplay their importance more than people up north). It meant there were elements who couldn't understand, sometimes in good times, and then in bad, why players didn't always want to come to Kent.

'Surely, aside from Lancashire, Yorkshire, Surrey, and Middlesex, this is the best set-up in the game.'

'No,' I'd point out, 'actually, we're quite a way down the pecking order. Canterbury is not the world's greatest ground. And actually, for a lot of players we're a long way away from home.'

On occasion, we were pitching for players at a price below the market value, thinking that obviously people would rather play for Kent for less money. I was asked if I would go with the relevant committee members to meet Ryan Sidebottom regards signing him from Yorkshire.

'OK,' I said, 'what's the deal?' – there were quite a few counties in for him – 'Are we being serious? Can we match them?'

I was told we couldn't pay what those other counties could, but we could offer him a chance to play for England and at Kent. They'd emphasise that Kent is a family club. Great – but is that going to pay the wages required? Is that going to swing a deal?

In business, you have to understand your market, know where you sit in the game. I always reasoned that the best place to start was reality. In fact, when a new treasurer later came in he summed it up really well. A breath of fresh air, he said: 'You have to know where you are shopping. We aren't quite at John Lewis but we're certainly not at the Co-op.'

Before that, one year I was sitting in a meeting when a plan was revealed to recruit 600 new members, this bearing in mind that year on year we were losing members, let alone gaining 600. Make no mistake; finding 600 new members for a county cricket club isn't easy. There are football clubs with crowds of 10,000 who would see selling 600 more season tickets as a major challenge.

I didn't want to ask, but knew I had to. 'Why 600?'

The 600 memberships, I was told, would equate to a certain amount of money, in turn equating to the players we could sign, and the chance to go forward as a team.

I pondered this revelation. 'So improving the team depends on recruiting 600 new members?' What kind of logic was this?'

The logic was that there were more than a million people in Kent; 600, it was felt, wasn't that many.

I couldn't help wonder why these 600 cricket-mad individuals hadn't joined us already. And also how the club intended asking a million people if they fancied a season's membership at the St Lawrence Ground.

People were trying their best but money was tight. I often thought that if you were looking for a business opportunity, a county cricket club is not the ideal place. It's a very hard sell, and Kent proved it. We were losing money every year for a long time, trying to recoup losses by selling off packages of land, paintings, anything to make ends meet. We basically survived off our Sky money and whatever came in through the gate. Year after year, Kent would wait for the handout from the ECB, via Sky, which meant the club had a heartbeat and everyone could get paid.

That's not to say there weren't some imaginative ideas. We played a home T20 at The Oval, the idea being we could attract a larger crowd than the 4,000 capacity at Canterbury. The problem was that while the plan worked – we got 6,000 spectators, our biggest gate of the year – it looked an absolute disaster. There were 18,000 empty seats.

Another idea was a player bonus structure linked to gate receipts. One executive considered that somehow we would play better if our money depended on bums on seats. We could only think about what would happen if it rained. Me and Simon Cook, our PCA representative, went to check out the numbers. The best four-day gate of recent times had been a game versus Lancashire when Freddie, always a big draw, was playing. Indeed, he had taken great pleasure in bowling me in our first innings. The game was also memorable for Matt Walker, closing in on a brilliant double century only to collapse on the floor on 197 with cramp and get run out. Over the course of those four days in July, the club took in the region of £6,000 in gate receipts.

Me, the coaches, and other senior staff would fight tooth and nail for the side, but it wasn't easy, and at times we had to be quite vocal. For example, someone might reason, 'If we get rid of a player on £70,000 who is having a bad year and bring in a lad of 18 on £10,000, we'll immediately save £60,000.' But that's not how cricket works.

'The bloke on £70,000 is a better player,' we'd argue. 'That's why he's on £70,000!'

But at times, captains and coaches lose those battles because for others involved in the decision-making process it's purely about finance.

In the middle of my captaincy, when the global economy was at an all-time low, it felt like any senior player out of contract might get moved on. Amjad Khan was by far and away our best bowler but his contract ran out and that was that. The club had no money and so off he went. Situations like that were hard to take. I was sitting there with only one thing on my mind: 'We need a bloody bowler.' We went into the following season minus half the team, and the club still expected us to work miracles.

I'd hear it all the time: 'We're going to win everything.'

'Well, I'll tell you now, we're not.'

I understood the position they were coming from. They wanted the club to have success. But as a captain you are so much at the mercy of the players you have. There's never been a good captain of a bad team.

The cupboard was so bare that in one game we went in with a bowling attack consisting entirely of triallists. We fielded players who we were never going to sign because they weren't good enough. We simply didn't have anyone else. It was just about surviving.

The shift in fortunes was so frustrating. Despite the backstage manoeuvring, we did manage to experience significant success. In 2007, we won the T20 Blast, and then in 2008 it looked like were going to add significant silverware. Everything looked so positive. We were riding high in the Championship, second in the table with two games to go, reached the final of the Friends Provident Trophy at Lord's, and again made it to Finals Day in the T20. It was essentially the year we had all been working so hard towards.

It turned out to be the year of everything and nothing. We lost our last two Championship games and were relegated. We lost the Friends Provident. And we lost off the last ball in the T20 final.

We were relegated by five points in a horribly concertinaed table, watched Essex celebrate on the Lord's balcony, and then waved Middlesex off to the T20 Champions League in Antigua.

Around the same time, our coach, Graham Ford, left. For the first time since I'd been at Kent, I felt a serious pull away from the club. I spoke to Chris Adams at Surrey about going there, potentially as captain. And yet for every pull I felt away from Kent, there was a stronger one holding me in place. For one thing, there had been the better times pre-financial crisis when we were all paid well and the club was able to sign decent players. When the tide turns, do you just walk away? I felt I should stand by Kent. I had experienced the good, now it was time for a different challenge, sailing the ship through rougher waters.

It wasn't easy, and there was more than one occasion where I wished I'd thrown myself overboard. I was proud of being part of the team – captain, coaches and backroom staff – guiding the club through that turmoil, but at the same time I knew, from a completely selfish point of view, I'd have been much better off going to The Oval, making runs on a better pitch at a county that didn't have the same financial worries. Instead, at Kent, my batting suffered. Like anyone, I only had limited reserves of energy. With 90 per cent going into the captaincy, that only left 10 per cent for the batting. I was still working hard at my game, but mentally I was nowhere near as fresh. Scoring runs was an issue. I always felt I'd just got too much going on inside my head. I started wanting to win too much, putting myself under more pressure because I was so heavily involved, unable to separate myself from the team and its goals. As a captain, I felt every moment of every day. As a player, on the other hand, once I was out that was it – I would play cards, do quizzes, whatever it might be. When mobile phones came about, they were a godsend. You could sit on them all day.

Eventually, it got to the point where it felt like the club was through the worst and I didn't feel like if I quit as captain I was leaving them in the lurch. I'd just had enough of being rubbish. James Tredwell was coming through, we'd had a decent year, and it seemed a good time to pass the baton on. As it transpired, it didn't quite work out as planned. Tredders was away a lot with England, it wasn't quite going as well as we all hoped on the pitch, and so I got asked to do it again. Except, somehow, now it didn't feel like a bind. In fact, if anything, it felt like I'd got a new lease of power. I had been asked to take the club forward, to be the driving force of that plan, and so it became easy for me to command how it should be done – with young players. I was the one putting the jigsaw together. It would probably only ever be completed way after my time as a player. When you're older and you start making everything about young players, you know your days are numbered, but at least I would be able to lay out the basic structure.

All well and good, except I then started batting like a muppet again. The only reason I ever wanted to play cricket was to score runs. What was the point of doing it if I was going to spend half my time batting like an idiot? I did a whole year as captain and then a couple of games at the start of the next season, and then gave it up again. I averaged more than 70 for the rest of that year, finishing with a 90 and two hundreds. It's never easy to give up on something or admit it has got the better of you, but in the end, captaincy and batting wasn't something I could do. I remember thinking the perfect scenario would be to ditch the batting and just be the captain! Especially at a time when I was essentially captain and director of cricket all in one, doing everything from leading the team to off-field business like working on who the club was going to sign. At that point, the day doesn't start at 10.30 and finish at 6. It feels like it never ends.

Nowadays things are different. The current chairman has been smart and brought in Paul Downton as director of cricket, essentially handing the cricket to someone with the expertise whilst his experience is on the financial side. Such a person takes a lot of the background noise off the captain. They act as a bridge between the coach and the captain. Before that happened, for years every county captain had exactly the same stories. At Kent, Matt Walker was homing in on club legend Frank Woolley's Canterbury record score of 270 when one of the oldest stalwarts of the club called up to tell Trevor Ward to declare.

'It's not right that this man Walker should beat Frank Woolley's record!'

Sometimes I would think, 'Just what on earth are we having to deal with here?' But that was how county cricket was: a professional sport with these older chaps, well meaning but occasionally slightly misguided, woven into the fabric. When I was 20, one prestigious member made all the young batsmen watch videos of Garfield Sobers in black and white. Again, heart in the right place, but an 85-year-old man telling us how we needed to copy Gary Sobers wasn't really what we wanted to do on a Friday night.

The world has moved on, and nobody embodies that better than Eoin Morgan. It was in New Zealand while captaining England A that I first got to see Morgs close up, both in the middle and the dressing room. What I found was a cricketer who never missed a trick. Morgs was quiet, but while some players are quiet because they are shy, disinterested even, Morgs was quiet because he was taking everything in. There is always a smattering of watchful individuals like this in cricket, and Morgs was definitely one of them. In New Zealand I could see that Morgs would always be my sounding board. While some saw a person who, they thought, just didn't care, the Eoin Morgan I saw didn't miss a trick. When the coaches asked who should be vice-captain, straight away I said Morgs.

'Really?' they'd say. 'He's very quiet. He doesn't say anything in meetings.'

But I saw somebody who wasn't willing just to say what people wanted him to say. And that's exactly the person you want in life. I made a point of valuing young players with an opinion when I was a captain. I could see that whilst Morgs wasn't like me in being overly verbal, he had a view on what was good and what was bad, and wasn't someone who was going to sit there telling you what you wanted to hear all the time. I thought that potentially made him a good leader, whereas others saw a person who was distant.

Those A trips are tricky: everyone wants to play for England, there is a lot of personal ambition, and as captain you have to manage that while trying to give everyone an opportunity. Morgs could see this dynamic, and if I asked him for advice he would always give me a good and honest answer. He really was excellent as an observer, a plotter, planner – skills he would reveal when he captained England to World Cup glory ten years down the line. Already in 2009, he was a spectacular player in the one-day game, a different class to everyone else. I knew then that, ultimately, the very best of Eoin Morgan would be seen by making him captain.

Morgs was never going to do anything he didn't think would benefit him and, by extension, the team. His single-mindedness was incredible. He wouldn't mess around trying to curry favour with coaches. If he thought they, or anyone else, was talking rubbish, he would give them nothing. Some people got him wrong in that regard, thinking he was cold. But if you spoke sense to him he would engage. He was his own man and I really admired him for that, especially as someone who had myself been sometimes misunderstood. There were times when I was seen as laid-back and relaxed. Sometimes that's viewed as a good thing. Other times it will be held against you – 'You don't care. You don't want it enough.'

Morgs certainly wanted it enough, and he wasn't going to let stagnation of imagination get in his way. Look at the two schools of thought with one-day cricket when facing a threatening bowler. One team might think, 'Let's not take him on', which can be translated as 'Don't take a risk, don't get out' – both negatives. Morgs's approach, however, would be, 'Let's try to be positive against him, let's knock him out of the attack, make his life hard work'.

Prior to 2015, when England failed abysmally at the World Cup and looked so out of kilter with more progressive one-day thinking, the more negative view was the one that prevailed. After 2015, the team went the other way. In four years, they utterly transformed themselves, to the extent that England winning the World Cup has to be one of the greatest sporting turnarounds ever seen. As ECB director of cricket, Andrew Strauss did very well there. He could so easily have changed both coach and captain. Instead, he just changed the coach, jettisoning Peter Moores and moving on to Trevor Bayliss. Morgs was then given license to execute the role the way he wanted to do it, which was to play positive cricket. That was confirmed to me when Bayliss's assistant, Paul Farbrace, rang me as Kent captain because they wanted to pick Sam Billings for the one-day squad.

'Morgs is adamant', he told me, 'that whoever comes in has to play their own way, so can you please get the message across to Sam that he has to replicate how he plays in county cricket?'

Again, it comes back to players. Yes, it helps if you have great coaches, great captains, but first of all it is about the players. To completely turn it round in four years, the ethos of the side had to be transformed. The approach went away from trying to turn Test cricketers into one-day cricketers. It constantly challenged accepted ways. When his team got bowled out, Morgs's greatest strength was that he stuck to his guns. He disagreed with those pundits who made out it was the worst crime since the Great Train Robbery not to bat out the fifty overs. I loved that. It's something I have never understood either. Why is it so vital to bat all fifty? If a team is 70 off the pace, why bring up the drawbridge and drag the game out? Losing is losing, fifty overs or not. You can lose off the last ball or lose with ten overs to go; you have still lost. That's where a good captain comes in. As a player you need a captain to let you know they are OK with what you do. So if you do run down the pitch and get out, you don't get the silent treatment when you get back. You don't walk back into the dressing room to people acting like you shot your grandma. It's more like, 'Oh, hard luck, hope you do better next time.'

Morgs also understands that coming into international cricket isn't easy. That's a time you really do need to know the captain is there for you – and he is very good at that. A good captain keeps backing his players, and Morgs, along with Trevor Bayliss, got that absolutely spot on. Similarly, Morgs isn't a shouter. He talks to people one on one. He supports them through thick and thin. I interviewed him after the World Cup and brought up a criticism the team received of bowling too short at times during the tournament. I asked him if, in hindsight, he agreed. His answer was clear: 'No'. He always defends his players to the hilt in public. Again, I like that. I always think the first sign of a manager or coach who has lost the plot is when they start shifting the focus on to the players. Then their days are numbered. José Mourinho is a case in point. I always used to love José for the way he would take the flack off his players, to the extent of making himself the story rather than them. Then, over the last couple of years at Chelsea, and again at Manchester United, he turned from defending them publicly to actually having a go. At that point, I had only one thought: 'That is the beginning of the end'. Once a captain or coach starts turning on players, they lose authority. Effectively, they are saying, 'It's not my fault, it's theirs.' How do they go back into the dressing room having done that? You never saw Alex Ferguson do that. Yes, a coach might say the standard wasn't good enough, urge his players to take responsibility, but when they start singling out individuals? Towards the end of Mourinho's reign at Old Trafford you could almost see the players waving goodbye. Player, captain or coach, remember one thing: win or lose, you could always have done more.

There is one player a captain can all too easily forget about – himself. Morgs, again, is all over that. He has got a healthy perspective on what he is doing. Away from cricket he likes his horse racing and his golf. That escape, that recognition of playing down pressure, is vital. The best captains, such as Kane Williamson of New Zealand, play pressure down. MS Dhoni is another. I love watching Dhoni in the middle of the chaos that is Indian cricket and the expectation that goes with it. He is unflappable. He has spoken about concentrating on lowering his heart rate and the benefits that brings both to him and the team. Williamson and Dhoni, alongside Morgan, Vaughan and Matthew Fleming, have all made outstanding captains because while they might have been churning inside, they never actually showed it. They never looked anxious. As a player, there's nothing worse than a captain coming up to you looking stressed and not in control, because that makes you feel exactly the same.

Decent coaches and captains have two things: an understanding of human nature and an understanding of the game. From that starting point, the most important consideration is how they communicate and get their point across. The terminology they use and their whole demeanour is so important. Look at Morgs before the Super Over in the World Cup final. There was none of that shouty, bullish, fist-pumping – 'We have to go out there and win!' There was no great rallying cry. What he actually said was, 'Let's just go and enjoy this.' That is brilliant leadership. You know as a sportsman if you are under pressure. You don't need someone telling you. It was so good to see that philosophy come good, and I hope people respect that so, when in the future, at any level, a team of kids is in a final, there isn't some muppet telling them 'This is everything'. I see it all the time at junior level, coaches talking about how important the win is. Really? Is it? It's not at all.

Morgs, with his single-mindedness, his adherence to a set of beliefs, epitomises the fact that generally speaking, the person who's been head boy at school is not the best captain. They can't always think outside the box, can't see the wood for the trees. The better captains are those who think differently, have a different angle on the game. Vaughan is born of the same breed. When he became captain he wasn't actually the obvious choice. On the 2002/03 Ashes trip, Marcus Trescothick was vice-captain to Nasser. The more they saw of Vaughan, though, the selectors realised that whilst he was very much his own man, he also had the team and people skills that would make an excellent successor.

Often the best captains are not the obvious ones. The same ethos applies in any world of work – sometimes you have to look a bit deeper for your choices as a leader. Otherwise we are still on that school playing field, doling out the captaincy to the best player, a person who often lacks empathy, because better players may have no care for why other people cannot do what they do. Other players have that bit of empathy because they have had a bit of struggle as well. Look at Eoin Morgan's career – he has been through the ringer. Alastair Cook, too, had times when he was struggling.

It's hard to be a great captain. It's a brave and possibly slightly deluded or disingenuous individual who claims to have been one. In cricket, there are some great tacticians who are terrible man managers and some great man managers who are terrible tacticians. There aren't many people who are good at both.

I certainly had an inauspicious start. Playing club cricket in Western Australia, I ended up captain and coach. Immediately, I dropped our wicketkeeper. He was 40 and I wasn't hugely impressed. Neither was he – he gave me a proper serve. What I didn't realise was that the guy I dropped him for had a serious drug problem. Putting his name on the team sheet was far from a guarantee he'd turn up. W.G. Grace would have been a more likely starter. That was slightly embarrassing and taught me to do a bit of research. A good lesson in leadership, you might call it.

But whatever you do as a captain, there's one thing you have to remember: cricket is like a game of chess. I wish I could think of something slightly more original, but the truth is that there is no better analogy. On the cricket field, as on a chessboard, all you are doing is moving pieces to try to somehow get a win.

And then, just when you think you've got the other lot in checkmate, some sod comes in and tips up the board.

Chapter 9

The Grind

A player can become very cynical about cricket. It's difficult for people on the outside to understand, but the county game in particular is a real treadmill, a grind, at times. It's hard actually to enjoy what you're doing because you are literally just getting out of bed, getting out of the hotel, and getting into the next game. If you are on a great roll, it's good fun. But all too often the games merge into one and it becomes a real slog. No matter where I was in my career, I still loved the part of the game that I always wanted to do – scoring runs. But wake up knowing you are in the field all day? I'd dread that. Time can really drag in the field. People used to say, 'Well, it could be worse, you could be in an office,' and I would stand there on a freezing cold afternoon, drizzle in the air, wind howling through my sweater, and think, 'Actually, the office is looking pretty bloody nice at the moment – comfy furniture, internet, phone, cup of tea …' The 'you could be in an office' analogy was completely the wrong one for me. Not that there was ever any chance of me going down that route. The real world of work was a mystery. I used to have a few standard lines for the questions that popped up regularly in interviews, such as what I would do if I wasn't a cricketer. A mate of mine worked in the City so I always used to say 'derivatives trader'. To this day, I have no idea what that job is. Either that or I would mention the futures market, because I had watched *Trading Places*.

It is, though, as a cricketer, sometimes very hard to fight feelings of disaffection. When he was playing for Glamorgan as an overseas player, I asked the Indian great, Sourav Ganguly, 'What are you doing playing county cricket?', because he never seemed to enjoy it.

He looked at me. 'If I had to do this forever,' he said, 'it would be like a prison sentence.'

The South African batsman Daryll Cullinan, when he was our overseas player, remarked to me once, 'You just can't be up for this every day.' And he was spot on. You do have some days where you just can't be arsed. And that's a fact. But it's one that no one who doesn't play county cricket week after week ever actually realises. Daryll said that on the days when he felt like that he just tried to get to 20 or 30, at which point he'd think, 'OK, I'm ready now.' There's nothing wrong with that. Everyone, in every job, does the equivalent. It has to be the case – there are some days when, whoever you are, you wake up tired.

The problem with first-class cricket is, it makes you very old, very quickly. I was playing sixteen four-day games a year from the age of 18, so by the time I was 25, I'd effectively played as many as someone who had experienced ten or twelve years of Sheffield Shield cricket in Australia, where there are fewer teams and they play half the number of matches. Some fight that feeling of overkill. Paul Nixon was such a great bloke, one of the biggest givers I've ever met. The difference between me and him was that he was ultra-positive, I was ultra-cynical. Every morning he would say to me, 'All right, Bob lad?'

'Not bad,' I'd reply.

'Well, how bad are you? Good bad? Average bad? Really bad?'

'I'm just not bad,' I'd say. 'I'm tired. I didn't sleep very much. I feel like shit. I could do with having a lie-in. I've got a sore throat. But I'm not bad – I'm still going to do the job.'

Paul had come to us from Leicestershire, where he would ask Darren Maddy the same question and receive the reply, 'I'm on fire! I am roasting!', hence Darren's nickname, 'Roaster'. What he found in me was the complete opposite. But I tend to think that, ultimately, more people wake up and think 'not bad' than 'roasting'. Other than being in a hotel with no air con, I can count on one hand the number of times I've woken up thinking, 'I'm roasting'.

That was how I saw it. County cricket was great fun but, like anything, when you do it a lot, it becomes a bit like Groundhog Day. That's life. Whatever you do, it can become overfamiliar. You take it for granted a little bit.

Let's face it, there are crap parts of every job. Yes, there is stress as a sportsperson, a lot of which actually we put on ourselves, but show me a job that doesn't have stress. It is part of life and you have to accept it. Thankfully, in my case, the good far outweighed the bad. And it's because of all that sitting around, travelling up and down the motorway, standing in a field like a dog running after a ball, that scoring a hundred was the greatest feeling in the world. The crap made the good feel even better. Preseason training, winter runs in the foulest of weather, you do all of that stuff solely so you can raise your bat for a hundred. I played in snow in one preseason game. Another occasion, I had ten layers on. Joe Denly and I would stand at mid-on and mid-off and often just think about other things we could be doing. But again and again, I'd trade all that misery in for a hundred. The cold days, the preseason meetings, the Core Covenants, the team building, the fitness training – all that was worthwhile if I was scoring runs or winning games. Right there is the sense of achievement. Yes, there is a lot of crap that goes with cricket, but the good times are immense, and that's why we play. When you work hard and it all comes together, it's a moment to savour, and I wouldn't have traded anything for that. There are those who went on a lot longer than me, years longer – Graeme Hick, Graham Gooch, Marcus Trescothick to name but three – but they made those extra sacrifices for the self-same reason – the addictive feeling of success.

In sport, longevity may come down to a simple question: Can I still do this and, if so, do I still enjoy it? If you are Roger Federer and still number one in the world, then the answer is fairly easy. If you are Roger Federer and your ranking has plunged to 150 and you're not getting anywhere in tournaments, then you must really love tennis to want to continue. Sachin Tendulkar, Steve Waugh and Jimmy Anderson are the Federers of the cricket world, going on and on while maintaining their position at the top. Alastair Cook and Shane Warne are perhaps even more extraordinary, performing at the very pinnacle of their sport for years and then, instead of retiring, going back to county cricket.

Family is also a massive consideration. By the time a player retires from international cricket, they will have spent months on end away from their partner and children. They are looking at their world from a different perspective. After the demands of the international game, it's a mental de-stress to go back and just play county cricket and have a bit of fun with it.

Of course, some carry on because they simply love the game more than others. But also you have to remember that they haven't spent a lot of time doing anything else. It's all well and good for a player to finish when they know they're going to be all right and find satisfaction in a similar or different field, and most cricketers do indeed fall on their feet, but that landing mat isn't there for everyone when the plunge through the trapdoor comes.

There is another issue. When I started, a good pro would finish on a similar salary to a teacher. They might have had a sponsored car and a benefit, but their lifestyle was fairly moderate. Gradually, as Sky became more involved, extra money came into the game and so a county contract increased. By the age of 18, I was being paid £8,000 for six months. At that point, as a teenager, no commitments, I lived like a king in the summer, and then in the winter I'd cash cheques down my local cricket club, not realising I needed the funds to back them up. In my naïvety, I thought you just gave the person the cheque and, hey presto, they gave you cash back.

It became clear I needed more security. I was opening the batting all season for Kent on £8,000 and that wasn't a long-term plan. I went in to see the chief exec knowing there was a wage ladder: second team, first team, capped player, England A, England. By then I had been picked for England A, which, according to the structure, meant a salary of about £30,000.

'What do you want?' he asked.

'Well,' I said, 'I know that the England A band is £30,000.'

He stared at me for a second. 'Not for you.'

He gave me a four grand increase instead. To be fair, England A had changed, becoming a development team as opposed to the England second eleven.

Around the same time, I got myself an agent. I wasn't particularly money driven but I wanted to make sure I got what I deserved. Yes, agents took money out of the game, but they gave players more power. Previously, counties had been able to bully players who were scared of rocking the boat and ending up in the water. Now senior professionals started earning over £100,000, a decent wedge – more if there was England money on top. Their lifestyle changed accordingly: bigger house, bigger car, better holidays, bigger mortgage. More and more players felt like they had to play for longer and longer to meet those commitments.

One day, though, it all comes to a sudden end when their contract isn't renewed. But the mortgage doesn't end, the payments elsewhere don't end – they carry on. In decades past, when house prices were lower, it was possible for a player to pay off their mortgage with a benefit. These days, not everyone has that luxury. Players with years of commitments ahead of them go from £80–90,000 a year to a last pay cheque in September and then nothing. That's it. 'Cheerio!' Done. It's a scenario no one thinks about when they're 20. At Kent, as a youngster, I would sit through every meeting about finance, anti-corruption, drugs, or whatever, and think, 'I'm never going to do any of this – it's so boring.' The Professional Cricketers' Association is very good at issuing advice, but what you need at that point is somebody to grab hold of you and, rather than make suggestions, actually put the financial protections in place for you. There would then be less pressure on players when they finish.

I was lucky when my time came that I had a pre-existing relationship with Sky compared to many of my peers who were left to consider, 'Right, what am I going to do now?' They'd gone from spending every day playing cricket in the summer, practising in the winter, chatting, playing cards, to suddenly being deemed beyond their useful life. That cricketing bubble is soon a mere speck in the distance. Those players that they spent every day with have gone too. It happens. I have experienced it myself, a situation where you are pulled up short – 'I used to share a dressing room with that person and I haven't seen them or even thought of them for months.' That's cricket. That's the harsh reality of professional sport.

It's crucial then that as a cricketer you revel absolutely in the good times when they come. All the counties used to play a lot of out-ground cricket, and as players we found it a lot of fun. When you play Championship cricket in a big ground with nobody there, it feels pretty soul-destroying. A festival atmosphere is something different. Southend was a case in point; a shocking dressing room but with great crowds and just a short wander down to the amusement arcades on the front, where we'd shovel coins into the slots, retiring before 7.00 pm when all the boy racers turned up in their souped-up Ford Escorts – you know, those kids whose stereo system is worth more than their car?

Scarborough was another favourite. Always a big crowd, who would often turn on Yorkshire if they weren't playing well. 'Wakey, wakey, Blakey!' would be shouted every time their keeper, Richard Blakey, dropped a catch. Chris Silverwood might be a respected coach now but back then, if he bowled a couple of long hops he'd be panned. They could give the visiting team a bit of jip, too. Probably one of the greatest shouts I ever heard was when I put the 5ft 4ins Matt Walker on to bowl at Michael Vaughan.

'This lad's a f***ing midget,' someone bellowed, and then, in unison, all 3,000 spectators started singing *Heigh-Ho* from *Snow White and the Seven Dwarfs*. Vaughan couldn't hit the ball, our keeper, Steve Marsh, couldn't catch it, and in the slips we were in hysterics. Every time Matt ran in, the rhythm of his run-up matched perfectly the speed of the song. A perfect moment in time.

Yorkshire was always a place where abuse was forthcoming. At Headingley, there would often be twenty people or so sat in a row on the Western Terrace, each with a T-shirt containing a single letter. The idea was a message of support for the home team, but whenever I played they would manage to rearrange themselves into 'FAT BASTARD'. I played there for England one time and dropped three catches. As I headed for the Western Terrace boundary I would see them shuffling around their letters. If I was lucky, they would just spell 'BUTTER FINGERS'. I would always laugh. It's a game of cricket. There's no point being moody and reacting badly. Wear a smile and it shows you're a good sport, just as it did with David Warner when he turned his pockets out at Edgbaston in the first Test of last summer's Ashes when the Hollies Stand were having a go at him for Sandpapergate.

I've seen the flip side of that Ashes coin. In Australian crowds there are those who sit there all day and call you every name under the sun.

'Where's your father, you bastard?' they shout, presumably in the genuine belief they are the first person to make this enquiry. Turn around and smile and immediately they think, 'Oh, good bloke!' Suddenly, I'm OK in their eyes because I'm smiling at them, when really in my head I'm thinking, 'Actually, you need to take a look at yourself. You're a 40-year-old man and you're sat in a crowd swearing and calling me out.'

Chelmsford, the home of Kent's big rivals, Essex, could be a feverish bear pit of an atmosphere. It would become Fortress Chelmsford for T20s. I was waiting to bat once, stood on the narrow stretch of grass between the field and the dressing room, when the home mascot, the Essex Eagle, came up to me and took its head off. I could see this poor fellow inside, exhausted, sweating.

'That's it,' he told me, 'I've been tripped up three times, punched in the guts, by a load of kids. I've had enough.'

For all the warnings you hear on the public address about bad language, how anyone caught using it will be kicked out of the ground, the reality is somewhat different. In that same game, one ball went straight through me in the field and all 4,000 spectators called me a fat bastard in one go.

One of the reasons I liked to captain was so I didn't have to field on the boundary in T20s. The vast majority of my T20 career was spent in the ring. I wasn't going out there at deep midwicket to be abused. Let the youngsters have a go. The day I stopped captaining the T20 team was the day I stopped playing. There was another reason. By the end, in the field I was like an old automatic car: put your foot down on the accelerator and nothing happens for five seconds. When the ball went past me, my brain would want me to do something, but there would be a delay before I could actually physically do it. It was painful, mentally as well as physically. For those, like me, who don't like fielding, the fear of letting people down is constant, as is knowing you can't do anything about it. As captain, I would often manoeuvre myself into extra cover, a little bit too close to the batsman so the ball would go past me a lot.

There's a school of thought in sport that you are a long time retired. Speak to some ex-players and they will say, 'Drag it out as long as you possibly can.' Even without Sky, though, I was of the opinion that you have to retire at some stage – and for me, that time had come. I finished my career at a time when it was hard for batsmen, especially opening batsmen. With Championship cricket bookending the rest of the summer calendar, pitches and conditions were very bowler friendly. Had I been scoring hundreds every week in the sunshine, maybe my view would have been different, but sport doesn't work like that. Every sportsperson goes through tough times, whether it's mentally or physically, and those occasions tend to come with a patch of real bad form. It is then that a player – especially one who has been round the block a few times – questions whether they want to carry on.

It's like anything – you may as well jump in and see where you end up. There's nothing worse than putting something off. You are going to have to do it eventually. You can't keep hiding. You have to finish, and then you have to start working out what you are going to do with the rest of your life. There comes a point where you know full well you have pretty much reached the end and are only taking up a young and upcoming player's spot. For all the talk of big name players and the gap they'll leave when they've gone, I don't think there's anyone who is actually missed that much. The club still goes on without them. I expect when Colin Cowdrey finished, Kent wondered if the side, the club, the very cement of the St Lawrence Ground, would simply crumble away. I had those thoughts too when, as captain, every senior player left, but actually the club *will* carry on, someone else *will* come along. When Ian Bell finally goes from Warwickshire, the club won't fold.

If I was going to leave, I wanted to give my successor a free run. I was entrenched in the club, wearing so many hats I could hardly see where I was going. We had a skeleton staff and I was basically director of cricket, coach, and captain, doing everything from running the team to thinking who the overseas player should be. As a captain, there's nothing worse than somebody on the sidelines telling you what to do. At that point it is your show. You are inclusive with opinions but ultimately, you are the one making the decisions. When I retired, I was very aware that Sam Northeast would want to put his stamp on the position. In any new job, few people want the old regime constantly in their face. It's natural that they should go in with new ideas, thinking they can do better than the person who came before. Every employee in every organisation thinks they are a better boss than their boss – until they have sat in the hot seat for a few weeks. Then they realise, 'Shit, this is hard. This is not quite what I thought it was.'

When I left the club, it was easy for me to completely distance myself. I did it from the point of view of what was right for the team and the players. Nowadays, I am happy to be spending more time back at the club.

Even if I'd wanted to, I wasn't one of those players who could leave the first-class game and keep playing on. Even now, Freddie could take a bat out of its wrapper and look pretty good, but that wasn't me. If I had to play in a joke game, I'd probably face some lollipops that I couldn't hit and then be terrible in the field. If I was to play a proper club game, I would have to really practise, get on a bowling machine, work out how to do it again. Cricket has lost all its magic in that regard because I wouldn't get any sense of achievement. Having played professional cricket for so long, it just wouldn't be much fun – that's the long and short of it. Fred replaced the adrenalin rush, the feeling of achieving something, with boxing and TV. I did the same with golf. Hitting some balls at the driving range was incredible, a straight swap of one technical challenge for another. If I needed to feed that side of myself, then golf was a three-course meal. It consumed that part of my personality. The Canadian podcaster and journalist Malcolm Gladwell once described golf as 'crack cocaine for old white guys'. I listened to that and thought, 'Yes, that's pretty much me.'

There's another good thing about golf: it doesn't last all day and the heating's always on in the clubhouse.

Chapter 10

Perspective

It's true that sport can consume a person. There was a time when my whole day surrounded how I was batting. My only concern would be about how I was playing. When I first met my wife Fleur I was in a bad patch of form. We were in the car and she asked me, 'Are you all right? You seem a bit down.'

'I could do with a few more runs,' I replied.

'Can I help?'

'Why do you think I'm falling over to the ball that's nipping back?'

'I don't know.'

'Well, you can't help me then, can you?'

And that was the end of us trying to help with each other's careers.

Right to the end, though, she was still asking me how many goals I'd scored. If I'd got out for five, she'd say, 'Well done!', thinking it was better than nought.

No matter how determined you are to make it in sport, it helps if you can also maintain an element of perspective. When all's said and done, it's cricket. A ball, a bat, and three stumps. Graham Thorpe had a great take on it, which he passed on to me as a youngster.

'You've got to flip perspective on its head at times,' he told me. 'Just stop for a moment when you're feeling nervous or anxious. You think you are doing the most important thing in the world. But think about something really bad that has happened to you, or to someone you know, and then see how worried you are about it. You cannot make accurate decisions when you are bound by anxiety or overly emotional. Flip it around and you can always think to yourself, "Jesus Christ, what are we getting worried about here? Does it really matter?"'

Thorpey put cricket to one side when he had more overriding personal issues to address in his life ahead of the 2002/03 Ashes tour Down Under. And it was there that I found myself going through my own particular learning curve on perspective – in the fourth Test at Melbourne.

Australia declared on a meagre 551-6, bowled us out for 270, and then enforced the follow-on, which left us with about twenty overs to get through before the close. Tres and Vaughan went out to open while I was batting number five, on a pair, having been skittled by Brett Lee first time round. At the MCG, players have a choice of watching from a little outside viewing area or the dressing rooms, which, in the bowels of the stadium, are essentially sport dungeons. Not being much of a one for watching, I chose the dungeon. From there I could hear that every ball Brett Lee was bowling was being accompanied by a shout of 'No-ball!' from a Barmy Army keen to remind the paceman of the fact he'd been reported for a supposed illegal bowling action early in his career. From their point of view, with a day's worth of beer inside, and the safety of a 100-yard vantage point, I can see they might have found their antics highly enjoyable. On TV down in the dungeon, however, all I could see was Lee getting more and more annoyed. The speed gun was going up and up. I was willing the batsmen before me, 'Please get through it!' They were trying, but wickets were falling at regular intervals.

It was like being in a torture cellar and in the end I decided the whole thing was too horrendous to watch. I wandered over to another TV showing a golf tournament. The American, Mark O'Meara, was being interviewed. He was talking about his game and how, when he was younger, his emotions were very much attached to his golf. If he was playing well, he was a good person. If he was playing badly, he was a pretty ordinary individual. While chaos reigned outside, I was sitting there watching this life lesson unfold before me. Minutes before, I was thinking the world was about to come to an end. Now my head had switched – 'What am I thinking about? This is nonsense.' It totally flipped perspective for me. I didn't want to escape what faced me; I wanted to embrace it.

'If a wicket goes down,' I determined, 'I'm not going to have a nightwatchman. I'm going out to bat.' Barely had that thought entered my head when Duncan Fletcher came down to the dressing room. He could see I was set and prepared to go out.

'Why aren't you having a nightwatchman?' he asked.

'Because I want to go out and bat.' Richard Dawson was down for the nightwatchman's job, but why should he have to face a barrage like that? To me, it was a nonsense.

Outside, the umpires were reviewing footage of a possible catch.

'You're not going,' Fletcher kept saying.

I was adamant. 'I am going.'

It was ridiculous. We just wouldn't leave it. We were going to end up with both me and Daws walking out.

In the end, the review was turned down and neither of us had to bat. Instead, I went out the next morning and got 50-odd. I recognised those few minutes listening to Mark O'Meara had prompted a mental shift. I went back to my more natural position of a 23-year-old just taking in the incredible experience of an Ashes tour, a position that was basically just 'How good is this?' – a standpoint I'd occupied at the start of the match. Back then, Alex Tudor had brought the drinks on after the first hour of play and pointed out to me, 'Do you know? If you were a footballer you would now be nearly three-quarters through the match?'

'Yeah,' I thought, 'and we've got four and a half days to go! And they get paid more!' But that didn't reflect my actual mindset. I was just thinking, 'This is the best thing ever. I'm playing against Shane Warne, Ricky Ponting, Justin Langer, in an Ashes series for England.'

I didn't have the baggage that some of the other players were carrying. A lot of them had been beaten up by the Aussies time and time again. I was devoid of scars. It was barely five months since I had arrived in the England team. The only thing I was carrying was innocence. When I first got picked I had no idea about my own game. I just went and batted. And I was in the same position when I went to Australia. In hindsight, I was nowhere near ready. I just thought England was a bonus. I was so young that I didn't expect too much of myself. I just thought, 'This is going to be an unbelievable experience. Nasser Hussain, Alec Stewart, they're the ones who get the runs. I'm just along for the ride.'

The Barmy Army were also a great reminder of perspective. The best supporters of any team ever, at no stage during that tour did they ever hammer us. Unlike most of the other England players, the Barmy Army never had a song for me – I don't think I was ever there long enough – but, make no mistake, they always delivered. They started out at Brisbane chanting, 'We're going to win 5-0!' In Adelaide, it was, 'We're going to win 4-1!' In Perth, 'We're going to win 3-2!' In Melbourne, 'We've got three dollars to the pound!' And then in Sydney, finally we gave them something to shout about. Never did they complain. When we were about to lose they were always still there singing. They were there through thick and thin. Mainly thin.

Naïvety is a nice problem to have. I was the same when I was a kid and a young emerging player. I thought I was invincible. In my mind I was going to play for England and that was it. And that was exactly as it should have been. If you can't be arrogant and over-confident at that age, you never can. I wish I could have carried that ignorance about my own game throughout my career. As it was, the older I got, the more experience I had of nicking off and getting out, the more aware I became of my failings and their consequences. The absence of naïvety then becomes a problem. Instead, it's easy to carry a weight of negative personal knowledge, mental pounds that can be hard to shake off. I always tried to stay emotionally quite level but in a bad patch of form, inevitably I'd be down. I'd try to switch off, but it was hard. Fleur would probably say I was worse than I think, but I know I would definitely carry the mood of the day home. When the light went off at bedtime was the worst, because that's when I would really start to mull over the negatives.

It's an odd thing, sport. I didn't go to work every day trying to find a formula for world peace. It wasn't like I was a brain surgeon with the weight of life and death in my hands. Essentially, none of what I did matters. And yet, actually, within that professional sporting bubble, it does. It really does. Within that flimsy sphere, all that occupies your mind is you, your game, scoring runs, and potentially playing for England. What then happens is a real flip over in pressure. The game gains a bigger significance. It's no longer simply about personal ambition. Now it's about paying the bills, making sure the kids are enjoying a good life, ensuring that when your career finishes you've got something going on and you won't be out on the street. When you start out, you don't have those things in your head, you don't wear those chains round your neck. Soon enough, though, they start clanking. At that point, you go from 'Bloody hell, I got here!' to 'Jesus Christ, I'd better stay!' That flip over tends to occur at the age of 26 or 27. When it comes, you might be playing for England or, as I was, trying to get back in the side. You might alternatively be a settled first-class cricketer. Whatever the circumstances, one thing is paramount: the ability to continue to play to a level that will, at the very least, get you selected for your county until retirement. For most players, the game is all they know. If they could guarantee everything was going to be all right by the time they retired, if someone could pop up and tell them, 'You know what? Everything's going to be fine', it would take an awful lot of stress away. Thankfully, for the vast majority of players, everything is fine. Sometimes it's important to remind yourself of that. But it's not always easy when you know your club's finances aren't great and the end can come with little or no warning – a quick message to see the chief exec in their office, and that's it, you're gone.

There are two schools of thought when it comes to ensuring there is no early full stop to a career. The first is to warp factor every day up, keep telling yourself how important your career is, in the belief it will make you concentrate. The second is to flip perspective to make the sport matter less. I always tried to relax as much as I could. Andrew Symonds was similar.

He played a lot of one-day internationals without finding his way. When the good times did arrive they coincided with a point in his life when he was enjoying himself more than ever. The more fun Simmo had off the field, the better he would play.

Simmo was always a joy to be around in a dressing room, if a little on the noisy side. A truly precocious talent, at Kent we got him on the way up before he showed himself as a real giant on the international stage. He turned up at Canterbury in his cowboy hat. Only right and proper; he's a real country bumpkin, a fisherman, a bloke from the sticks. Straight away we could see what a great lad he was, someone who played hard on and off the field. His version of touch rugby had to be seen to be believed. It was a very hard 'touch' indeed. He was as Australian a person as I have ever met. We used to room together early on. He'd have a few beers and then he'd feel the need to put on John Williamson, a great hero of Australian music, similar to Slim Dusty, celebrating the outback culture. The fact I was no great fan of John Williamson was of no consideration to him.

'Any chance you could turn that off?'

'No mate, this is proper music.'

Simmo did things his way, which tends to be a mark of a great player. In a game against Yorkshire we had lost two early wickets when he strode to the wicket. He offered hope of turning the situation around, especially when he hit three fours in a row off Steve Kirby. At the fourth attempt he ran down the wicket at Kirbs and got bowled. It was Simmo all over. Who else runs down the wicket to a 90-mile-an-hour bowler? That shot had to be premeditated. There just wasn't time to think once the ball was on its way. We were in real trouble now because our overseas player had gone. Everyone in the dressing room was livid at Simmo for losing his wicket that way. When a player gets out like that and walks into the dressing room, you'd think they'd just shot someone the way some players go on. It's like they stink or have a virus – no one goes near. I never used to bother when people got out. I'm there to score runs and don't always do it. The way I saw it, who was I to comment when someone else doesn't? If anything, I thought Simmo's dismissal was quite funny. I wasn't going to ignore him.

'What were you doing there, dibshit?'

'I just found myself halfway down the wicket having a slog.'

'What? So you didn't premeditate it?'

'No, I just ran at it.'

It was almost as if he had no control over himself – just a pure natural talent. And that talent was only burnished by his love of all facets of life.

Simmo was only following what others had done before. Gary Sobers, the best of them all, once told Charles Colville that if he had gone to bed at eleven o'clock every night he would never have got a run. I was someway short of Sir Garfield, but I was certainly aware of the need to relax. At the same time I tried hard to develop a central mindset where I always backed myself to play. Both were positive mental moves on my part and generally they produced results.

The same as a bad trot gets you down, when you're scoring runs and in a good patch of form, you're a much nicer human being. You're walking through town and the sun's out even if it's raining. You've got the soundtrack to *Mary Poppins* going through your head rather than that scene in *Notting Hill* where Hugh Grant plods through the seasons in an attempt to mend his broken heart to the background of *Ain't No Sunshine* by Bill Withers. What you really want, though, is a level plain. That's where, for me, having kids made a massive difference. A two-year-old couldn't care less what kind of day I'd had. I'm not necessarily advocating that cricketers should go out there and procreate to become a better player, but children definitely deliver balance, and that is one of the best things any sportsperson can have.

Look at the greats of the game – how many of them were as intense away from the pitch as on it? Actually, very few. Intensity is the last thing a player needs, especially in the hours leading up to play. Take England's opening Test in that Ashes series, at Brisbane. You know the one, where Nasser famously won the toss and had a bowl, and then Australia proceeded to look totally untroubled in racking up a huge first innings total. Me and Freddie didn't play at the Gabba – he was injured, I wasn't picked – and the truth is, had we batted first we would have lost anyway. We didn't lose the Ashes because of that decision – one that, contrary to popular myth, many people thought was a good call on the day (there were plenty who did a little bit of a job on Nasser, letting him take all the blame) – we lost because not only were they a better team, but they had a relaxed mindset. That first morning we'd been out warming up for half an hour, doing endless stupid exercises, swinging our legs around like puppets, everything so intense, before the Aussies even arrived at the ground. Eventually, they appeared. They just strolled across the outfield into the dressing room. They had discovered that the best way to deal with pressure was to try to relax as much as they could. Forget all the theories about the benefits of warm-ups and training when you're under pressure. All the Aussies did was come out and have a few taps. And there we were, virtually having a full-on net session. If the Ashes had been about who warmed up longer, then we would have won 5-0.

Nearly twenty years on and, as I covered the World Cup, I was given a fascinating insight into the fact that the way the world's greatest players dispel pressure hasn't really changed. Interviewing players before matches, and especially at Old Trafford for India vs Pakistan, revealed to me that, without doubt, the best players and teams are those who are most relaxed. Look at the Indians before that game – the biggest, in terms of its significance on and off the pitch, in world cricket. It is a fixture of no half measures. Both teams carry with them the expectations of a nation. Inside, the Indian players would have been churning, so, so nervous. But they made a real point of looking relaxed, smiling and laughing. Same with the England boys before the semi-final with Australia. I was doing my bit out on the pitch and all around me they were talking about anything other than the game, which, sadly, included taking the mick out of my golf for ten minutes. Point is, when everything around you is carnage, you must somehow try to play it down. The opposite way brings nothing but more pressure. I once had a coach who told us every day that we were playing in a final. His team talks were always massive, rousing, Churchillian. I'd sit there and think, 'Bloody hell, could you possibly heap any more stress on this team?' Same with pre-match practice. I, for one, just didn't understand the obsession. I couldn't help agreeing with one player who refused to go on to the field until the start of play, reasoning he was going to have to concentrate for six hours, so why should he have to do so for seven?

Pressure comes from telling yourself that something matters too much. The last thing you need is a coach who makes that a central part of their approach. Unfortunately, and really it's only human instinct, when players are struggling they tend to put themselves under more pressure anyway, without the coach weighing in. They train even harder, and have bowlers trying to knock their heads off from 18 yards. In that mentally confused state, they are taking a level of pressure and ramping it up even more. It's like being on a treadmill at 15mph, knowing you're going to burst, and, instead of slowing down and having a breather, turning it up to 20. It's not a good move. At Kent, I would see young lads sat in the dressing room crying their eyes out because they'd nicked off for a low score. I probably wasn't the most sympathetic person. In fact, me and the bowler Mark Davies named it the League of Criers. Mark had played most of his career at Durham and thought southerners were so soft – 'What is it with all these lads crying, Keysy?' It's what comes from a player allowing themselves to be overwhelmed. The real key is to go the other way. Graham Thorpe, again, was spot on with the psychology when he told me how, if he was struggling, he would make a point of thinking to himself,

'I've got a pretty decent life, my kids are all right, it could be a lot worse.' By so doing he would free himself up, feel less nervous, and therefore better able to make good decisions. He was no longer turning playing cricket into something it wasn't.

It should be pointed out, of course, that the amount of analysis cricketers are subjected to these days is far more than me and Thorpey experienced – one of the reasons it's harder to be an international batsman than it ever has been. I played for England at a time when Twitter hadn't been invented. Nowadays, everyone has got an opinion, and it's not unusual for it to be highly vitriolic. Whereas in the past a player might not buy a newspaper if they'd had a bad day, nowadays the conversation is everywhere. An international cricketer exists in a goldfish bowl where everyone is on the outside watching, coming up with issues, real or imagined. It's not easy in those circumstances. Even on the pitch there's no escape. Drop a catch and there it is on the big screen again and again, slowed down, magnified, frame by frame. Right now, such is the level of technology that an observer could find a chink in anybody's armour, the only exception, in my view, being the truly brilliant Kane Williamson. For that reason, the international stage has become a very different place for players. They can try to switch off but somewhere down the line they will glance up at a TV, switch on their phone, and there will be someone talking about a shot they played, their technique. They may be able to ignore it, but it's not easy if those voices are coming from players who in their time were the best in the business and remain the sharpest cricket brains around. At that point the modern player has a choice to make – stick with what got them where they are or go down a different route. They need to find strength. But in the midst of a media maelstrom, they can be forgiven for losing perspective, making rash decisions that, in calmer, more reflective times, they may well have given a lot more consideration. We live in a world of immediacy and sport is one of the most glaring examples of that fact. Cricketers are demonised, football managers are sacked. Forget overnight; people go from hero to zero in a matter of nanoseconds.

Jos Buttler has the right idea. On the end of his bat handle he's written 'F*** it'. Every player should do that. Before they do anything, bat, bowl, whatever, they should sit back and think, 'What is the worst that could happen?' Life will go on. Some people, nurses, doctors, soldiers, don't have that luxury. In sport, we are fortunate to be able to switch that perspective. It's a game of cricket. Remember that.

Jos might have the right idea when batting, but you can never account for the other bloke stood 22 yards away. I wasn't fond of batting with players who were intense. Paul Nixon, the wicketkeeper, would come in at number six for Kent, which meant if I was still there I'd got a few runs. Nicko was a great bloke but not necessarily when he came out to the wicket with four Red Bulls on board. On arrival, he'd smash my glove a few times.

'Right, come on! Run hard! Ones into twos! Twos into threes!'

And I'd be thinking, 'Mate, how about f*** off? I'm going all right. I don't need to be running like an idiot. I'm here for the long haul.'

Other times, I'd play a ball and a batting partner would come down the wicket.

'Keep going! Keep going!'

Again, I'd be thinking, 'What else am I going to do? I really don't need you to say that.'

I once batted against Jimmy Anderson on a bad wicket at Old Trafford, one of my best defensive displays. Jimmy was quicker than people realised. He was also way more skilful – and that's bearing in mind how skilful everybody knows he is already. Jimmy was the only bowler where I never knew what was going to happen next. Like a great magician, he never showed a batsman what he was doing. I couldn't see him change the position of his wrist or the ball in his hand, couldn't see what way the ball was going to swing. With Jimmy, you saw the ball and hoped you could react. Hard enough at the best of times, but on this occasion at Old Trafford, it was a quick pitch and the ball was seaming everywhere. I batted against him for a whole session with Brendan Nash at the other end. Brendan was a Jamaican Australian who had played a bit for the West Indies, so he was hardly inexperienced, and yet he was so intense. After every ball it was the same.

'Keep going mate! Keep going!' In my head I was thinking, 'I've got enough to worry about without you.'

After about an hour and a half of him swishing at every ball, he came down the wicket. 'Come on! Switch on!'

I'd had enough. 'F***ing switch on?' I thought. 'How about you just f*** off down your end and go about your own business?'

Verbally, I was a little more restrained. 'Mate, just chill out. I can't deal with this. I've got enough to worry about without you on at me like a Jack Russell nibbling at my toes.'

There's nothing worse than being told what to do by someone else. Players think their batting partner wants feedback and we really don't. I didn't need someone to say, 'Oh, by the way, you're falling over to the offside.' I knew if I was falling over. 'You look after your own game. I don't want a coach at the other end.'

That's why Dave Fulton was great to bat with. He wouldn't tell me what to do any more than I would him. We enjoyed the battle together and worked together as a partnership – 'Let's try to get 100 runs this session.'

In the middle we would talk about anything but cricket. We might even just stand together for a bit, give each other a quick 'Good luck', and that would be it. Other players, though, would relive every ball of the over, or arrive at the wicket desperate to know what was going on. Martin van Jaarsveld was a seriously good player for Kent, one of the best the county has ever had, but would come in at number three always wanting to know what the bowler was doing, how the pitch was playing, chapter and verse on everything. I never knew what to do in the face of this grilling.

'He's bowling outswingers,' I'd tell him, just for something to say.

Andrew Symonds felt the same. He told me how he was batting in a World Cup game when Mike Hussey arrived at the wicket. Simmo couldn't have been more laid-back, while Mike was a bit the opposite.

'All right, Simmo?' he greeted his batting partner. 'What's going on out here? Is it swinging?'

'Have you not been watching the TV?' asked Simmo.

'Yes, but what's it like in real time?'

'It's the same as it is on the TV, mate.'

Simmo was never that chatty between overs – mainly because he was always blowing out of his arse. He was an athlete who was never fit. He was fit to play, which, as anyone who has played sport will know, is a different thing altogether. Everyone was thinking I was unfit and yet here was this bloke, supposedly a great Aussie athlete, sucking in air. If we had to run to any great degree, that was it – deep breath, deep breath, deep breath, glove tap, 'Good luck', and back to his end. I'm not sure who started it, but most players tapped gloves – except Rahul Dravid, who, at Kent, would always want to tap your bat. He would stand there for thirty seconds, not say a word, quickly wish me well, and then I'd stand at the other end watching him play. Rahul's mind was elsewhere, purely on his batting. What I was doing was irrelevant. He was too busy plotting his next move, his next 150, how he was going to take each bowler down.

The trick about batting as a partnership is always to respect the person at the other end. Yes, your neuroses might be firing, but at the same time you need to understand that the bloke at the other end might not need to be burdened with them. Bowlers are a case in particular. You could hit three fours and at the end of an over they will still only talk about the other three balls they faced.

'Did you see that shot, Keysy?'

And I'd be thinking, 'What about the three fours I've just hit? Jesus Christ!'

Other bowlers were more concerned for their own well-being. Mark Davies was as scared as anybody I've ever seen about fast bowling. All he would talk about as he was waiting to bat was how fast it was, to the extent that someone would bowl a bouncer out in the middle and back in the dressing room, he would duck. He was living every single ball. When he finally came out to bat, it was with only one concern: 'Keysy, will you take the fast bowler?'

That's not to say I wasn't capable of occasionally letting emotion get the better of me. I came back from that Ashes tour looking like I had a bit of potential and immediately was shipped out on the Academy tour to Sri Lanka, which unexpectedly turned out to feature a fair deal of aggro. Sri Lanka had a batsman called Michael Vandort, from quite a well-to-do background, which appeared to mean the umpires would never give him out. It wound me up, and wound Rod Marsh up even more. At one stage, I caught Vandort cleanly at second slip only for him again to be given not out. After all that had gone before, it was too much. I had a go at the umpire, and was then myself given a dodgy decision when I batted. I threw my bat, walked off, and was sent to see the match referee. My mood lightened considerably when it turned out to be Graeme Labrooy, a former Sri Lankan player I'd heard of, but only because of the Australian comedian Billy Birmingham's infamous *Twelfth Man* tapes, where his take-off of Channel 9 commentator Max Walker refers to him as Graheemy Labrooy.

Labrooy was chewing me out for throwing my bat and all I could think of was Birmingham's spoof Tony Greig telling him, 'His name's f***ing Graeme, Max.' Check it out on YouTube. It still makes me laugh today, so you can imagine what I was like when faced with the man himself. I was getting a bollocking, but inside I was wetting myself.

Such incidents were few and far between. Generally, I was one for the quiet life. If I could apply a needle to the balloon of intensity, push the need for stepping back a little and bringing mental relaxation into the equation, I would try to do so. Wholly unexpectedly, I was reassured by an England great of the black-and-white era that he too was no fan of that all-consuming preparation and warm-up. Colin Cowdrey was a gent. A Kent legend, he would always ring a player up to congratulate them when they got their first hundred. Although when it happened to me, I didn't believe it was him.

'Hello, it's Colin Cowdrey here.'

'Yeah, f*** off mate.' I was convinced it was Min Patel having a laugh.

'I've rung to say well done.'

'Yeah, whatever, mate. Next.'

Fortunately, Colin forgave me my transgression and later, me, Ed Smith, Dave Fulton and Matt Walker – four underachieving batsmen – were invited to his house. Colin was a truly lovely man, regaling us with terrifying tales of facing Dennis Lillee and Jeff Thomson when he was flown out, in his forties, twenty years after his Test debut, to shore up England's battered batting line-up during the Ashes of 1974/75, the same series when Thommo smashed Bumble's box, which my fellow Sky commentator has dined out on ever since – not the box, the tale.

Club legends are always worth talking to. Their experiences are often uncannily closer to yours than you may realise. Trouble is, when you join as a young player you don't necessarily know who these legends are. I was sat next to Matt Walker during a game at Maidstone and couldn't help but be diverted by this old fella on the other side of me talking about bowling as if he knew everything about it. He struck me as something of know-all. I was just about to have a word when I finally twigged that it was Derek Underwood.

'No, please Derek, do go on.'

Anyway, back to Colin. The skipper, Matthew Fleming, had organised the outing, thinking meeting the great man might give us a kick up the backside. Matthew never felt that we practised hard enough. His answer to everything was that players should arrive earlier and practise more diligently.

'What time would you get to a ground to get ready for a game?' Matthew asked Colin, in the sure-fire belief he was going to say something like 8.00 am.

Colin gave the matter some consideration. 'Well,' he pondered, 'the hardest thing, especially in London, was judging the traffic so I didn't miss the toss.'

It was possibly the best line we four had ever heard.

Of course, for some, perspective is a little more unreachable. They are tasked with carrying a heavy burden, be it of anxiety or depression. Steve Harmison was a freakish talent. He was someone you knew was going to be the best bowler in the world; it was just a matter of when the penny dropped. For sure, Harmy had a rare gift. It was a gift I also felt he didn't necessarily want. Cricket took him around the world when what he really yearned to do was stay close to home.

Me, Fred and Harmy sat around in Zimbabwe once talking about what we might have done had we not been cricketers. Fred was in the army, I was in the police, and we were both saying how lucky we were to be playing cricket for a living. Harmy, on the other hand, was talking about how he'd be working in a factory, as he had as a teenager with Alan Shearer's old man. As he spoke, we saw this glow come over his face.

'Surely this has to be better than working in a factory?' we asked.

'No, no – I loved it.'

For Harmy, touring was the downside that came untidily wrapped with the gift.

'We're going to give you the ability to bowl at 90 miles an hour, an engine that can bowl all day.'

'Great!'

'But, by the way, we're also going to make it so that you don't like being away from home, dread getting on a plane and hate being overseas.'

I knew from the start that touring was a real struggle for Harmy. He and Fred had been on the Under-19 tour to Pakistan and Fred had told me how, three days in, Harmy had knocked on his door and told him he was going home. Actually, he stayed a few weeks longer but as a first experience of travelling abroad (Harmy had barely been further than Newcastle at that stage) it left him scarred. From a close-knit community and family, he struggled. That anxiety, that homesickness, was a constant presence. He had so much invested in his life back in Ashington. At the England Academy in Adelaide, I was 18 years old and living it up. Harmy was married with a kid. He had much more responsibility than me and Fred. His was a very different world. He didn't want to be mucking around cooking for the coaches and all that nonsense.

Harmy had no real interest in being at the Academy and didn't pretend otherwise. He always had a trump card up his sleeve. Whereas for the rest of us, the main threat the coaches had was to send us home for bad behaviour, he would have welcomed nothing more than a seat on an early plane. It meant a slight difference in attitude. We'd be working on fitness, stepping around him in the gym while he'd be sat there laughing. We had to do a 5-mile run out to a pier along the beach and as we were running back, Harmy would be walking past with an ice cream. The only threat the coaches had with Harmy was to keep him out there longer!

The thing with Harmy was, when we played, he always stepped up to the plate. When he crossed the boundary rope on to the pitch, finally he could he escape his overwhelming emotions of wanting desperately to be back home with friends and family. He had the biggest heart. This is what kills me about reputation and how the wrong one can follow people around. Yes, Harmy could have trained harder, but as a player you could not get the ball out of his hand. Steve Kirby would be injured, Chris Tremlett, Alex Tudor the same. Harmy? You couldn't get him off the field. In practice games we'd always play a team of twelve so if a bowler wanted a rest after a spell he could just go off.

Harmy would refuse. When I captained the team in Canberra, and proceeded to put the opposition in on the flattest pitch in Australia, Simon Jones went down, Tudor went down, Kirby went down – and Harmy bowled all day. He never rested. That continued throughout his career. I saw Harmy bowl 15-over spells against us at Kent, and that is going to hurt – fast bowlers carry pain as a matter of course. As a coach, give me that every day of the week over somebody who trains their nuts off, does everything right, says what I want to hear, but when it comes down to it, bowls five overs and walks off. Harmy is one of the kindest, most loyal people you could ever meet and had one of the greatest gifts in the ability to bowl fast, but his love for the game only really extended to playing. Once he was over the line, he would always give his all, like a performer who lives for the stage, but the training, being told what to do, ordered around, didn't always sit well with him.

In many ways, Harmy is a more understated version of Fred. He comes from the same place of loyalty and honesty. He doesn't want to pretend to be someone else. Cricketers know that when you speak to a journalist you speak a good game. You don't lie; you might think your team has been utter shit, but what you do is put a bit of spin on it. Not Harmy. Harmy was honest. After England lost the Ashes in 2006, Nasser asked him, 'What are you going to do now?'

'I'm going to go back to Ashington,' replied Harmy, 'to relax and sort myself out a bit.'

Everybody was going to go home and relax, but anybody else would have said, 'I'm going to go back and work at my game, do everything I can to improve as a player and help England win games of cricket.'

As ever, Harmy was the only one being honest. Everything is trial by media these days. Look at politics – people don't know the policies but they know the personalities. We are living in a vacuous celebrity culture. But Harmy, like Fred, would never portray anything other than exactly who he is.

While Harmy, with his attachment to all things home, would have done anything not to be there, whenever, wherever, we toured, he would never ever burden anyone with his problems. I could, of course, tell he was down, and knew he didn't find it easy, but he was always the same great company, as hopefully me and Fred were for him. He just wanted us there. The one upside for him being on tour was having friends around. Off the field, we'd all knock about together, Harmy's attraction to home meaning his DVDs all had a north-eastern flavour. He had DVD wallets full of *Spender*, *Crocodile Shoes*, Jackie Charlton biographies, and *Auf Wiedersehen, Pet*.

The life of an England cricketer on tour is basically a lot of time spent shopping, walking around, having lunch, having dinner. I once read Steve Waugh's diaries and he would go out visiting all sorts of places. Me, Harmy and Fred were three people who were never going to make the most of opportunities like that. We couldn't think of anything worse. We would be quite happy sitting there in a café sharing a basic thought – 'England is the greatest country in the world. We're not going to see all this other stuff.' In South Africa, players would get up at two o'clock in the morning to go on safari. I would rather chop my leg off than do that. I've never been bothered by sightseeing. I'm still the same. What's the point? It's all on Google. I went to India to cover the World T20 for Sky, doing pieces with cameraman Ben Wilkinson and production manager Liz Thorne. Me and Ben were pretty much the same, but Liz was the opposite, wanting to make the most of the country. My heart sank when I heard this – I wanted to make the most of the five star hotel. Instead, I had to shoot a piece at a religious festival where they stage the 'ceremony of paint' – basically, they hurl paint over everyone present. When I was given this piece of news, I had a single immediate thought: 'That's the last thing I want to do.'

A few more thoughts arrived seconds later. 'I don't want paint thrown on me. I'm not religious. I don't want to travel three hours out of Delhi on Indian roads.'

Liz, on the other hand, was thinking, 'What an opportunity: a paintfest – great pictures.' Not only that, but the festival happened to be only half an hour short of the Taj Mahal, number one on her bucket list. Ben and I could see what was coming.

'Anyone fancy going to the Taj Mahal?'

We were both unresponsive. You could have literally walked there from where we were but neither of us had any interest in going, so poor old Liz didn't get to go to the Taj Mahal.

Thing is, people are forever getting their cameras out taking pictures. Although I've enjoyed travelling, I just don't need to go and see everything. You get a much better view on TV.

I used to joke with Liz. 'What are the great wonders of the world for you?' I'd ask, and she would reel off some of the most renowned sights on the planet.

'Mine would be my iPhone, WhatsApp, free messaging, and YouTube,' I'd say. The mind boggles at the greatness of human ingenuity that they can create this thing, a phone, I can spend my entire time on and miss everything else.

I was always at my happiest just chilling out. In Johannesburg, me, Fred and Harmy just walked around the mall talking about football, which I knew nothing about. The shopping centre wasn't the greatest fitness regime. We would spend a lot of time drinking caramel frappuccinos, which only later did we find out were about 1,500 calories a pop. Then it would be Nando's and bed. Occasionally, I'd have a look round the shops, find whatever dark-coloured top I could, but that was it really. It was a very unglamorous existence. None of us really played golf, so it was just about killing time. Sometimes we'd go to the cinema. Harmy was scared of horror movies. *The Ring* was out at the time. I told him it was a comedy, thinking it would be funny to get him properly frightened. In the end, it was me and Freddie who ended up terrified while Harmy was hardly fussed at all. I went into the next Test match thinking, 'Jesus, I haven't slept properly for days.' I couldn't close my eyes. I was so worried about this horrific girl coming out the TV.

Harmy had other ways of ensuring he was rarely alone. He always liked his darts, for instance. He always knew how to get down from 301 in nine darts with a good finish. I was never that keen on darts. I always ended up on double one, sick of the whole thing, desperately trying to finish the game. Harmy was just bang, bang, bang! It was never a contest really. But there was only so much he could do to take his mind off what was happening at home. Christmas Day on the Ashes tour, me and Harmy spent it together. Other players' families had flown out but Harmy's wife Hayley had just had a baby. Harmy had seen nothing of his new daughter other than a blurry picture on a phone – mobile technology wasn't what it is now. It would be several more weeks before he got to hold her. While other players enjoyed some family time, we spent Christmas in McDonald's and the casino. It was the Boxing Day Test the next day so it was the natural leisure choice of all great athletes. As much as we tried to enjoy ourselves, it was pretty depressing when everyone else was with their families.

Of course, me and Fred couldn't be with Harmy every minute. One way or another, he had to front up to his issues on his own every day he was away. In that pressure cooker of international cricket, where everything is magnified, your success amazing, your failures very low, he somehow negotiated a way to exist. Back then, no one talked about mental illness, anxiety, depression. In Harmy's case, to most people he was 'a bit down', and he just had to get on with it. Now, thanks to the openness and honesty of Harmy, Marcus Trescothick before him, and several others, the PCA is actively engaged with mental illness in cricketers. There will be players today receiving help precisely because of how those people have spoken about less enlightened times. And there are plenty of others now thankfully aware of the signs to look out for in teammates in the dressing room.

Thinking about those in cricket who have battled demons down the years – that is perspective.

Chapter 11

Nasser

Harmy and I made our debuts in the same Test, against India at Trent Bridge in 2002.

Before play, Nasser presented us with our caps.

He shook my hand, 'Well done, Kent.'

He shook Harmy's hand, 'Well done, Durham.'

And walked off.

I suppose I was lucky he talked to me at all. Before the game I did an interview with the *Daily Mail*. I didn't think anything more of it but then a couple of days later I opened the paper to see a large picture of me looking moody and a big headline about gambling and beer, and how it had nearly ruined my career. I should have realised the journalist was up to something because he wasn't asking me much about cricket. It was all about going out, the social side of things. I had done a bit of media training but I didn't think there was much the reporter could get up to and, if anything, I had played everything down. But even then, he made a massive big deal about it in the piece. When I actually got into the dressing room at Trent Bridge, Nasser revealed how his wife had been reading the article to him.

His first thought, he told me, was, 'What on earth have I got on my hands here?' Especially with Fred already being in the team.

An emotional embrace and a box of Roses was never going to be Nasser's way. When it came to his style as captain, no one was ever going to say, 'He's a bit like David Gower, isn't he?'

While, over the years, I grew to love Nasser – in fact, I'd go so far as to say he's one of my favourite people in the world – as a captain he was hard. He would bollock people – a lot. But that was Nasser, the bloke who toughened up English cricket, and did so by necessity. He expected high standards and to achieve them he felt, if needed, he had to be hard on his players.

Nasser is an incredibly intelligent bloke. He knew where England had gone wrong over the years – he'd seen and experienced those errors close up. He knew there needed to be a revolution and he was the one who started it off. He was the one who took England into that new era. He was like a wartime leader, slightly Churchillian, the one who was at the heart of the action, planning, scheming, sorting everything out. He'd been asked to do a job and was going to do it the best he could, to put everything into his game and his captaincy. As with Fletcher as coach, if that meant he didn't have time for small talk and pleasantries, then so be it.

So while some might have felt Nasser's cap-awarding ceremony was unnecessarily brusque, it didn't bother me one bit. Nasser was under pressure because he was going to bowl first. Those are the days when as a captain you can look like an idiot. He had enough to deal with without us, although the tongue-lashing I received later did come as a bit of a surprise.

Back then, I used to hate going in the slips because I simply couldn't concentrate for long enough. I'd been booted out of there at Kent two or three years earlier for just that reason. However, Tres fielded at slip, which meant there was a vacancy. Fletcher was walking round the dressing room looking for somebody to fill the spot.

'Who does first slip?' he asked.

Freddie immediately piped up. 'Keysy will do it.'

It was the first I'd heard of it. 'What?' I thought.

But Fletcher wasn't the sort of bloke who wasted time talking.

'Key,' he asked, 'you OK doing slip?'

It was the first thing the coach had asked me. I wasn't going to say no. Out of the corner of my eye I could see Freddie laughing. He just wanted me to stand next to him so we could have a bit of fun.

Thankfully, I managed to catch Rahul Dravid off Matthew Hoggard early on. It all seemed simple enough and soon Freddie and I were chatting to Stewie, telling him stories about the Academy and all the things we got up to. Then, in the middle of an over, I heard Nasser's unmistakable shout.

'Oi, Key, you fat c***! I didn't put you there to chat to your fat f***ing mate all day. F***ing concentrate!'

I'd had a few volleys in my time but this was right up there with the most abrupt of them.

'Jesus Christ!' I thought.

Fred looked at me. 'Don't drop one now, whatever you do.'

I'd come in for Marcus Trescothick, who had a broken finger, opening with Michael Vaughan. It helped that I had Harmy there. Walking into any alien situation with a mate is always going to be better than on your own but here was everyone I used to watch as a kid, to the extent I was slightly in awe of some of them. I'd seen Nasser, now captain, get 207 against Australia at

Edgbaston, Alec Stewart make a hundred in each innings against the West Indies in Barbados, and Mark Butcher smash that incredible 173 not out to beat Australia at Headingley the year previously – and now here I was, sat alongside them playing for England.

These were players of a different generation, one that had been left battered and bruised. They had war scars from campaigns against Australia and the West Indies in particular, the great teams so prominent in their heyday. Some had been there when the England team officially slipped to the bottom of the Test rankings following the home defeat to New Zealand in 1999. The tide was starting to turn in international cricket just as they started to retire. A lot of the great fast bowlers were done, while at the same time, a new era of English players, mentally unblemished by past failures, were coming through. I didn't think about how the presence of this influx of youngsters must have felt to the old guard. It's only when you yourself get a bit older that you realise it's not that easy to relate to a 21-year-old. That's not to say there was a separation amongst the players. It was more just a natural situation of young and old. In those circumstances, in any walk of life, you tend to gravitate towards the ones you know. In my case, that was Freddie and Harmy, but equally, everyone in that dressing room was welcoming. Stewie, in particular, was very generous with his time. Ask him anything and he would always try to help. Craig White was also great at putting new players at ease, as was John Crawley, while Dominic Cork was just as big a character as he'd always seemed from the outside, more than happy to give Nasser a bit of chat, whereas we youngsters were all a bit scared to say anything back to him.

Actually, we needn't have been. Nasser would always back his players. He understood when someone was struggling, and if someone was in a bad place he wasn't going to have a go out there on the field. When Harmy lost his run-up at Perth in 2002/03, he backed him to the hilt. Nasser only reacted badly if he thought players weren't performing as they should or if they were being lazy.

English cricket owes Nasser a lot. He's an unsung hero. It was the boys who came after him who went on to reap the rewards of his actions. There's every chance there would have been no landmark victory in the 2005 Ashes without Nasser. He never received that adulation, the open-top bus ride, the party in Trafalgar Square, but he fought so many of the battles that led directly to those players revelling in that life-changing success – and he did so without anyone even knowing. He never shouted it from the rooftops. So while Nasser wasn't one of those people who was going to tell you 'Well done' all the time, that didn't mean he wasn't fighting your corner. Also, this was international cricket, not the school playground. You have to be resilient. You can't expect someone to be tough on your behalf. If you aren't doing what the captain wants, you have to learn to take a bit of stick, to be put under pressure, and you have to learn how best to deal with it.

What Nasser and those players of the nineties went through is unbelievable compared to the way the England team is now. When Ray Illingworth managed the team, he repeatedly criticised the players in his charge in national newspapers. Imagine that? Opening the paper and there's your team manager telling everyone what he thinks of you. You could see how that generation, without central contracts, had to be the thickest skinned. It was such a volatile time, with players in and out of the team all the time, and only the toughest survived. Nasser got rid of all of that and brought solidity to selection. He also brought values of integrity, respect and loyalty.

I wouldn't have seen that side of Nasser as a player because I didn't socialise with him. Two days before a Test match, Nasser was starting to focus on the game, what he wanted to do and how he wanted to do it. I and a few of the other lads, on the other hand, might have been down the casino, or out having dinner, not thinking too much about what's going on. As captain, you are in the same team as your players but experiencing it in a completely different way.

Similarly, the unpredictability of life as an international cricketer had taught Nasser's generation to be focused wholly on what they had to do. Call that selfishness, if you want. It wasn't really. It was simple self-preservation. These were players whose international careers had been spent constantly looking over their shoulders. When Fred came back and played regularly for England, he did so in an era where, thanks in particular to Nasser, who had been at the coalface of the push for central contracts, that was becoming less and less the case. Nasser is a saviour of English cricket. I'm not sure I'd favour a statue to that effect – the cost of the nose alone would be prohibitive – but it would be nice if it could be remembered occasionally.

Nasser is equally professional when it comes to his job on Sky. He has enormous pride in what he does and takes great care. He does so much research to make sure he's right before he says anything. Nasser, for sure, is one of the best to work with. He doesn't waste words, but if you ask him to help you with something, he'll do everything he can. He is also one of the funniest people around. He will argue with every single thing I say, which I love. It's much more fun that way.

One of the great characters, I am so glad to have had a second chance to understand the real him. Nasser was very intense as a player and I always wished I had got to know him better, but I was in my twenties and he was in his thirties. We were very different people. Now I'm in my forties and he's in his fifties. Age, as they say, is a great leveller.

Chapter 12

The Red Handkerchief

It's my first memory of cricket. It's 1989 and we are on holiday in Portsmouth. On the TV, I see a batsman playing in the Ashes. He has a Gun & Moore bat, is chewing gum, has a glare of steel, and occasionally mops his brow with a red handkerchief. He doesn't get out.

Thirteen years on, nightwatchman Richard Dawson has just got out. I am walking out to bat on the third morning of the fourth Ashes Test at Melbourne.

'That's Dawson's career over,' says the man with the red handkerchief.

I consider this. 'F***,' I think, 'he's right!'

Then he adds, 'Who's next?'

Two balls later, I was bowled by Brett Lee.

I had encountered Steve Waugh in between those two occasions. At the end of the 2002 domestic season he'd played a few games for Kent, replacing Andrew Symonds. The difference was when Simmo came to Kent, no one was really that bothered. But when Steve arrived, the committee couldn't wait to lay out the red carpet. They wanted a real good fuss made of him.

Steve was going to stay in Simmo's old house. I stayed there myself on occasion because I lived an hour away from Canterbury and it was convenient for me to stop over. The night Steve arrived, me and Simmo ended up going out before a bit of a party back at his flat. There were people all over the place. When Steve turned up at the door it looked like a bomb had gone off. Next morning, a mate of mine emerged from one of the bedrooms in his underpants, and there stood in front of him was the captain of Australia. At no point was there any sign of a red carpet.

Steve found it funny. The committee, though, found it an absolute disgrace. Me and Simmo got an absolute shoeing from them.

I soon found Steve was never a man to waste words. When he said hello, he was never going to follow it up with 'How are you getting on?' It was simply, 'All right?' And I loved him for that because it was exactly how I expected him to be.

He had come to Kent looking for form. He'd not played first-class cricket for five months and had a Test series against Pakistan and then England coming up. To bat with him was a dream come true. I hung on to his every word. For me, he was a cricketing god who could do no wrong. He always knew what to do. At least I thought he did. We were batting together in a one-day game against Somerset, and were set a difficult target on a tough pitch. Steve was blocking at one end and I wasn't scoring that well either. The rate was creeping up. We met in the middle every now and again, as batsmen do, trying to work out if we were going all right. Of course, when you're with Steve Waugh, you leave that kind of decision-making to him.

'Shall I have a bit of a go?' I asked, after he'd patted back another over.

'No,' replied Steve. 'It'll be all right.'

He had a look in his eyes that told me, 'We're good here. No problems. We'll get it done.' It was Steve Waugh, after all. What could go wrong? Everything was going to be fine. But then, yet another over would go by with him just knocking it back. The run rate was now over eight, and this wasn't like nowadays where that kind of target is easy; this was before T20.

'Tugger,' I proposed as another six balls came and went, 'shall I have a crack?'

'No, don't worry,' he said, in that familiar Aussie drawl. 'I'll come good.'

He had that icy gaze that just made me think he had it all under control. But at the same time, another over would go by, and another. In the end, I felt I had to have a hack – and immediately got out. When I got back to the pavilion everyone was looking at me.

'What's going on?' they asked.

'It's OK,' I said. 'Tugger says it will be fine.'

We ended up losing by 118 runs. But there was something about Steve that made me, right to the last, believe we were going to win it.

By 2002, and barely believably, Steve had been playing Test cricket for Australia for seventeen years. Over that time, the team had changed massively. In his early years wearing the 'baggy green', Steve had been part of a struggling team. But throughout the nineties and into the noughties, it had morphed into a highly formidable machine, capable of crushing any side on the planet – which it usually did. To my mind, this presented a problem for Steve. When Australia became so great, his strength, his ability to come in to bat with the team at 100 for 4 or 50 for 3, the ball going everywhere, was no longer needed. Steve was the man for making runs in adversity. He had something about him, an aura of invincibility, the guy you would want to bat for your life. Every sportsman wants to be regarded as being mentally tough. Steve was the embodiment of just that: a tough man who got tough runs. He was the man to get Australia out of a hole, the man for a crisis. Now, though, he was coming in on the back of Matthew Hayden and Justin Langer smacking the ball everywhere, followed by Ricky Ponting and Damien Martyn. His modus operandi was no longer required. His lifeblood no longer available. These guys were men of brilliance: Hayden, the bully, so big at the crease; Langer, the opposite, smaller, but equally as good; Ponting, one of the all-time greats; Martyn, on his way to another 50 before you knew it. It was almost sickly how Hayden and Langer were in the middle. Walk past most batsmen and usually you hear them saying things like, 'He's swinging it', or 'This guy's fast', but with those two it would be, 'How much fun is this? We're smashing them everywhere! It's like playing in the back garden!'

More often than not, Steve was entering the fray with his team, not at 50-3, but 350 for 3. His juices just weren't flowing. Before Sydney, he was in no nick whatsoever, scoring only two 50s, and the press were into him, asking questions about his place in the Test side, the suggestion being he was only surviving because he was captain. Steve had already been dropped from the one-day team and the world he so loved seemed to be slipping away. Not that he was ever going to disappear from any format – one-day or Test – without a fight. A return to the one-day team was definitely in his sights. The World Cup was coming up and, with the England-Australia one-day games rather oddly being played between the Tests, he wanted to force his way back in. He played in a one-day warm-up against England for New South Wales, a big chance for him to reaffirm his value to the side, only for Michael Slater to steal the opportunity by getting a hundred at the top of the innings. Steve eventually arrived at the crease with less than 30 needed. He had nowhere to go in terms of a statement innings. Boxed into a corner, there was nothing he could do. Except he didn't see it that way. He hit 24, with three sixes to win the game off Ronnie Irani. That was it, game won. From nowhere he had created a huge storyline all around himself. The entire crowd was on their feet chanting 'Steve Waugh! Steve Waugh!' I was staring, unbelieving, at this scene, thinking, 'Who does that?'

Steve, clearly, was never a man who was going to go quietly. Nevertheless, the final Test at Sydney was effectively his last Test match. If he didn't get runs, that was the end of it. Australians are brutal. They're not like us in England where we allow people who have given good service to go out on their own terms. In Australia, they just get rid. And back then they could do so with impunity. They had some big cabs waiting on the rank – Darren Lehmann, Martin Love, to name but two.

On the plus side for Steve, his bowling was going OK – he'd got me lbw in our first innings. Butch had done a little better, making a brilliant century, and with the ball starting to bounce off a length and the odd one going through the surface, it looked like we'd got a good score, especially when Andrew Caddick then got the ball seaming around, and all of a sudden, Australia were 56-3.

Hmm – 56-3. For once, Steve Waugh was coming out to bat with his side under pressure, and he was in no mood to prevaricate. There were two sessions left of the day's play and straight away he played a cut shot for four. From then on, everything was hitting the middle of his bat.

'This', I thought, 'is what I have grown up watching. This is the Steve Waugh I remember.'

Sydney, as opposed to Melbourne, which is basically a massive bowl full of 90,000 people shouting abuse, is a ground where the crowd is right on top of the players. It is much more of an amphitheatre, and as Steve got closer and closer to a century, the crowd were all over what was happening.

When the last over of the day arrived, bowled by Richard Dawson, Steve still needed five for his ton. He took three off the fourth ball, and then Adam Gilchrist took a single to get him back on strike. The noise level by now was unbelievable. But Nasser wasn't going to make it easy. He slowed play right down, sorting out the field, Steve taking the opportunity to reach into his pocket for the famous red handkerchief to mop his brow. I was watching all this from point, happy because I was effectively out of the game; with the off-spinner Richard Dawson on, there was no way the ball was coming to me. My head was playing every scene I remembered of Steve as a kid: him tearing his calf at The Oval, hobbling to a hundred practically on one leg; him standing nerveless, immovable, utterly dominant at the crease. And now here he was, in perhaps the ultimate moment of his own brilliance, right there in front of me. That red handkerchief right there in front of me. I was still a young man – the Steve Waugh of memory wasn't distant. He was front and forward in my mind. Alive, never more alive, than right there at the SCG.

Had I been captain, I'd have told Daws to lob it up, bowl a pie. Steve was going to take the delivery on whatever, and with two men out on the slog sweep there was always a chance he could be caught. In the end, Daws bowled a dart, which Steve latched on to and cut past me and Caddick for four. If a jumbo jet had taken off from the outfield, the roar at that moment couldn't have been louder. I was stood 5 yards from Daws in the aftermath and the whole SCG was chanting Steve's name. Like a battle chant, something from a film. We both looked around and, as one, said, 'How good is this?' Not that we could hear each other. We just saw each other's lips moving. It was the most amazing moment of sporting history, one of the most incredible in cricket. To think that there, somewhere in the middle of all that, was a single person receiving such a welter of adulation, was unbelievable. And again I was reminded that true triumph comes only from adversity. In the second Test at Adelaide, Nasser had insulted Steve by setting the field back for the other batsmen and then bringing them all in when he was on strike because he was playing so badly. I saw the look of contempt for Nasser on Steve's face when he did that. But had he not suffered such a bad trot, such ignominy, none of it would have meant as much.

You can be known as a great player, but to be known as mentally tough, to have performed when your side needed you most, that is the ultimate accolade. To stand up when the chips are down, that is what we all want from our sportspeople. I don't care what job you are in, surely you want to be known as the person who can be counted on when the odds are stacked against you. In cricket, that person was Steve Waugh. The way someone plays cricket tends to be uncannily reflective of the way they are as a person. Look at David Gower, a man born with grace. You could see that when he was presenting – a whole manner of chaos going on in his ears, directors and producers flapping, and yet he himself was totally unflappable. With Steve Waugh, every shot, every mannerism revealed a grittiness. His brother Mark was different again. He was a flamboyant character. Batting was an art to him. To his brother, it was practical, pragmatic.

Ed Smith once asked Steve about mental toughness. He told him he had exactly the same sort of fears and doubts as everyone else, he was just better at silencing them. You never would have guessed that was the case when you looked at him. There was never any suggestion of any doubt at all. If those doubts did exist, he always won the battle.

After I made my 47 at Perth in that Ashes series, Steve was asked what he thought of me as a player.

'He doesn't give a shit about much and is real relaxed,' he replied. 'I like that in a bloke. It stops him getting overawed.' It was a great compliment coming from him.

I felt overawed.

Chapter 13

Serve and Volley

Steve Kirby played for Yorkshire. He burst on to the scene from nowhere and made his debut at Headingley against Kent. His first ball was a quick bouncer at Dave Fulton and he finished his follow through inches from his face, giving him a right volley. To be fair to Steve, he hadn't singled Dave out for treatment. Everyone he bowled at came in for bucketloads of abuse. That night we went out to watch the rugby league on the ground next door. Steve came along too. We couldn't believe what a nice guy he was. Our captain, Matthew Fleming, part of the Fleming dynasty that included a merchant bank and James Bond author Ian, went up to him.

'Very well bowled today, Steve,' he praised him. 'Congratulations on your debut. I hope you have a long and prosperous career.'

'Thank you so much, Mr Fleming,' Kirbs replied. 'It's an honour to play against somebody like you.'

We tried to tell Matthew that Steve wasn't such a nice guy when you came nose to nose with him on the pitch, but he couldn't understand what we were on about.

'What a lovely guy,' he kept saying.

Next morning, Matthew, who hadn't yet faced Kirbs, went out to bat and he immediately ripped a bouncer past his face.

'Get back to your pot of gold, you rich c***,' he told him. It was one of the great lines.

Kirbs came out to Australia on the Academy trip. His mouth accompanied him but this time he was keen to leave a different kind of impression. Rod Marsh was staging a meeting with the squad and, after everyone else had finished speaking, Steve piped up.

'Just so you know, Rod,' he stated, 'I'd run through a brick wall for you.'

As it turned out, Kirbs didn't bowl a ball for several weeks of that trip through injury. After a fortnight of not being able to do anything, Rod shouted across to him. 'That f***ing wall looks a long way away now Kirby!'

The aggression Kirbs showed on the pitch was just part of his schtick. I scored a hundred against him on four occasions. Each time, the shout went up, 'Round the wicket, umpire, call an ambulance!'

No one was deemed too good for a classic Kirbs sledge, although he wasn't always guaranteed to get it right.

'I've seen a better batter in my fridge,' he told Mike Atherton, which didn't quite have the same cutting quality as what he'd meant to say – 'I've seen a better batter in my fish and chip shop.'

Kirbs was such an incredible character. When I captained him in Canberra on that infamous flat pitch, I talked to him about staying one side of the wicket, bowling as if there were six stumps.

'Imagine there's another three outside the original three,' I told him. 'That's where I want you to bowl it. We'll have everyone fielding on the offside. Do you understand the plan, Kirbs?'

'Yeah, no worries.' He bowled a slow full toss and got hammered over the leg side.

'Kirbs,' I enquired, 'what was that? We need to stick to the plan. Stick it outside off stump and bowl to the field.'

'Give me the ball,' he said. 'I'm going to bowl him a beamer.'

Mad as a cut snake, as the Aussies used to say.

As a batsman, I always used to enjoy it if a bowler had a go at me, and I would always come back at them. It never bothered me because my view was that the bowlers who sledged the most were also the most insecure. It was all a front. And the thing was, if you got runs they would always have to stop. Dominic Cork, naturally, was different. He would have a go whatever score you were on, probably to fire himself up more than anything. Freddie, meanwhile, was one of those who favoured giving you a bit of a look, one that asked, 'What are you even doing here?' without ever needing to say it.

As a captain, I understood some players were better left alone. You didn't sledge them because it would just get them going. Warney was a case in point. A handy batsman, he famously always wanted to get a hundred. On one occasion we had Hampshire in trouble and he came out and played his usual counter-attacking innings. When he got to 90, Dave Fulton strolled past him. 'Have you ever got a hundred, Warney?' he enquired. He thought he was being clever, reminding Warney of the milestone, distracting him from the job in hand by putting it front and centre in his head.

'No,' he replied, 'I've got 99 a few times but gassed them all.'

As the bowler ran in for the next ball, he turned to us in the slips – 'I've got a few poles though!'

From that moment on, Warney just laid into Fults. 'Thanks, mate. I was going to throw it away there. Thanks for making me concentrate. Thanks for helping me.' He got his hundred. To be honest, once Fults had wound him up, it was never in doubt.

Start a fight with Warney and you knew about it. Steve Waugh was the same. No one tried to switch him on when he was at Kent – aside from Kirbs. When again we played Yorkshire, they had agreed amongst themselves that nobody should sledge him. Kirbs didn't listen. In he steamed, giving him the usual volley. He might as well have uncapped a volcano. Every time Kirbs walked back to his mark, Steve was following him, abusing him.

'Who are you? This is my ground. I love it here at Headingley. How dare you talk to me.'

Kirbs was telling him to shut up but by then it was way too late. Everything he did was only going to make it worse. Waugh smashed 146.

I knew only too well what a mistake Kirbs had made. I had seen first-hand, in Adelaide, on the Ashes trip, how Steve Waugh would try to pick a fight to give himself a jolt. Fred was injured but, as twelfth man, was fielding at leg slip. As he did so, he burped. Waugh gave him an absolute volley.

'You're a fucking rude prick, aren't you? Who are you anyway? The twenty-eighth man?'

I was at short leg and Fred and I looked at each other. We didn't know what to do. Especially me – Steve Waugh was my hero. It was the one time me and Fred were lost for words. In the end we mumbled a meek 'F*** off' and left it there.

That Australian line-up was just incredible. Why would they ever be intimidated by anybody? They were streets ahead in every discipline. For the Boxing Day Test in Melbourne I was at third slip. It was the best seat in the house. I didn't have to do anything - they never nicked it. Andrew Caddick was abusing Langer, getting into him, trying to rattle him, telling him he wasn't up to it. Caddick, such a good bowler, so underrated, could be a fiery customer and it wasn't uncommon for him to have a word, but I was just thinking, 'Why are you getting into Langer? What's the point?'

Caddy was insistent. 'I think we're getting to him,' he kept telling the rest of us. Langer got 250 over the course of nearly ten hours.

Everyone used to say the same: the true greats, the likes of Brian Lara, Shane Warne, Steve Waugh, leave them because it just gets them going. Sachin Tendulkar was a little different. It didn't so much get him going as not even touch the sides. I was stood at silly point in a Test match when Nasser started sledging him. The little master had a habit of making the opposition wait, forever stopping the game if he thought there was someone or something behind the bowler's arm, and this occasion was no different.

'Oh, Sachin's in charge. Sachin's running the game. Let's all wait for Sachin,' Nasser noted sarcastically. Sachin wouldn't even look at him. Like most Indians, he didn't say a great deal. He just let his bat do the talking. He got 190.

Others believed that sledging volatile characters would work in their favour. At Kent, Steve Marsh had an usual approach. A real gutsy bloke, who lived life hard on and off the field, he was of the mindset that if you sledged Wasim Akram, he would bowl quicker and quicker, trying to hit you on the head. I know what you're thinking: Why would anyone want to wind up one of the world's most venomous fast bowlers so he aimed at your head? But wait a minute, there is some logic to Steve's thinking. He felt that Wasim bowling bouncers was preferable to Wasim bowling the length balls that so often got batsmen out. Certainly, Marshy's method wound Wasim up. Trouble is, cricket operates with two batsmen, not one. If a rabbit like Alan Igglesden was batting with Marshy, he was quick to point out to Wasim that it wasn't him doing the winding up, desperate to make sure Wasim knew he shouldn't be the one on the end of the onslaught.

Andrew Symonds was another who was never going to be told there was only one way to skin a cat. Encountering England wicketkeeper Jack Russell in a one-day match against Gloucestershire was a case in point. Jack was nothing if not quirky, to the extent he would call out the name of the fielder when he hit the ball. 'Two to Keysy.' 'One to Walker.' Out on the boundary I'd hear him shout out, 'Go! Keysy isn't moving!' Unbelievable. He would talk the whole time. One thing every player knew not to do to Jack was sledge. It would just make him concentrate more, and for a man already exceptionally good at concentrating, that wasn't a particularly good approach. Simmo, however, had other ideas. As Jack strode to the wicket in a one-day game, we reminded each other to keep it low-key. Simmo was having none of it. 'F*** that!' he stated, and headed, Cruise missile-esque, straight for the Gloucestershire limpet, meeting him halfway.

'Just me and you, Jack,' he intoned, 'you little shit.'

He gave Jack a volley all the way to the crease. And, just as we'd warned, it made him even more impossible to dislodge.

It was never anything personal with Simmo. He just had the Australian point of view. I'd been on the end of Australian sledging myself. Matthew Hayden never shut up when I turned up on that Ashes series Down Under. He was obsessed with my helmet, how it looked, how I wore it, how it sat on my head. To me, it was just a helmet. I couldn't for the life of me work out what the hell he was on about. Justin Langer, meanwhile, would call me Joe Bugner – and more people than I'd like have smiled in recognition when I've told them that. The Aussies weren't alone in the mindless abuse department. South African all-rounder Andrew Hall once told me, 'Shut up, you fat bastard,' enquiring, 'If I covered myself in chocolate would you eat me as well?'

All I could think was, 'How on earth has he even thought that up?'

Hall's captain, Graeme Smith, was another. He would sidle up when not much was going on and stick the odd unpleasantry in. But insults are just pointless, pathetic.

Steve Waugh was cleverer. Famously, he described sledging as 'mental disintegration', but that didn't come from inane jibes or calling people names. Steve worked with knowledge. His modus operandi was to take existing wounds and open them even wider. Arrive at the crease and Steve would remind you of past failures, to the extent he pretty much painted them fresh on a canvas in front of your eyes. He'd set the field identical to the one when you were last out. And on the off-chance that didn't resonate, he'd kindly explain it to you.

'Remember this?' he'd ask. 'You should do. This is what it was like when you last got out. You know the same thing is going to happen today.' And more often than not, it did.

Steve's was the one voice in the field you really didn't want to hear. At Perth I walked out to bat on the fastest pitch I'd ever played on. Brett Lee had just been brought back into the team and before I went out, Vaughany and Tres were debating whether he was quicker than Shoaib Akhtar. I was listening to this thinking, 'Oh my God! I could do without this. I'm going to have to face him.' I didn't really want to hear an argument about who was 95mph and who was 96. As I took strike, I was genuinely worried about how I was going to face Lee. As it turned out, his first ball was fairly innocuous. Second ball, however, he bowled me a lightning quick bumper.

'That's more like it!' growled a voice from gulley. Steve Waugh. More chilling than any silly nonsense about the fit of my helmet.

The best form of sledging, the one where I've seen it really affect players, is when you can get a batsman visibly thinking about their technique. Warney, naturally, was the master. He'd talk to the guy next to him in the slips – 'Jesus, have you seen his grip?'

At which point, you'd be thinking, 'What's wrong with my grip?'

He would, quite openly, pick your game to pieces.

'Jesus, Keysy's falling over a bit here.' Or, 'Have you seen where his bat's coming from?'

I'd be stood there, trying not to look bothered, thinking, 'Christ, is that right?'

I didn't realise that I myself was a bit chirpy in the field until I retired, at which point, a lot of people contacted me on Twitter and said they would enjoy the fact they weren't going to get called a 'clubby' (a club player) from mid-on. I would get bored, so I used to chirp to keep myself interested. But I was never an emotional player, so I never lost it out on the field. I never crossed the line or said something I shouldn't. My chat would always be calculated. I did more of the Warne-type thing of trying to rip apart someone's technique. I always thought sledging was about trying to make someone think about their game. If they had any sort of insecurity, I wanted them to feel that I knew it. Having said that, I never minded Warney commenting on my game from second slip. It felt pretty good to have someone like Shane Warne talking about me!

Other players never seemed to get the point of sledging as a subtle method of disrupting a player. André Nel, the South African paceman, never shut up. Do it all the time and it is just noise – what's the point? Because we had South Africans playing in our side, we would try to get inside his head in a rather more calculated manner by our South Africans telling him that they knew certain of his countrymen thought he was no good.

'They told me you're a pea-heart and you'll give up in a minute.'

That's giving an opponent something to think about rather than just dishing out abuse. Nel may have thought it was rubbish but the seed had been planted.

David Warner is another who clearly has trouble drawing the line. As soon as he took his spat with Quinton de Kock off the pitch and into the pavilion at Durban, he had lost that battle. It doesn't matter what's been said, lose control of yourself and you lose, full stop. That's the same in any walk of life. It's a sign of weakness, not strength. I always believe that whatever happens on the pitch you should always say well done afterwards and smile.

There is a need to keep standards as high as possible, while at the same time recognising that a degree of confrontation is always going to happen. The game knows that, which is why the South African bowler Kagiso Rabada received only one demerit point for jumping up and down in front of Joe Root when he got him out at Port Elizabeth. It was the fact that he had accumulated four demerit points in two years that meant he was then banned for the final Test of the series.

It should also be said that people often see sledging when there's none there. When Jos Butler told Vernon Philander to 'Get out the f***ing way' while keeping in the recent South Africa series, that's the stuff that happens in top-level sport all the time. People always think the batsman is the innocent party in these exchanges, but actually, half the time they're the ones giving it out. Philander got in Jos's way, I'd say on purpose, and Jos told him to move. Cricket operates on a basis of vigilante justice. I never complained once to a match referee, or anybody else, about sledging. I would just get my own back, and I would do it subtly.

The trick is to maintain the competitive edge, to encourage personality and character in the game, while accepting a responsibility to uphold the image. Maintaining some decorum has to be the way. You can't go back to the time when Merv Hughes was accused of spitting at people. You can't go back to the time when people would just dish out mindless abuse so openly. Be subtle about it, try to get one over the opposition, but then expect the same back. Then, at the end of the game, shake hands and get on with it. We have to remember that if players are seen to be behaving badly in international sport on TV, then it will soon infect the lower echelons. It's something club cricketers need to remember. In all honesty, sledging in club cricket is worse than in first-class cricket. Players at that level, right down to the juniors, see sledging on TV and try to replicate it without ever really understanding what it's about. They think they're being big and clever when actually they're being nothing of the sort. It's club cricket, not the MCG.

The fact is that if people in club cricket did what Rabada did, then eventually somebody would turn round and smack them round the head with their bat. Even worse, kids see bad behaviour and just assume that's what you do. I'm very clear with my kids. If I saw my daughter do something I regarded as out of order I would take her off the field. She wouldn't be allowed to play again until she had learnt her lesson. There's nothing wrong with people trying to uphold respect and the laws of the game every now and again. As long as a player is punished for their actions, and there is consistency in that punishment, then everybody can move on. I felt the punishment Rabada got was absolutely right. I agree the next game was worse off for not having him in it, but the fact he was the best bowler in the South African side was irrelevant. If he was a bit-part spinner, the same rules would apply.

Yes, the game is better off for emotion – no one wants to have a game full of robots – but if you lessen the standard of behaviour and keep allowing things to happen again and again and again, it just lowers the bar.

I accept completely that people lose their cool. I did so on many occasions, especially with umpires, who I'm sure could find me hard work. I got demerit points, mainly for being a sarcastic so-and-so rather than for out and out abuse. Essentially, I would try to demean them. If an umpire made a wrong decision and didn't apologise, I would spend the rest of the time trying to belittle him, trying to put him under an element of pressure.

'Let's have him lbw – again,' I'd say if a batsman had survived a strong appeal.

I would also not ask that umpire's opinion on anything else all day. I would make a point of approaching the other umpire instead.

Trying to get one over on the umpire passes the time, more than anything, and with certain officials you knew you had a better chance than with others. At Kent, I once tried repeatedly to get the ball changed because there was nothing going on for us in the field. In the end I went up to the square leg umpire.

'Your colleague says we can change it if you think we can. He reckons it's gone out of shape but he needs your final say-so. If you say it's out of shape now then we'll just get it changed.'

'Did he actually say that?' he asked.

'Yes,' I told him.

And, rather than being bothered to walk to the other umpire, he took my word for it. We got a new ball and ended up getting a few wickets because it started moving around.

I considered it fair game to put umpires under a little pressure. I would always say to players, 'When an umpire gives a batsman not out, never say something like, "Oh, was that missing leg?", because it just reinforces their decision. Much better to ask, "What's wrong with that?" – make it clear you think they've messed up. Or if you do discuss it, give them the wrong reason why it might not have been out. Try to create doubt in them.'

People might think trying to manipulate umpires is the height of injustice, but actually it's all part of the game. Umpires are there to make decisions. Everything is in their hands in the end. That's why I never walked. I used to go mad if Kent players walked. As far as I was concerned, players who walked didn't care enough.

The way I saw it, I'd suffered bad decisions and no one had ever called me back. Never once when I had clearly not hit it did I hear the umpire or opposition players say, 'Come back, mate – on second thoughts, you were nowhere near that one.'

Yes, umpires may have apologised later for getting it wrong, but they never said anything at the time. In the bar it would be, 'You didn't hit that, did you?'

'No,' I'd confirm.

'I'm sorry about that,' they'd say.

'Well,' I'd ask, 'why didn't you call me back before I walked off?'

A few people walked in first-class cricket, but not many. Umpires are paid to do a job. No one else is doing my job for me, any more than I'm doing theirs for them. I don't deliver the mail for the mailman. Walking is a bygone era. It's meant to show sportsmanship, is it? I bet those same people who walk appeal when they know an opponent is not out.

To be fair, umpires in England are very good. Most of them have played and understand where cricketers are coming from. The poor umpires are the ones who don't understand, are too officious, and treat you like a school kid. Younger umpires, who I would have actually played with or against, would often come in like they had swallowed the laws book.

'Do this, do that.' I'd just want to go to war with them. But gradually they remembered that they were players once, that occasionally people were going to do the wrong thing, and instead of getting the rule book out they could just say, 'Hang on, mate, slow down, you're better than that.'

Over the years, I got to know the different personalities, the range of characters. Peter Willey, the ex-England batsman, for instance, I wouldn't muck around with. One, because he was hard as nails, and two, because he'd seen it all as a player himself and knew what I was doing.

Umpires could also be one of the great sources of help. Graham Burgess, the ex-Somerset player, when I got down the other end, might say, 'You need to be playing a bit straighter.'

The sight of Ray Julian, meanwhile, might not be greeted quite so keenly. Ray was the biggest lbw man in the world. Word was, his car had the registration plate R LBW AY. I'd find myself occasionally standing with him at square leg.

'All right?' I offered once, imaginatively.

'Yes thanks, Keysy. Had a great game last week. I had Mushtaq Ahmed bowling at my end. I gave loads of lbws.'

And I'd be thinking, 'That's great. I bet those batsmen were pleased.'

Ray would stand there, a smiling, grinning assassin, as he dismissed you leg before again.

But, as with all umpires, he loved the game – his heart was in the right place even if his finger, depending on your point of view, wasn't.

It's important to remember that a cricketer has a different relationship with an umpire than, say, a footballer does with a referee. In football, you might have a couple of words with the ref in ninety minutes. In cricket, it's perfectly possible to end up at square leg with an umpire for four hours a day or more. That's a long time. I headed for square leg once and, as ever, greeted the man in the white coat with, 'All right, mate? How's it going?'

'Not great,' he said. 'My wife has just left me.'

'Brilliant,' I thought. 'Do I look like an agony aunt? I could be in for six hours of this.'

I looked over to Ed Smith. 'Swap,' I said to him.

Poor Ed. 'Oh my God!' he told me at lunch. 'I feel like Dear Deidre.'

Sometimes it's yourself who needs to keep your mouth shut. Craig White, such a nice bloke, and a very under-rated all-rounder who would probably have played a lot more for England had it not been for his time overlapping with Freddie's, was getting a bit of attention from Matthew Hayden who, despite Craig bowling at 90mph, kept dispatching him into the seats over mid-on at the MCG. From my vantage point I concluded that Hayden's tactic was to go back to a length ball from Craig he could have gone forward to, and then launch the next one for six. At the end of an over, I went up to Craig.

'I've got a theory for you,' I said. 'Whenever he goes back to your length ball, the next one he launches for six.'

I don't think my timing was that great. 'When you can do that,' Craig explained to me, 'you can tell me how to f***ing bowl.'

Point taken.

Chapter 14

Warney

We were playing Hampshire at the Rose Bowl – a new umpire on the circuit, Steve Garrett, was officiating. It was the last day and Shane Warne was the man charged with bowling us out, and, as usual, he wasn't going to miss a trick. While he was bowling, he would walk up and down in the rough, appeal in it, everything. Short of pitching a tent and living in it, he was in there all the time. It was obvious what he was doing. When Warney switched to the other end, that rough would be his greatest weapon. Land the ball in there and, allied to his prodigious talent, it could go anywhere.

I was pointing this out to Steve.

'Can you tell Warney to get out of the rough?' I asked him. 'He's digging a hole, then he's going to bowl at the other end and it's going to spin square.'

'Yeah, yeah,' he assured me. But at no point was the required reprimand passed on to the Aussie great.

'Steve,' I repeated, 'can you tell Warne to get out the rough, please?'

Again, an assurance of action was followed by absolutely nothing. Warney was giving it all the theatrics, the big noises, the oohs and ahhs, after every ball. His usual repertoire. It felt as if Steve was intimidated by him.

After about the fifth time Warney acquainted himself with the rough, I'd had enough.

'Steve,' I said, 'either you tell him to get out of the rough or I'll tell him. You know what will happen if I tell him. He'll have a go at me, I'll have a go back, and we'll have a big argument. All things considered, it would be much easier if you did it.'

He looked at me. 'Yes, Keysy,' he said.

As Warney walked up to the wicket to bowl his next ball, I saw Steve take a big breath. There was a brief pause, and then he said it.

'Steve, can you get out the rough please?'

Steve! It was an interesting approach and one that I felt was unlikely to receive a positive response. Warney turned round with a look of utter bemusement on his face.

'Shane Warne, mate,' he told Steve, 'how the f*** are you?'

And that was it.

'Well I suppose he's just going to walk in the rough all day then now, Steve!' I said. 'Let's just leave him.' We laughed about it.

And that was the thing with Warney. Contrary to popular belief, he was an intimidating bloke on the field without meaning to be. There was never anything malicious. The mere fact he was Shane Warne was all it needed. He's actually one of the nicest blokes going – but at the same time, he is Shane Warne.

I had seen this lesser understood side of Warney before. When me and Freddie didn't play in the first Ashes Test at the Gabba in 2002, Warney and Glenn McGrath clocked us before the game and called us over. This was Shane Warne, the same bloke I'd watched at school, and Glenn McGrath, possibly the most consistently brilliant bowler of all time. They stood there and chatted to us about all kinds of stuff – how we were going, what we'd been up to, everything. It was a big myth about Warne and McGrath being nasty. They played very hard on the field, and gave you nothing, but they were two of the most generous people with their time that I have ever met.

As a player, I had first encountered Warney when he went to Hampshire in 2000. By that time he was already established as a unique talent and I wanted to learn as much about facing him as I could before I found myself with a bat in my hand 22 yards away in the middle. Our overseas player at that time was Rahul Dravid, about to become an Indian legend and also one of the nicest blokes ever.

I was keen to ask Rahul about Warne, who he'd already faced several times in his career. Back then the overseas players in county cricket were the greats. Dravid was no different, clearly a prodigious talent. He spoke in a way no one else could, had knowledge no one else had. He talked about how Warney bowled into a blind spot. To a right-hander, he would drift the ball in, to the extent that, by the time it pitched, the line where you'd originally placed your foot would be so off kilter, and your head so off side from the ball, that you'd lose it. He'd put it in your exact blind spot, just the same as when you're driving and you lose a vehicle in your left wing mirror.

We weren't ungenerous at Kent and offered Rahul an education of our own. For the first two weeks at Canterbury, he didn't want a car, preferring to travel with different players so he could get to know everyone. He taught us how to bat, and in return we taught him how to swear. That was the extent of our side of the exchange. He went from saying 'Jeez!' and 'Shucks!' to a full array of Anglo-Saxon expletives.

Either way, when we came to play Hampshire on a turner at Portsmouth, Rahul's advice meant I strode to the wicket armed as best I could. No words, though, can every prepare you for the moment you first come up against Warney, his brilliance further emphasised by the fact that when the ball came out of his hand you would first hear the click of his fingers and then the ball fizzing through the air. It was as was annoying as it was mesmerising.

It transpired that I had to bat for eight overs at the end of the first day after we had bowled Hampshire out. All I wanted to do was face Warne so I could say I'd done so. The result? I got out third ball exactly as Rahul had described it.

Later, me and Rahul went into the nets. From that point against Warne I changed my guard to leg stump to make sure I always played with my leg to take into account that awful drift. I also knew never to go across my stumps because he would get me lbw. These were things I'd never ever have thought of had it not been for Rahul. He was a different class, making an unbelievable 130 in our first innings, county cricket replicating Test cricket as, on a turning wicket, one of the greatest batsmen faced one of the greatest bowlers, to the extent that Warney even stated at one point: 'Just me and you here, Rahul. Let's see what you've got.' It was a masterclass with two great cricketers.

We ended up winning the game and second time round, I made a fifty. I didn't score a run off Warney but I did defend him like my life depended on it, and because of the lessons Rahul had taught me, it worked out. It was one of those moments in my career where I just thought, 'I am going to look back on this with the fondest of memories.' It felt an incredible privilege to be there, facing Warney, at that time – the kind of thing you would tell your grandkids about.

I've seen a lot of great players but Warney is the only one who had 100 per cent belief in his own ability. When Shane Warne had the ball in his hand he was at home. He believed he could do anything, a genius who, like the greatest performers, was at his best on a stage. Once he was up there he commanded every inch of it, such was his presence. As a batsman you faced him in mental as well as physical isolation. With others you could hang on to something. You might be able to work out their plan, see that they were trying to bring you wide and then trap you in front lbw. Not Warney. The plan was never shared. It couldn't be. No one could ever guess, let alone know.

I might have survived on that occasion, but I found it an exhausting experience. He'd made me feel as if I was batting left-handed even when the ball hit the middle of the bat. I would play a perfect forward defensive and he'd look at me in utter incredulity as if to say, 'What have you just done?'

He was ultra-competitive and had this incredible knack of making every delivery feel like an event, like something was going to happen. He would make you feel like your best forward defensive was a disaster waiting to happen. Forget sledging; Shane Warne could make you think you were the worst player in the world without ever telling you were the worst player in the world. You'd leave one and it would sail harmlessly over off stump, but he would make such a song and dance about it that he'd make you doubt your own eyes – 'Was that a bit closer than I thought?' Warney didn't appeal to get you out, he appealed to put you under pressure. And he was absolutely right in doing that. When someone plays no shot to a spinner, everybody should appeal. I would tell my players at Kent that all the time. You want the batsman to doubt whether leaving the ball is a sensible option. You want them playing a shot, because that way you might get a catch off the pad, glove, or whatever. Doubt is the bowler's best friend and batsman's worst enemy, and that's what Warne worked out. He would bowl around the wicket at me, and I would kick it away because it was so far outside leg stump, and he would react as though I was a millimetre off giving my wicket away. He knew the effect his shouting and wailing would have on the umpire as well. He put umpires under so much pressure just by being himself. But, like so many others who played hard, Warney never crossed the line. I never remember a time where I thought Shane Warne was out of order.

Thing was, Warney read the game better than anyone. As much as he had a gift for bowling, his real talent was seeing the game exactly as it was. He could see straight through a batsman, work out exactly what it was they were doing wrong, and formulate a plan for each and every player who came before him. For a batsman, his ability to work you out, to bowl to a plan, to set a field, was what set him so far apart.

His memory was just ridiculous. He had information about players in his head all the time. We had Niall O'Brien at Kent, an Ireland international. We were playing a Pro40, a dead game with nothing much going on, when Warney took out midwicket and put in two backward points. The very next ball, O'Brien reverse swept and got out. Warney at that point had around 700 test wickets. He had bigger fish to fry than Niall O'Brien in a barely breathing Pro40. And yet it was him who had instigated this situation. He knew exactly what O'Brien would do and acted accordingly. A few years later, I was sitting playing poker with Warney when he brought it up. All I could think was, 'How on earth, with all the wickets you've got and all the players you got out, do you remember an incident like that?' Every opponent was the same. A batsman would arrive at the crease and straight away Warney would move the field accordingly. If it was our own Dave Fulton, for example, he would immediately put a man in behind the keeper because he knew Dave liked to ramp it over him.

Tactically, the man was a genius. Graham Thorpe always said he was the only bowler who would give away boundaries to get you out. He'd seen it himself. In a Test match he gave Alec Stewart two long hops in a row, which he happily waded into and hit for four. Of course, Warney was was just setting him up. Next came the quicker one and that was it. Alec, stumps rattled, was on his way back to the pavilion.

Some players were easier for Warney to fathom than others, Carl Hooper being a case in point. In his pomp in one game, the West Indian had counter-attacked against Warne, who couldn't work out when he was going to use his feet to come at him. At lunch, Warne had a word with Aussie coach Bobby Simpson.

'I can't work him out,' he told him. 'I can't get a read on when he's going to do it, whereas everyone else, I know exactly what's going on.'

Bobby had some words of advice. 'Run up as if you're going to bowl,' he told him, 'but don't release it.' The plan worked brilliantly. In a flash, Warney worked out that when Hoops tapped his bat and looked down, he wasn't going to use his feet. When he stared at him, he would. That is all the ammunition a bowler of his genius needs.

Replicating Warney wasn't easy. In the Ashes, all we had was our fitness trainer and third team club spinner, Nigel Stockley. The shout was that, bearing in mind that right-armed leg-spinner Warney always used to bowl from middle stump, if you got Nigel to bowl left arm, with no stumps, it was the same angle. So there we were, preparing to face one of the most skilful bowlers in the world through the medium of Nigel Stockley, with the stumps out of the ground.

Some might have thought Warney's natural competitiveness would be reined in a little by county cricket. Nothing could have been further from the truth. Warney used to amaze me. Long after he'd finished with Australia, he would bowl all day in a game where Hampshire were miles behind. Possibly his desire to carry on came down to that side of him that was forever unfulfilled. He was such a great captain, but never got the chance to show it with the Aussies. He was the skipper Australia never had. There's no better cricket brain in the world.

When Warney took on the Hampshire captaincy, he was phenomenal, someone who made everyone on his team, and probably a few on the opposition, perform so much better. Play against Hampshire before Warney got there and it wasn't the same. When he arrived he made those same players feel 10 feet tall.

He cared so much for winning games. If he felt his team was on the end of a bad decision, he wouldn't just let it go. Even at breakfast the next morning, he would query the umpire on it – 'Can you talk me through that dismissal?' One time against us, he was given out lbw. He'd gone over towards the leg side as he looked for a run, heard the appeal, ignored it, and then realised he'd been given out.

'You f***ing what?' he shouted, and walked off, spitting expletives as he went.

Warney loved Hampshire in the same way he loved captaincy and cricket. He would deliver ball after ball, barely be able to walk that evening, literally hobbling, and then the next day turn up and do exactly the same thing. At the same time, he gave so much to everyone else. I would ask him a question about cricket and he'd sit down with me for an hour giving me his views. He would do that for plenty of others as well. Just look at the help he gave Kevin Pietersen when he came into the Hampshire set-up. So many people assume that, because he's an Aussie, Shane Warne is anti-English, but that isn't the case at all. He is a believer in positive cricket. He would make exactly the same point about an Australian as he would, say, Alastair Cook. If he thinks someone is being negative, he's going to hammer them all day about it. He believes the game is about entertainment. Actually, he has given more to English cricket than we'll ever know. Would Chris Tremlett have turned out to be the bowler he was, so destructive on the Ashes tour of 2010/11, if it hadn't been for the help and guidance he received from Shane Warne?

At Kent we had a young spinner, Rob Ferley, in our team. When we played against Hampshire he wanted to quiz Warney about bowling and asked me what to do.

'Just go and ask him,' I said. The upshot was, Warney invited him down to Hampshire for a coaching session.

After Warney retired, we had another young spinner, Adam Riley, aged just 21. I rang Warney and asked if he would mind having a word with him for five minutes.

'Any time,' said Warney. 'Just get him to ring me in the morning.'

Next day I gave him a call. 'I've got the lad next to me now,' I told him.

'Put him on,' said Warney. An hour and twenty minutes later, I got the phone back. Riles had got the biggest smile on his face. We were faced with bowling Surrey out to win the game and as we went out to play I asked him what he thought.

'I'm going to bowl defensively to an attacking field,' he said, a classic Warne move. Riles ended up getting six wickets and winning us the game.

I knew what it was to use Warney as a touchstone. He was the greatest captain I ever saw tactically, and the only captain I'd try to copy, to the extent that Peter Willey, the umpire, always used to laugh as I set the field – 'There you go, copying Warney.' But I make no apologies for that. Shane Warne was genius, absolute genius. He was like *The Matrix*, seeing a code, not a person. And the minute he saw that code, he could just break it down. The world's first sci-fi cricketer.

There were other sides of Shane that no one ever saw. Poker was big in county dressing rooms round about his and my time. We had a four-day match at Hampshire, the start delayed by rain, and straight away we were into a game: four Hampshire players – Sean Ervine, Dimi Mascarenhas, Warney and Shaun Udal – as well as me, Matt Walker, Dave Fulton and Min Patel. We got this huge game of poker going. The cricket match itself was on an hour, off an hour, and every time it rained we would run straight back in and carry on. We started at eleven in the morning and didn't leave until midnight, game after game, with pizzas, beers, all sorts. Finally, we all got up to leave only to find Warney tidying everything away.

'We can't leave all this for the cleaners,' he said. 'They shouldn't have to clean up after us.'

We turned up the next day and did the same thing all over again. Eventually, because it had rained so much, we ended up trying to negotiate a result. I always wanted to win in a negotiation so I refused anything that Warney came up with. It became a recurring theme over the years. I got on well with Warney, but as captains we'd argue endlessly over declarations. On one occasion, we were 300 ahead of Hampshire with a day and a bit to go when Warney wandered up.

'Any chance you're going to declare?'

'No way. Not in a million years.'

'How safe are you?' he continued. 'How many runs do you need? How scared are you?'

He didn't change my mind. I still wasn't declaring.

We got up to 400 ahead, with Warney still bowling. After each ball he was turning round and looking at me on the balcony.

'How many more runs do you want?'

Another over would go by. Up he'd shout again. 'How many more?'

I'd be sitting there thinking, 'Jesus!'

After the game, which ended up a boring draw, he told me, as he was bound to, 'You have to be prepared to lose to win.' His teams believed they could bowl anybody out on the last day even if they needed only 200.

'Yes,' I would explain to him, 'but that's because you're in the team. If you were in my side I'd declare on 250. You're the best bowler who ever lived. We haven't got Shane Warne in our side.'

Kent declarations weren't a matter of great joy to Warney, whether I was involved or not. The year before, Dave Fulton was captain and famously set up a ridiculous run chase against title leaders Nottinghamshire in the penultimate game of the season. We got bowled out and Notts took the Championship there and then, meaning they avoided a showdown with second-placed Hampshire in the final game of the campaign. Warney, understandably, was seething and had a go at Fults in the press. Now there we were, one year on, all having a game of poker. Fults was talking about what a good declaration it was. Warney was having a go at Fults. And I was watching, lapping it all up.

Again, it showed his view. Not just positive cricket, but taking the positive options when they were there. As a commentator, I thought Warney was pretty hard on Alastair Cook when he was England captain. Initially, I thought that was because he's an Australian, but then actually I saw he was equally as tough on Ricky Ponting, Michael Clarke, anyone he thought was playing negative cricket. It is Warney's central belief that cricket is a positive game. Anything negative, he will analyse and, if necessary, take down.

Positive, desperate to win, he might have been, but he never crossed the line. There was no one more respectful of the game than Shane Warne. He'd have a go, sledge, whatever, to try to get in your mind, but, as with Freddie when he took a hundred off the Aussies at Trent Bridge in 2005, he was always the first to say 'Well played'.

Problem was, so often he played better.

Chapter 15

The Speed Merchants

The fastest bowler I ever faced was Shoaib Akhtar. Not for nothing was he known as the Rawalpindi Express. I faced him in a celebrity Lashings game – Lashings being a superstar team that raises money for good causes. It was a full house at Canterbury and he was bowling at the speed of light. It was as if he had a reverse catapult for an arm. He would hyperextend himself and then this whip action would fire the ball at you at 95mph-plus.

Shoaib really was like nothing on earth, and as a batsman it was easy to get into a negative mindset that built him up and treated him as such. It was for that reason that Matthew Hayden developed a counterpunch. He made a prediction before an Australia series against Pakistan that Shoaib could, and would, only bowl twenty-four balls at top speed. Naturally, it became this big thing, Hayden versus Shoaib, and when finally Shoaib lined up at the end of his run for the first ball of the series, everyone was wondering what was going to happen. In roared Shoaib and pinged a bouncer at Hayden. He ducked under it, looked at Shoaib, and went '23'. Over the next few overs, he counted him down to none.

The difference between 85 and 90 miles an hour-plus is massive. That's why Test cricket is fantastic, because it tests courage. Once that ball reaches 90mph and beyond, it's not just about not getting out, it's about not getting hurt. Are you going to stand up to this thing coming down at you like a bat out of hell? I've seen plenty of players subconsciously back away, and that is the ultimate sin in cricket. A coward is the one thing no one wants to be known as in life, and sport is no different. If you are seen as being scared of fast bowling, that reputation is going to follow you round.

Nobody really likes excessive speed. At its most basic, playing the fast ball is obviously about reaction time. But it goes beyond that. All a batsman can really do when the pace gets excessively high is blank their mind out and trust that they are going to get out of the way. You really do have moments when fast bowling forces you to trust your instinct. You can't think your way through fast bowling. And to some degree, I liked that. I found it simpler than facing medium pace or spin because I didn't have to consider what the bowler was doing. There was a clarity. I watched the ball and that was it. There was nothing else I could do.

Fidel Edwards was a case in point. When I was batting with Fred in pursuit of victory at the Old Trafford Test in 2004, he was bowling as quick as I'd ever seen. Watching him from the England dressing room side-on in the pavilion before I went in, all I could see was the ball being released, disappearing, and then reappearing nanoseconds later as the keeper grabbed it above his head. Me and Fred are both pretty tall, and at tea we talked about the difficulty of getting underneath the bounce, concluding that we simply had to trust in our reactions to get out of the way. Think about short-pitched bowling too much and that's when you get hit. By the time you've had that internal conversation, 'Am I going underneath it? Am I going to sway?', it's too late. With the ball travelling at 90mph, the brain can't process the debate. This isn't *The Andrew Marr Show* on a Sunday morning, it's full pelt international cricket. It comes down to trusting in instinct, the same as putting up a hand if somebody throws a punch in your direction. To me, this was what Test cricket was all about – facing fast bowling against the West Indies.

Embracing fast bowling doesn't mean I didn't get hit occasionally. The South African fast bowler Makhaya Ntini caught me on the head at The Wanderers. He had a tricky action, quick, and also coming from an awkward angle, which made facing him hard work. He hit me in the last over before lunch. I was a bit shaken. It doesn't hurt when you get struck on the head, if you're lucky, but I spent the whole of the break thinking, 'What on earth am I going to do now? I can't see him. I can't pick up the angle. The ball that hit me came from nowhere.'

There was only one course of action. 'I'm just going to have to be brave – take him on and risk getting out.'

But then that imp on the shoulder pipes up. 'Hang on; you can't play the short ball. You can't do this. It's not going to work.'

Ntini bounced me the first over after lunch and I pulled him for four. Then he bounced me again and I pulled that for four as well. And that was it – I was OK. Those are the defining moments in your career. Zak Crawley got hit on the head by Kagiso Rabada in the recent South Africa series. I know Zak well and I know he's a tough kid, but it's a bit different being hit on the head at Newlands in a Test match with the world watching than by someone in county cricket. In those moments you have to compute – 'Right, stand up and be counted. Don't take a backward step. Don't look scared. Don't look like you're worried (even though you clearly are). Right – ready? Let's go.'

Test cricket cares nothing for your perception of what you are. All your bullshit, all the stuff you've done before, disappears once that ball smashes into your skull at 90 miles an hour. At that point it is just you and what you are made of. They are the great moments both to watch and to be in the middle of.

Shoaib might have been the fastest, and Ntini possibly the most awkward, but Harmy was the best, the most evil, fast bowler I ever faced. With a lot of tall bowlers, their short ball is quick, but their full ball is slower, a little bit floaty. Harmy was as quick full as he was short.

Against the odds, I got my first hundred against Harmy. None of us really knew him at that stage. We knew he'd been on the England Under-19 tour to Pakistan the year before when he'd got homesick and come home early, and that was about it. We soon got to see what he was all about. He turned up to play for Durham at Canterbury on a bad wicket and from nowhere this gangly lad was belting it down at the speed of light. He starfished Carl Hooper in front of his face – so called because the batsman is caught front on with arms and legs sticking out all over the place and his bat in front of his head – which no one did, and from that moment on we all knew this was something special. In the dressing room we were all, 'Oh my God! This is rapid!'

When it comes to fast bowlers, word gets around very quickly. And in Harmy's case, justifiably so. I played an Under-19 game with him in which he got a Pakistan batsman out lbw. The ball had struck the lad with such force he had to be carried off the field.

Talk about spotting talent – one ball from Steve Harmison was all anyone needed to see. Coaches could analyse him, stick pads all over him, watch his action, go through the motions, but why bother? Within a minute you knew this was an England bowler. And if you'd said, 'This lad could get to number one in the world', you wouldn't have been far off either. From the moment I saw him bowl, nothing would have changed my mind that he had what it took. When Duncan Fletcher saw him close up in the nets for the first time, he thought the same. Harmy didn't bowl that well in his first couple of Test matches and was dropped, but Fletcher still knew he had something special on his hands. He would have been thinking, 'Ashes 2005, this is the man.' He knew you can't teach pace like Harmy had.

As it transpired, by 2004/05, Fletcher had a bowling unit at his disposal that had something for every occasion. Simon Jones was rapid and accurate. He could bowl 93mph off his short run while, amusingly, petrified of fast bowling himself. Whenever Simon batted in the nets, he would give the bowler the evil eye, making it crystal clear that if they bowled any bouncers at him he would be right back at them knocking their own heads off when it was his turn with the ball in his hand. He was such a nervous character. Without fail, before he bowled a spell in a match he would leave the field to go to the toilet and do some stretches. It was like watching Jane Fonda or Linda Lusardi. He was the same on the field, except while other bowlers might do a quick calf stretch, with Simon it was a full-on Downward Dog or Warrior 1. I'd look out the window and there he'd be lifting his leg above his shoulder.

Simon was one of England's best-ever bowlers but will never go down as such because injury plagued his career. Infamously, he ruptured a knee ligament when his spikes got caught in the surface attempting a sliding stop at the Gabba in 2002. I remember that incident well – because I was twelfth man. Everyone in the stadium was going, 'Oh no! Poor Jones!' Everyone in the stadium, that is, except me. All I was thinking was, 'Forget "Poor Jones". What about me? I've got to field all day now. Come on! Get up! What did you think you were doing diving on that surface? Everybody knows what it's like.'

I hated, hated, being twelfth man. It's a terrible job. These people who like being twelfth man, there is something wrong with them. All you can do is what you're supposed to do – catch catches – and then if you drop them it's not like you can go and score a hundred to make up for it. You've got to do all the fielding and you never get a chance of redemption. It's a nightmare. I once got in trouble at Kent for paying James Tredwell to be twelfth man when it was my job. He wasn't on the staff at that point and was on a daily rate. I gave him £40 to do all the duties. The captain, Matthew Fleming, gave me a serious bollocking. I pointed out I was probably paying Tredders more than he was.

'I think he's done well out of it!'

He was having none of it.

Joking aside, it was such a shame for Simon. Bad luck was his constant companion and stopped him and the rest of us seeing his ultimate potential. He had the ability to reverse swing the ball and was one of the best in the world on a flat wicket. Again, he knew his strengths, having grabbed the chance to learn how to reverse swing the ball off Waqar Younis. Waqar was only at Glamorgan for a year but Simon took every opportunity he could to swallow the tricks of the trade. I always felt Jonah never realised just how good he was. I hope, looking back, he does now.

Matthew Hoggard, meanwhile, started out like Jimmy Anderson. He was quick and then became one of the masters of swing bowling, immaculate with his length. Hoggy played on being eccentric, but was actually a bright lad, a shrewd cricketer. He wouldn't necessarily speak up in meetings but he would have a good read on every situation. Because he wasn't express like Flintoff, Harmison and Jones, he had to be smart. There were quite a few guys around who could run up and bowl 85-mile-an-hour swingers, but there weren't any who could do it with Hoggy's brains behind the ball. Add in that Yorkshire grit and he was just going to keep going all day. He knew his limitations, stuck to what he was good at, and off he went. Michael Vaughan summed Hoggy up perfectly when he described him as the guy sweeping the shop floor. He wasn't front of house, but he was a hero nevertheless.

Fred? Well, Fred, as discussed elsewhere, had everything.

As great a captain as Michael Vaughan was, as good a coach as Duncan Fletcher was, they weren't anything without those four.

Players from the 1980s and 90s will argue that bowling was faster in their day. It may well have been – no doubt those West Indies pace attacks were quick, and it looks horrific – but you can't tell me that bowling is the only thing that hasn't evolved, that it hasn't changed/morphed/improved over the past thirty years. All modern batsman can't be rubbish, and yet if we argue that bowlers haven't moved on, that the challenge doesn't remain, that it has been somehow watered down, then that must be the case. What has actually changed is intent. That's why bowling doesn't look as fast as it did. Watch great players who play fast bowling positively and it's as if they take speed off the bowler. They don't, it's just that they stand their ground and hit the ball. They are playing with intent. A bowler never looks as quick when that happens. As soon as a batsman starts ducking out the way, they look so much faster.

It's not just a matter of technique; there is a key mental process at play here. Adopt a positive mindset and the brain works faster. Adopt a negative one and the brain slows down. There is no proven scientific basis for me to say that, but, in my opinion and experience, if you are thinking positively, if you are looking to score runs, being positive in defence as well as attack, the bowling does not feel as quick as it does if you are batting like your life depends on it. In that negative frame of mind it feels like a bowler is sending it down at a thousand miles an hour.

Even Shoaib couldn't do that.

Chapter 16

Murali

Murali and Fred had a deal. It went like this: If Fred didn't bowl bouncers at him, Murali wouldn't bowl doosras back.

It was a deal that came from a place of friendship. Murali had played for Lancashire before he came to Kent.

The agreement worked fine in county cricket, but, of course, they then came up against each other in a Test match – with Nasser as England captain. At which point, Nasser delivered the edict that nobody was allowed to be nice to Murali.

'Yes, he's a lovely bloke,' he told the team, 'but let's stop smiling at him, because he's always smiling back at us – "Hello! Hello!" We've got to ignore all that. In fact, we've got to ignore him, full stop. We shouldn't like him and he shouldn't like us.'

But that wasn't easy for Fred. He and Murali were best mates. And, as ill-luck would have it, Fred was bowling when Murali came out to bat.

Nasser wanted Fred to hit Murali on the hands to intimidate him. But Fred had his special deal. A deal he could never tell Nasser about. Instead of the short delivery demanded by Nasser, Fred came running in and bowled a length ball, which Murali promptly smashed out the park.

Nasser was seething.

And still the short ball didn't come. Next up, Fred bowled Murali a slower ball. Again, it disappeared into the distance.

This perhaps might not have been quite so bad were it not for one thing: Murali was using Fred's bat.

Murali had forgotten his, so Fred had lent him his, which he was now using to smash him out the ground.

I can see where Fred's misgivings about laying into Murali might have come from. Forget the deal, Murali is probably the kindest human being ever.

One year he insisted Fleur and I go on holiday with him.

'You must come to Sri Lanka, Flair!' He always called her Flair – I tried telling him.

We made the right noises but weren't really planning on going. Murali, though, kept asking.

'Have you got your tickets?'
'Not yet,' I'd say. 'I'll do it.'
Two weeks later, he asked again.
'How's it going with your tickets?'
'I can't get any,' I lied.

Another two weeks passed and a letter arrived. I opened it to find two tickets to Sri Lanka inside. He had bought them for us.

We landed in Colombo on Christmas Day and he picked us up for a look round. We ended up in the beautiful resort town of Bentota, joining Murali and his brothers out on the sea on aqua sausages. England were touring so there were a lot of holidaymakers around. Next thing, just as we were enjoying a pleasant relax, Murali was organising a 20/20 game, rounding up eleven English guys and girls to play the locals on the beach with a tennis ball.

'Murali,' I objected, 'do you mind? I'm on holiday here!'
'Shut up fatty, you've got to play.'

The bloke was unstoppable in every single way. He just wanted to make everyone happy. We were in Beckenham once.

'Don't your parents live here?' he asked.
'Yes.'
'Let's go round.'

My mum and dad love cricket and so I put Murali by the front door and rang the bell. My mum had just come out of the shower, hair all over the place. She answered the door and there was Murali – 'Hello, Mrs Key. How are you?'

One of my first nights out with Flair, I mean Fleur, was with Murali. It was after a day/night game at Canterbury and we ended up at Churchill's nightclub in the town. Murali loved a night out, his tipple of choice being Bacardi Breezer. He was drinking it like it was going out of fashion, heading to the dance floor, where everybody was copying him as he did his Bhangra dancing – this Sri Lankan fellow with massive eyes, arguably the greatest bowler in the world, right there giving it all his moves. Afterwards, we went back to his place and he made us a curry. It was no ordinary curry – these were the hottest spices we'd ever had. Fleur and her friend walked home virtually in tears. It was a great summer as the three of us knocked about together.

Whenever I saw him down the years, Murali would always ask after Fleur.
'How is Flair?'
'Good, Murali.'
'You're very lucky to have Flair.'
'Why's that, Murali?'

'She's very pretty. Too pretty for you.'

'Cheers, mate.'

'No, no. You don't understand. You don't have face for ladies.'

I thought this was a little rich. 'Well, what about you?' I'd say. 'It's a good job you've got 800 wickets.'

Murali had first come to Kent in the mid-nineties with fellow Sri Lankan Aravinda de Silva. At that time, although he had more than sixty Test wickets, nobody really knew who he was, and he was quickly vanquished to Leicester to play club cricket. There, again because he was relatively unknown, he found himself placed in the second team.

'What did you get?' I asked him after his first game.

'A nine-fer.'

'So you didn't tell them you should be in the first team?'

'No, no. I was fine to play second team.'

Just the loveliest bloke. We'd go out for a meal with him and he'd sneak off and pay the bill. He'd help out other players for hours throwing at them in the nets. When he arrived at Kent he brought with him four Sri Lanka World Cup-winning shirts signed by the team just in case that season's beneficiary might want them.

By the time Murali returned to Kent in 2003, we were good friends. Because he was big mates with Freddie, we were all part of the same crowd. Also, I had made a hundred against him a couple of years earlier when he played at Lancashire, so he had a bit of respect for me. He thought I could play, although that innings was before his doosra really came good – it would just go straight rather than spin the other way. I could pick him, so I could play him without too many issues.

That game happened to start the day after 9/11, so there was a very sombre atmosphere throughout. It was the last game of the season but no one really cared – there were much bigger things going on in the world than a dead rubber between two county cricket teams in the wind and rain of northern England. All of a sudden, cricket didn't have a whole lot of meaning. Nevertheless, Murali thought of me as a good player. The feeling was reciprocated. Arriving at Kent, he placed two balls down on a length in the nets, one for the doosra, one for the off-spinner, and proceeded to bowl at and hit them nine times out of ten. That was the level of his accuracy. Murali's value on the pitch was never less than immense. We went from being bottom of the Championship to second. I was glad to be on his side for once, never forgetting the incredible fizz of the ball coming down the wicket at me when he'd played for Lancashire.

The downside was his driving. It was as if he hadn't noticed he was no longer in Sri Lanka, weaving in and out of traffic while various teammates cowered in the passenger seat. We'd get our own back by inviting him to play Drink While You Think, where one person says a famous name and then the next has to name a celebrity with a first name starting with the first letter of the previous celebrity's last name. If that person can't come up with one straight away, they have to start drinking while they come up with an answer. You'd be right in thinking you never saw it in Toys R Us. Murali's trouble was, he knew no one but cricketers, so he'd end up very hammered very quickly.

His batting was equally unpredictable. While Murali could always slog a few, go out and hit a couple of sixes, his running wasn't always the best. He was at it again, smashing some much-needed runs in a tight game, when he hit the ball to point and called his partner, Martin Saggers, through for the run. We were watching from the balcony as Murali got halfway down the wicket before screeching to a halt and sending Saggers back. The point fielder picked up the ball, threw at the stumps at the batsman's end, and missed. It was a balls-up, but Murali had got away with it.

'Well done!' he was shouting at Saggers. At which point, square leg picked the ball up and threw it to the bowler. This, really, is where it went wrong. Because Murali had forgotten to run back himself.

I was in hysterics. Dave Fulton, the captain, not so much. Murali was on his way back to the dressing room and so everyone adopted the standard 'unlucky mate' face for when a colleague is out. Except me. I was cracking up behind a newspaper. And except Murali, who came in absolutely wetting himself. It summed him up: he never took anything too seriously. He had a real childlike innocence, which allowed him to say whatever he wanted. Mal Loye, the Lancashire batsman, was known for always worrying about his stance. As he got set at the wicket in one game, Murali took a quick look – 'Shit stance you have, Mal Loye,' he told him matter-of-factly, and walked off.

Fair chance the swear word had come from us. Murali didn't speak much English when he first came over. As with Rahul Dravid, he taught us all these great lessons in cricket and we taught him the full range of English expletives. We would go and watch friends playing club cricket and Murali would be getting excited, shouting the c-word left, right and centre, even in front of Fleur.

'You can't walk round saying that,' I would have to tell him. 'You need to use some other words as well.' Problem was, the other ones we'd taught him weren't much better.

Whatever words he used, he was merciless when it came to taking the piss. He would spend every waking moment taking the mickey out of me, calling me every name under the sun. It was the way he was. If he did something, he did it full-on. He was such a cricket nut that you'd go round to his flat and he'd be sat there watching Teletext for the county scores. He wanted to know everything that was going on, a complete cricket badger.

Murali is not only the most generous of men but the humblest. In Sri Lanka he is heavily involved with the Foundation of Goodness, an incredible organisation that helps the under-privileged across the island. The Foundation was based right on the beach, not far from Galle, only to be wiped out when the tsunami hit in 2006. Me and Fleur had visited three years earlier when we'd gone over on our holiday. It was an amazing, and moving, sight. There were thousands of children there and the Foundation workers were handing out school clothes to them, books, other necessities. I heard my name mentioned on the PA and, totally unexpectedly, found myself presenting books to dozens of little kids. Murali asked Fleur to do the same. They were bowing at her feet. She couldn't help but burst into tears at the sight.

Fortunately, while the Foundation buildings were lost, everyone escaped unscathed when the wave came. The complex was rebuilt and continues to perform wonderful, life-changing deeds, with Murali remaining at the heart of the cause, injecting endless funds and delivering a global profile.

When he gave a masterclass for Sky, revealing all the tricks of his remarkable trade, with typical humility he didn't want anything for it. Sky insisted on paying him, at which point he made sure the money went straight to the Foundation. Murali has done so much for charity, but never with any song and dance. When George Michael died, there were stories of him quietly helping all sorts of people. I see that as the ultimate selflessness – no PR, no furthering of a career, nothing. Murali is exactly the same.

Both he and Shane Warne are better people than they were cricketers, and that is saying a lot.

Chapter 17

The Times They Have a Changed

When I started, many players couldn't care less about one-day cricket and I was one of them. I hated it. All I wanted to be was a Test player. The one-day game was a chore, a distraction from the proper stuff. Practising one-day skills? There was no such thing.

Now we have a situation where players get all the way into Test cricket without ever really completing their education. When the England batsman Ben Duckett struggled against Ravi Ashwin in India in 2016, he appeared not to have a clue he had a problem with high-quality off spin until the ball was halfway down the wicket. It's hard to understand how that can happen, but it does. That is the measure of the change in the game that has occurred, the dominance of different formats, especially T20.

At Kent, we were in the First Division of the Championship for most of my career. One-day cricket in any format had no appeal to us because all our focus had always been on winning the Championship. If anything, it was an inconvenience. But I remember a friend of mine who knew his cricket stating that in years to come, T20 would be the biggest domestic tournament. He wasn't far wrong.

At the outset, we had precisely zero interest in T20 and would finish down the lower reaches in the league stage. Andrew Symonds was a master of 50-over white ball cricket, but when it came to T20, no way did he treat it with any measure of gravitas. He would walk out on to the pitch and openly state, 'Let's get this over and done with.' He wasn't alone. Most of us saw T20 as a three-week holiday in the middle of the season – 'I'll have a slog and if I get out, who cares?'

When times were lean at Kent, however, and I was captain, the hierarchy said that we needed to turn that around, that we needed to focus on the T20 more than anything else. I argued all the way.

'T20 isn't even 15 per cent of the season,' I reasoned. 'Where does that leave our four-day game? We haven't got the luxury of not concentrating on four-day cricket, because it's four-fifths of what we do.'

That wasn't petulance. It wasn't a refusal to move with the times. Truth is, there's nothing more soul-destroying than bad four-day cricket. It's a long, slow day if you're not competitive. Also, when it comes to the actual physical nature of the two formats, it's far easier to go from the long form to the short form of the game than the other way round. With a handful of notable exceptions, those who have gone from white ball to red ball cricket are few and far between. In reverse, the skills are more relevant. On the other hand, it was apparent T20 wasn't something a county could or would ignore. All of a sudden, grounds were full, India won the World T20, and the IPL popped up. The same Andrew Symonds who couldn't give a monkey's about T20 was now fetching a million dollars in the IPL auction.

When at Kent we did actually apply ourselves to T20, started to take it more seriously, straight away we got through to the quarter finals. A year later, we won the tournament. Until then we'd never really thought about being realistic challengers. By that point, T20 had become a firm favourite, bringing kids and families back to the game. It was a major sporting and social occasion, something people could take in after work on a Friday night or have a bit of fun with on a Sunday afternoon. Its reach was incredible. If someone had told me when I started out that I would play in front of 25,000 people at The Oval in county cricket, I would have laughed in their face. The only time that sort of crowd happened was in a 50-over Lord's final, and even they became so devalued they wouldn't sell out. Now the Lord's final doesn't even exist.

T20 has changed all that. It has created a unique cricketing experience. I would say, bar the final, the atmosphere at a Lord's T20 is as good if not better than any of the games I saw there in the World Cup. As a commentator, it always amazes me how good the atmosphere is for T20 cricket. If you were trying to pitch a new sport to someone, T20 would be the one. There is always drama (T20's explosiveness makes it a format that allows big personalities to be big personalities), often a close finish, and even if the game is a little one-sided, there is still lots of entertainment. In T20, even where we think it's not a close finish – a team needs two off the last over, or wins with two overs to go – that is very close by 50-over standards. Occasionally, there will be an unbelievable 50-over game like the World Cup final, but they are rare. All of a sudden, 100 overs seems an awful lot of time to reach a result. And that's without four-day cricket, where we often know the result the day before. T20's hit ratio for a great finish is up there at 80-plus per cent. The other formats are down at 10 per cent.

For the smaller clubs, long pushed out the door of the Championship party, T20 gives them some element of hope. Twenty overs a side is a leveller. The longer the format, the less chance of luck playing a part, the less likelihood that one person can influence the game. In four-day cricket, fifty overs even, a team has got time to recover and come back into contention. In twenty overs, one person can have a good day and that's that. Afghanistan could beat England in twenty overs. In Test match cricket, they are years away from being able to do so. That's why spectators like T20 – because it's volatile. Look at Carlos Brathwaite in the 2016 World T20 final against England. Bang! Bang! Bang! Bang! Four consecutive sixes off Ben Stokes. And that was it, won, from what many would have judged a near impossible position. From a Test perspective, that's like a bloke getting two hat-tricks. It just doesn't happen because the game is too long and there is the ability to recover. A team can be 150-8 and scrape up to 300. In T20, that's it, you're done. T20 is also a great way of dragging spectators into cricket. If they then go on to like four-day cricket, great. If not, who cares? They are still, one way or another, fans of cricket.

The question now is not so much whether T20 is a flash in the pan, but whether the Championship can survive. County cricket has become a microcosm of the world game. As much as we all like to think our sport is about togetherness and embracing different cultures and environments, it is actually about money. As with football, you might get the odd Leicester City coming along and doing something incredible but the chances of that happening are becoming fewer and fewer. The clubs with the money can get the best players, employ the best coaches. A winning environment comes after all that is in place, not the other way round.

County cricket was much closer in the early days of my career. Leicestershire won the Championship twice. They had a number of England players, such as Alan Mullally and Chris Lewis, and were a very good team. They weren't alone among what we now see as the 'lesser' counties. Derbyshire had Dominic Cork, Dean Jones, Devon Malcolm and Phillip DeFreitas. Northamptonshire had Curtly Ambrose; Gloucestershire had Courtney Walsh. Top players were happy to head to those counties, which meant the challenges were much more spread out. Now the power is concentrated among the few. When, late in my career, I returned after a gap of several years to Trent Bridge for a one-day game, I was seeing a different world. The same for Lord's, Edgbaston, and, in particular, The Oval – Alec Stewart has taken that club to a level of professionalism other counties simply cannot match. However, even then, the Surrey model is not based around a smattering of bums on seats for Championship games. The Oval is a vast commercial venture. It makes its money from T20, Test matches, one-day internationals, events, conferences, allied to a great spot in the middle of one of the world's most vibrant capital cities. No disrespect, but only a handful of counties can come near to matching that.

Four-day cricket as a business is completely bankrupt. It makes no money and costs a hell of a lot to put on. Compared to other formats, it simply makes zero financial sense. A big game in the T20 can bring a county £50,000 in gate receipts. Three hours' work for fifty grand! Take that formula to The Oval, with its 26,000 capacity, and you can see how it multiplies.

Championship cricket really has only one card up its sleeve. The TV rights for the game are linked to Test cricket, and Test cricket can only survive so long as there is a production line of players from the Championship. County cricket exists only because of the money from Test cricket, the England Test team only because of the Championship conveyor belt. They are the ultimate odd couple: worlds apart, but unable to get divorced because they are so utterly reliant on one another. As it stands, Test match crowds, while dropping around the world, are healthy enough in England to keep rings on both fingers.

Meanwhile, everything else is changing apace. Not so long ago, if a batsman scored runs in one-day cricket but couldn't play the four-day game, their time was limited. Nowadays, players are signed on white ball contracts only. While for me the long game will always remain the pinnacle, it has to be accepted that there are players who simply don't want to play four-day cricket, and that will only become more and more the case. As initiatives like The Hundred come in, more money is ploughed into the abbreviated version, so there will be players, as there already are, who sit there thinking, 'Why am I bothering with four-day cricket?' They get criticised for that mindset but what people outside cricket don't always understand is that a four-day season isn't always fun. Those players who think, 'You know what? I can make a living without this' are not lazy or unambitious. It's just that standing in the field for a day and a half and then nicking off for a low score is not a barrel of fun. They can do without that. That's why they don't want to invest in the four-day game – they don't see it as being enjoyable. As it is, even with the introduction of The Hundred, 80 per cent of the playing year as a first-class cricketer will still be spent playing the four-day game. Do they want to spend their days doing that? Remember as well that today's teenager has grown up with T20 cricket. It is not an interloper, something to get used to and accept, like the rest of us have had to. For them, it is not just part of cricket, it *is* cricket. Ask kids now what they would rather play and most would say T20, because that's all they have seen. Maybe, if they progress in the game, their ambition will be all about scoring hundreds in Test cricket. But getting there takes up so much time and focus that they can hardly be blamed for seeking a different option.

Bizarrely, considering my disinterest in T20 at the start, the format did see me reclaim my place in the national team, called up for the World T20 in 2009. I had worked to get back into the set-up, done the hard yards, been on A tours, so when the call actually came, typically, I was in the worst form of my life. I couldn't get past 10 in county cricket. As tends to happen, I got picked for what I'd done rather than what I was doing at the time. Indeed, I was in such bad nick that, while I was down to open, they opted for Luke Wright up top instead. It was a time when still, internationally, we didn't quite get the format. I played in one game, an ignominious defeat to Holland, and that was it. The good thing about that campaign and getting it so wrong was that it paved the way to putting into action a plan that would actually deliver England's World T20 victory in the Caribbean a year later.

When it came to T20 on the big stage, I was always going to be best placed in a pod.

Chapter 18

Blue Sky Thinking

Throughout my career, the laws of cricket never failed to amaze me. On the second morning of one match in my last year as a player, the groundsmen were cutting the pitch. My first thought was they were cheating. We'd been seamed out on a green pitch and now they were cutting it? Suddenly a thought occurred to me – they must do that every morning. That was after roughly 300 games.

So there I was last summer at the World Cup final. In all honesty, I was having a bit of a quiet day.

Broadcasting doesn't always work out the way you think it's going to. Prior to the start, I was supposed to do a piece with a couple of players over at the nets, but nobody came. Then, between innings, I was meant to do something with Warney on the pitch, but we weren't allowed to go out there. Even at the end, when the plan was for me to go into the England dressing room, we found that wasn't possible. In the end, I spent the game watching from our little Sky room with, among others, Ian Ward, Andrew Strauss, Stuart Broad and Bryan Henderson, who had the role of producing the coverage for Sky and Channel 4. Not bad company. It felt like one of those experiences that charities put up for auction.

I always find 50-over cricket a real slow burner and the World Cup final, despite its importance, was no different. I thought it was boring for the first four hours – my main contribution to the gathering was the occasional yawn – but then, of course, it sparked into life in the most extraordinary of ways. As England desperately tried to stay in the game, with nine needed from three deliveries, a throw from a New Zealand fielder hit Ben Stokes's outstretched bat as he dived for the crease. In a one in 10,000 chance, it ricocheted away to the boundary. It was like a scenario from one of those *You Are the Umpire* books – you know the ones, where the ball hits a passing seagull before being deflected to mid-on for a catch – and my initial instinct was to call dead ball. I had no idea it should count as extra runs. I could have sworn the ball was dead when it hit the batsman. Fortunately, I wasn't the one trying to make sense of this rush of events on commentary. I would have made entirely the wrong call. The extra four runs made it six off the ball and effectively took

England to a Super Over. Ah yes, a Super Over. Remind me, how does that work? Again, thankfully, I wasn't on the mic. As a commentator you haven't got time to get the rule book out and start thumbing through it. You have to get on with it.

Actually on air were Nasser Hussain and the former New Zealand keeper turned pundit Ian Smith.

Just think how difficult the final minutes of that World Cup final were for them to negotiate. There were several key moments that would have been all too easy to call wrong. In all honesty, no cricketer, I don't care who they are, really knows the laws of cricket. But Nasser and Ian negotiated their way through that maze of confusion with great skill and authority. Nobody could have done it better. If, like the rest of us, they didn't know what the hell was going on, then not for one second did they show it. Both were unbelievable throughout the World Cup, no better illustrated than at this intense moment of incredible drama. In the mad tornado around them, they were the calm eye of the storm.

I wasn't too dissimilar. There were others around me who had a much bigger stake in the game. The final was the culmination of a four-year plan for England to win the trophy and confirm themselves as the best one-day side in the world. Andrew Strauss was at the heart of that project. Usually the coolest and calmest of men, as England strived to make the plan a reality, he was now a few feet away from me cheering and shouting. I didn't join in. I've just never been like that. Rarely have I celebrated anything spontaneously. I would watch England football matches down the pub with my mates and when England scored they'd be jumping up and down while I was sat there thinking, 'What on earth are you doing?' That's not to say I don't appreciate the great drama that sport throws up, but I feel I almost have to fake the celebration that goes with it. When we won the Youth World Cup in 1997, it felt amazing but no way could I bring myself to jump up and down. I've always found it weird when grown men jump up and down. For me, there's nothing better than sitting back contentedly, taking a deep breath, and taking something in. There are some who know me who will call this being a miserable so-and-so, but for me it's just appreciating something in a different way. I have also been around Sky long enough to know that as a commentator or pundit you have to keep a level head.

My relationship with Sky may well go back long enough to when viewers were fortunate enough not to see me in high definition. After we won the Youth World Cup, I was asked to work on Sky's coverage of England's Under-19 internationals. There was no training. No one said, 'Look into this camera, say this, say that.' What happens is they give you a mic, Charles Colville asks you some questions, you answer them, and that's it. If you get asked back, they like you; if you don't, they don't. Simple as that.

The other thing in my favour was I turned up just at the point where Sky were having studio guests for practically every game across the planet. Night after night, I found myself offering up my opinions on the likes of Bangladesh versus New Zealand. It reminded me of the jetlag I'd experienced during the relentless venue switching of the Tri-Series in Australia in 2002/03, except this time I'd only travelled a few miles to West London. Of course, only a small part of the time, pre and post-match plus the lunch and tea intervals, is spent actually talking about the cricket. The rest is spent sitting around drinking cappuccinos in a desperate attempt to stay awake. Boxing Day tests were the hardest. At 8.00 pm on Christmas Day, I would have to drag myself off the settee. I like Charles Colville, but sometimes there are places you'd rather be, people you'd rather be with.

The worst part of doing the overnights is the point you have most people watching also happens to be when you are at your most tired. During the 3.00 am lunch break you might have come up with some diamond observations and no one would ever know. When you are struggling to speak two hours later, that's when everybody is getting up and switching on the TV. You need to be on it, only to find your tongue went to sleep an hour ago. Everyone has to start somewhere, though – Ian Ward had done those sessions before I did – and what I liked more than anything was that, after being up all night, I'd occasionally be a guest on the highlights show as well. That meant recording lunch and tea fillers for a game where I already knew the result.

'I shouldn't be surprised if Dale Steyn gets an eight-fer in the afternoon session,' I'd say. I'd look like a genius.

Those initial years of long nights were absolutely priceless. I didn't realise at the time – I love talking about cricket so I had nothing on my mind other than giving my view – but while it was happening I was learning a trade. What seemed like a convenient, interesting and enjoyable way to earn a bit of cash in the winter was actually giving me a skill that meant that when I did finally come out of cricket, I was fortunate enough to end up working more solidly at Sky.

It's not like I had an inbuilt knowledge of how these things work. Other than catching the highlights occasionally, I never used to watch cricket at all. My cricket viewing tended to be confined to VHS videos such as *England's Caribbean Crusade* from the early 1990s or *Botham's Ashes* from a decade previously. When Sky came along, my mum refused to have it. She claimed we watched enough TV as it was, and that was with four channels, let alone the dozens more that having Sky would have added.

I was lucky to have that apprenticeship – Sky don't generally do the overnights anymore, unless it's a match involving England. It's not quite such a common occurrence to see a vaguely recognisable cricketer wandering blearily from Sky HQ in West London at seven in the morning.

The leap from studio punditry to live commentary is a big one, but having knowledge of the set-up helps smooth the transition. At Sky, the absolute key moments of a game only come your way when you have had that full apprenticeship, and that's because, just the same as on the pitch, cricket is a game of subtleties. A commentator has to reflect the tone of the game. Take England's World Cup semi-final against Australia. England won that game so easily, and so the voice has to match that ease of victory. If the winning run comes from a wide down the leg side with five overs to spare, then shouting and screaming about it isn't a great idea.

Then there is the size of the occasion. Winning a game in the Blast is not the same as winning a Test in the Ashes. That Ashes triumph is going to be played forever. The broadcaster needs a top commentator on air to get it absolutely right. Commentary is essentially two things. One is calling the game. The other is getting the big moments spot on, because they will be watched again and again, a part of sporting and cultural history. Look at Nasser's measured outburst of emotion when England won the Ashes down under in 2010: 'Put the beer away. Put the champagne on ice. Twenty-four years of hurt in Australia. Finally they are beaten at home by England.' Nasser never wastes a word on air.

Nasser was on commentary again when Ben Stokes played perhaps the best innings any of us will ever see to drag England over the line in the 2019 Ashes Test at Headingley. 'What an innings! What a player!' he cried, as Stokes smashed the winning boundary. And again, he got it absolutely spot on. That was exactly what the whole country at that moment was thinking. Not only that, but it revealed his own joy and excitement at having been witness to a once-in-a-lifetime spectacle.

Ian Smith and Bumble always say 'Don't over prepare' when it comes to words on air. That takes not just a lively brain but a confidence that the filter between it and the mouth won't be needed. It is rapidity of wit, thought and analysis sent straight down the microphone. Athers combines both fluency and research. He is a great observer of cricket. I'll watch him commentate and then go and write a piece for *The Times*. The way he operates is a masterclass in cricket coverage, researching everything days out from the match itself. He is incredibly intelligent and has a way of articulating what we all see in such a simple way. He's very matter of fact about the way he sees the game.

I wasn't surprised to see how methodical Athers is. Early in my career I watched him bat for Lancashire against us and get 152 at Canterbury. I noted how he was always conserving energy. He was in for the long haul. His body language and demeanour was never one of intensity. He looked so relaxed, to the point you barely knew he was there. I watched that innings thinking one thing, 'That's exactly how I want to be.'

That ambition was nothing new. As a 16-year-old in second team cricket, I would try to copy him – 'I'm Athers today.' I had a Gray-Nicolls Powerspot precisely because of him. I desperately wanted to replicate his lethargic way of batting, like he was on cruise control, except when I tried, it just looked like I was lazy and wasn't trying. John Wright absolutely volleyed me for it – 'Oi! Keysy! Your footwork is going nowhere. You don't look interested.'

'I'm trying to be like Michael Atherton.' It didn't change his point of view.

More than anything, it was Athers' mental toughness I wanted to replicate. When he saved England at Johannesburg in 1995, scoring 185 not out, and facing 492 balls in an innings lasting 643 minutes, I listened to him at school batting out the last day at The Wanderers with headphone wires going up my arm. Yes, you can be a great run scorer, but to be renowned as mentally hard, that's the ultimate trick. That classic passage of play with Athers versus Allan Donald at Trent Bridge in 1998 is one of those moments that we as players all want to be remembered for. A batsman would give anything to be in that situation and get through it. Athers did. And that toughness is what people of my generation recall most fondly about Athers. It says everything about him, though, that whenever England are playing South Africa and need to bat out time, and a producer suggests looking back at that 185, or Athers versus Donald, he doesn't want to talk about himself in that regard. Ask him about that scrap with Donald and he'll say, 'Yes, it was pretty fast,' and that's about it.

Both Athers and Nasser have an authority to talk about whatever they want because of what they went through in their careers. They were hard-as-nails players, stubborn, uncompromising in a lot of ways, and that's why, out of a generation of talented cricketers, they were two of the very best. They had to be like that to survive. They faced the best spinners, the best pacemen. They had a brutal era to come through and they came out the other side. Now, in commentary, both pretty much recreate how they batted. Athers will sit back in his chair and call the game, while Nasser looks more fully engaged with the proceedings.

Both are often used by Sky to do the more in-depth features, whether they be documentaries or interviews. Athers tends to be used for the pieces that are more contentious. If it's a complicated issue, such as corruption, Athers gets the nod. Plus he's got a real love of history, so when we go to South Africa, he'll be the one saying to the producer, 'Let's tell the Basil D'Oliveira story,' or he'll be going through the museum at Lancashire. As much as he was a great player, he has a keen journalistic side as well, where he wants to get in there and get the story.

There is another element to Athers – he's the biggest stirrer I know. Whenever there's an elephant in the room where no one wants to mention something because it might be slightly difficult, Athers is the one who will barge in and take great delight in the awkwardness of it all. Make no mistake, though, when Athers needs to be switched on, he is exactly that. Athers can go from taking the micky, having a bit of fun, to getting the moment absolutely spot on.

Ian Ward, meanwhile, is the best TV sports presenter by a country mile. A totally underestimated skill, Wardy can handle live TV, with all the chatter down the earpiece, the unpredictability, like he's been doing it all his life. I turned up at Sky at the start of an India vs England one-day series, with Wardy just about to go on air with me as the guest, and just as the titles rolled we heard the producer's voice: 'We're not going to get the rights. We're not going to be able to show the game.'

My initial thought was one of mild panic. 'Right, OK! What do we do now?'

At that moment, when something goes wrong, as can happen when you are dealing with India, where it always seems that the rights are never quite as straightforward as elsewhere, Wardy has to think of a whole new top of the show. More than that, the entire team has to think of something to do for the whole day. Dermot O'Leary does a great job on *X Factor*, but fact is, he is looking into an autocue reading rehearsed words. We might turn up at Sky and it rain for six hours. The *X Factor* is many things but it is never rained off. At that point, you have to find things to talk about. Those occasions cannot be scripted and actually, more often than not, are the most enjoyable part of TV punditry – for the guest, anyway! Normally, the show is on a schedule: the presenter needs to hit the toss, the anthems, the start. That's where they earn their corn. When a rain break comes, I enjoy it as we get to expand the points we are making. In some ways it feels more like a podcast.

But there is so much more to Wardy's ability than quick-thinking. He is the best presenter because he is so adept at making it all about his guests. His role is to make Athers, me, whoever, look good. Not the easiest of jobs in my case. As a viewer, I see Bumble deliver his opinion in his usual polished, professional and knowledgeable way. He looks great, but I know that the ease with which he is talking has been set up by Wardy. Not everyone does that. Watch some presenters on TV and you can see it's all about them – 'This is my moment to shine'. They will ask their guest a question, which is actually a statement to which they can say little more than 'Yes, I agree'. Sit across from Wardy during a rain break and you can see him weave a way to get you to talk about something that you know about while he takes a back seat. Same when he interviews players in front of the Sky video cart at the end of the day. It's not the questions he asks so much as the way he asks them. Wardy can be probing but does so with an underlying empathy and understanding. If a team has been bowled out for under a hundred, he is going to ask pertinent questions, but they will come from the place of a man who knows these things can happen. He understands that players are only human, and as such they share the same emotions as the rest of us, be they elation, disappointment or sheer brutal tiredness after a tough day. He has an ease of personality that allows honest, frank and humorous discussion. It is never about making himself look like the expert. No one knows the answers to the questions he's asking better than himself, but he's totally selfless in that he always allows the person opposite to be the one doing the talking.

Sometimes we will have to mention what's coming up on Sky as a whole, ranging from sport to drama to comedy. Wardy, of course, is the ultimate pro. He particularly likes golf, to the extent that whenever he's reading a golf promo he will embellish it slightly. If he is required to flag up a tournament at Portrush, for example, he will add 'the notoriously tough Portrush'. It's sickening really how effortlessly he does this kind of stuff. When it's my turn, things don't always turn out so well. Football isn't, in all honesty, my bag and so I have a habit of reading out a simple promo such as Manchester United versus Leicester City as Manchester United vs Leicestershire. As you can imagine, these things tend not to go unnoticed by fellow commentators.

When you compare the days of Peter West introducing Test cricket from a rickety box on a bit of scaffolding five minutes before the start of play, to now, with a team of presenters whose ability and skill is revealed through character and interplay as well as a digest of informed opinion, then it truly feels, as it very much is, a different millennium. When you see Bumble actually talking to people in the crowd through their earpieces, it's just insane. But that comes not just from technology, but from getting the mix of commentators absolutely right. If there's a quiet period in play, Bumble will say, 'Give me some earpieces', and that's it, he's off. 'I'm liking your hat, mate. How are your sandwiches?' He is so good at it, and it is exactly what is needed in those moments. Nobody can do that as well as he can. Anyone else who tries is just going to look like a poor imitation. He is passionate about protecting the game and making sure everybody loves it. How does he do that? With great knowledge mixed with incredible humour. When you're working in a team with Bumble, you can't ever take yourself too seriously. He doesn't have a TV persona; he is exactly the same all the time. When we're travelling around with Sky, we play cards. The England players join in too because everyone so enjoys being around Bumble. We play a game called nomination, and if you don't get a hundred points, you have to do a forfeit. The idea is that the person who fails to reach the target should suffer a degree of embarrassment. Embarrass Bumble? That would be impossible. If he doesn't get a hundred points, and the forfeit is to shout 'I'm a banana!' as loud as he can, he will bellow it twenty times. On a plane.

Bumble is the Yoda of commentary – so much knowledge, and a very distinctive way of talking. I have been trying to work out if there's anyone who has had so many different jobs in cricket. He's been a player, an umpire, a coach, a columnist, and a broadcaster on radio and TV. I'm sorry I missed him as an umpire – that was before my time as a player (when I started out, he was England coach) – which is a shame because I'm quite sure he was just as entertaining with a white coat on as he has been in every other walk of life. The man has just got funny bones. He's got incredible stories, he can do all the voices and, like all the best comedians, he's got great timing. He can turn any situation into a bit of fun. I've been on a boat fishing with him twice for pieces with Sky. I hate sailing, know nothing about fishing, but he loves both – and yet it's always him it goes wrong for. It's always him who gets his line tangled, gets in a fluster. I'm not sure he's caught anything on TV yet. We did another piece where we were at Victoria station looking at a steam train. I couldn't help but wonder what on earth I was doing there, which I suppose is why it works as TV, but he loves steam trains, was so into it. And that's Bumble. He has a fascination with so much – such a good observer of life.

Bumble has, without doubt, become one of the most recognisable names in English cricket. He gets spotted everywhere and has always got time for people. Better than anyone I know he can relate to every generation. He can entertain my kids the same as he can people in their eighties. In his early seventies himself, he is still incredibly relevant. He gets Twitter and is prepared to embrace the changing face of the game. He's not one of these people constantly harking back to the 1960 and 70s. He can look forward as much as back. Bumble would talk as admiringly of Kevin Pietersen when he came along as he might have done about Colin Cowdrey in the past. His experiences in cricket are second to none. He has worked with some great players and talks about the game with so much affection, and that comes through with his commentary.

He is also one of the best judges of a cricketer. If a new player comes around, Bumble will be one of the first people whose opinion I'll seek. He knows an awful lot about the current crop of players. He goes to watch them live as well as on TV.

Similarly, he is always prepared to pass on his knowledge of commentary. It's something that never really gets taught and so Bumble's the one we all go to. Why wouldn't we? This is a man who never misses a beat on commentary. He's called some of the biggest moments in world cricket but is equally unparalleled when it comes to the more mundane passages of play. In the box, there is the lead commentator, whose job it is to call the game and reflect the tone of the play as it happens, and then the co-commentator, who is there to add insight. Commentary is a relationship, but Bumble makes it very easy for the person alongside him. If nothing is going on you can put the mic down, pass it over to him, and watch him go. The last thing you should ever try to do is compete, because you will quickly get found out.

In real life, and as a commentator, Bumble is also incredibly generous. At the World T20 in 2016, when Carlos Brathwaite hit Ben Stokes for four consecutive sixes to win the game, Bumble was commentating on that last over. Off his own back he made a brilliant call. When Brathwaite hit the third six, he passed the mic over to Ian Bishop – a great gesture; as the lead commentator you are the one who is supposed to call that final over, and especially the winning moment. As it is, Ian Bishop will never be forgotten for his 'Remember the name!' line as Brathwaite dispatched Stokes into the stand for the final time. Bumble just understood that the right thing for that moment, for a West Indian win, was to have a West Indian voice. That was selfless commentary. A lot of people would have wanted that moment for themselves.

I first worked with Bumble at T20 finals day. He was brilliant, incredibly welcoming, and I watched a genius at work. T20 is what took Bumble to that next level of popularity, and that's because he was the first one who really got what the coverage needed to be. It wasn't about analysis, picking up on the negatives; it was about celebrating the positive side of the game.

T20 suits Bumble as he's an innovator. He will always try to find a different way to do something. In New Zealand, Wardy was interviewing him when he walked over the boundary rope and started playing cricket with the crowd. He is perfectly capable of behaving in a similar manner back on home turf.

Sky can do an interview with Sir Alastair Cook and it won't get as many views on social media as Bumble doing a 'pitch report' on a patch of pavement outside a pub in Birmingham.

Bumble is a great reader of a game, but there is nobody better at predicting what will happen than Warney. So often he'll get a hunch – 'He's going to sweep here and get out', 'He's going to chip one up in the air'. He's the master at making those calls, an incredible eye for detail. I had just finished a stint commentating on a Test match, my first one, England versus India at Southampton, when Warney rang me. Moeen Ali was bowling at the time.

'Watch Pujara,' he told me. 'He's the only batsman who runs down the pitch after the ball has come out the spinner's hand.'

I watched and he was exactly right. 'You can use that,' he told me. 'You can freeze it on the touch screen and show how different he is in his approach.'

He is also, as you might expect, slightly mischievous. Sitting around behind the scenes, there's nothing much more fun than Warney laying into Nasser and vice versa, an argument that's probably started after Nasser has raised a time where, as captain, he considered he'd got the better of Warney. There'll be this great verbal ruckus going backwards and forwards.

For sure, when you've got Bumble, Athers, Warney, people like that, at Sky, it's a pretty ruthless dressing room. Whenever players retire they miss the dressing room more than anything. In doing so, they maybe forget the tougher elements of dressing room life. But the Sky commentary team is one of the great dressing rooms because it's brutal, in a good way. Feet are kept firmly on the ground because nobody takes themselves too seriously. If you do, you get told pretty quickly.

Sadly, one man who formed such an integral part of Sky's coverage for so many years is no longer with us. Bob Willis was the kindest of blokes. We would sit together for hours and hours at the Sky studio watching whatever game it might be. He wouldn't say a lot at times, but if you asked him a question he was so bounteous in his answer. He would try to give you as much as he possibly could. More than that, though, he was one of the funniest men. People saw how cutting he could be on air, and he was like that in real life. He held an opinion but so often it was made with such great humour. All you could do was sit there laughing.

Bob was very matter of fact about everything. As a cricketer, especially when I first started playing, if he was on Sky, my first thought was, 'Oh shit, here we go! If I play badly he's going to eviscerate me!' But then, when I got to know him, that all subsided because I was truly able to see what a lovely bloke he was, and also how much he cared.

As a pundit, you have time in between games. It's easy to take that for granted whereas Bob was never less than 100 per cent properly researched. He hadn't played county cricket for a long time but knew everything about the game, what people were averaging, what their attitude was like, their weak and strong points. He knew what players were doing. He knew if they could bowl or bat, always speaking from a place of authority, not just because he was a great bowler for England, but because he genuinely knew what was happening across the grounds of the country. He was doing the same research as we all do now. Which is exactly how it should be – if you think you can turn up on TV and blag your way through, you will soon be found out. Bob was known for strident opinions, but they all came from an educated place.

He also knew how to deliver a line. Sit opposite him on *The Verdict* and you knew he was going to have something in his locker, be it 'Prior dire' if England wicketkeeper Matt had endured a poor day, or the classic 'More hookers than Soho' if England had been a little over-enthusiastic with the bat. Whatever he'd thought up was there, ready and set to go. But he never let on what he was going to do before the broadcast. Everyone knew he was going to come out with something, but he never gave his opinion, his lines, away. With me, he'd rather be asking, 'How's the golf going, Keysy? How are the kids?' It was always very engaging – and then the camera would roll, and BANG! It would all come pouring out. I'd be sat there in hysterics because I knew this was one of the nicest blokes you could ever meet. People would say to me, 'Why were you laughing? He was being horrible.' And I would say, 'He's the gentlest bloke in the world. You have no idea how good a person he is.'

The Verdict, or *The Debate*, as it is these days, was Bob. And that's why it's so hard to go into that show now. His absence has left a gap, one that is not easy for any of us to get used to. The reason the show is able to carry on is because its guests are steeped in honesty. And, like Bob, they all come from a place of wanting the best for English cricket. Sky has pundits who may occasionally be harsh but who essentially do as much as they can to show English cricket in a good light. Bob was sometimes seen as being at the other end of the spectrum, but actually, what he was doing was making everyone accountable – because he too wanted the national team to experience success. Not everyone does that. Many broadcasters are so sycophantic towards what they are commentating on. Sky is not like that, and Bob was always an important part of that approach. Let's face it, sometimes people just want to hear someone say it how it is, and you could never accuse Sky of not doing that with Bob Willis. It was another way they challenged the received way of covering cricket. It's such a shame Bob never got to see just how much the public loved and respected him. The outpouring of both after his death was amazing.

It was Barney Francis, Sky's long-serving sport executive, who really took cricket coverage forward to another level. He launched T20 both as an event and on TV, and was responsible for winning rights to all cricket for Sky Sports. Innovation was his byword. Doing an interview? Instead of the studio, why not meet your subject in an environment they enjoy – golf course, fishing, a café – to get a more personal insight? A quick wrap-up at the end of the day's play? Why not a whole show looking back at the major talking points in detail?

After Barney, Paul King headed up Sky's cricket coverage, coming up with the Sky video cart, the touch screen technology. Then came Bryan Henderson, who came up with the T20 pod, one of THE great innovations. It's brought so much more to the commentary, positioned us, quite literally, at the heart of the game. Sit in a soundproof commentary box and it's very hard to feel the atmosphere. Before his final commentary stint on India vs New Zealand at Old Trafford in the World Cup, Ian Smith went out and stood on the balcony for a couple of overs. At that point he realised the whole place was in chaos. All the Indian fans were cheering, the noise was terrific. You don't get any of that in a commentary box, whereas in the pod you get everything. Commentary is about going with the game and the atmosphere. Sometimes, when there is a small crowd, it is harder. You might have a really close game but nothing in the ground is saying so. In those cases, it is up to you to use the mic to deliver the tension of the action, the brilliance of performance, for those at home. Thankfully, those occasions are few and far between. In most cases, the pod becomes part of the event, part of the game, even, with the odd ball entering at speed from the flash of a player's bat, and it is easier to let yourself go and become swallowed up by the vibe.

Hendo also came up with the masterclasses that would eventually become commonplace across sports broadcasting, the first one being Warney talking through his bowling expertise, all done live, with no script, just one great bowler and an excellent presenter in Ian Ward. That 'Let's do it' attitude still prevails. One day they might just say, 'Why don't we go to the indoor school and do something with Tres against left armers?' At that point, we'll wander across with two cameras, no idea if we're going to be allowed into the indoor school to do it, let alone if it will make good TV. But it doesn't matter. The producers are just, 'Come on, let's do it!' The tragic thing for me is I find myself watching, introducing, taking part in these masterclasses, thinking, 'Bloody hell, I wish I'd known that at the time.' I was doing a piece with Kumar Sangakkara and he was talking about how standing lower in the stance to spinners helps the batsman to pick up the ball better. I was astonished. Why did nobody tell me that twenty years ago?!

Hendo is very good at seeing not just the big, bold moves, but the 1 per cents that continually push Sky's coverage forward. He's not shy in coming forward with advice, which is all any of us want. For example, if Nasser introduces the toss with 'I'm out here in the middle with the two captains', he might say, 'Where else would you be for the toss?' Same with pointing out that telling an interviewee 'Thanks for doing this' makes no sense – it's precisely where they're meant to be at that given time. He is always challenging us to be better broadcasters, to think outside the box, not get stale. He loves nothing more than for all of us to take a risk. That's why he's so good to work with – he's prepared to give praise and criticism at the same time.

Right now, those people will be thinking of the next innovation. And, as ever, it will come without diminishing the integrity of the broadcast. But innovation doesn't just appear out of nowhere. If, fifteen years ago, someone had suggested a commentator talking to people in the crowd, be it down a mic, or through a headset, they'd either have been laughed at or carted off to a lunatic asylum. Not now. The Sky attitude is just 'Go for it'. They are not set to one way of doing things.

And that is the thing – the game is evolving so quickly. Being out of the dressing room for just two or three years, you are slipping behind in terms of knowledge, methodology. As a pundit and commentator, it is incumbent on me to remedy that, be it talking to Jos Buttler about how he plays a certain shot, or Ben Stokes about his attitude to batting. As a broadcaster, you must constantly evolve with the game; otherwise, you are going to be left behind. You will be talking about the game as it was played ten or fifteen years ago. Move with the times. It's not all right to be sitting there repeating 'When I played, it was like this'.

I like also the fact that the people in charge have got a view. We are not, for instance, allowed to say 'And there it is!' when the winning runs come. That's not always easy, but they are right – we shouldn't be peddling clichés when there are more novel and interesting ways. The producers are constantly trying to move the coverage forward.

The fact is that people like Nasser, Athers, Wardy, Bumble, are among the best broadcasters in the world, not just of cricket but of sport, full stop. And that sheer weight of knowledge in the Sky commentary box allows the opportunity to look at things from the coaching as well as the playing and captaincy point of view. If Jonny Bairstow, perhaps, is talking a leg stump guard against in-swingers, Athers might point out the danger of that policy.

Jonny, or any player, could watch that and learn from it. In South Africa, the batsman Rassie van der Dussen stood watching Nasser do a piece to camera about playing spin and he was absolutely spot on to do that. It's not just criticism, it's criticism with a solution, which is a much better way to be. We can get far too caught up in the negative. So much of TV and life is about pulling people apart for their flaws. What we're all trying to show is answers to problems, and that might apply as much to a batsman in Kent Under-15s – different guard to an off spinner than a leg spinner – as someone in the Test side.

Sky has carved a role in which it offers impartial analysis in a way that is supportive to the game. Everyone is pulling in the same direction, and players respond to it on that basis. That's not just those in front of the camera. The people behind the scenes, the sound engineers, producers, directors, are all part of the equation. I soon realised just how much these guys are fans of cricket and how desperate they are for England to succeed. They are probably bigger supporters of England than I am! They are the ones jumping up and down when they do well. They are not necessarily doing the job they do at Sky for any other factor other than they love the sport. Everyone is invested in it heart and mind. I've been at Test matches with Athers, Bumble, Nasser, Bryan Henderson and Ian Ward, and believe me, they are always debating something. It is always great value – heated, funny, micky-taking. I have sat there with just one thought: 'This is why this job is the best job in the world, because I get to have a laugh and listen to this lot. People would pay a small fortune to sit down at a function with this line-up and here I am, some mediocre international cricketer, if that, sharing these amazing times with some of the true greats of English cricket.'

But of course, that conversation, and the subtle micky-taking it always entails, isn't hidden from public view. It is heard on mic, or in studio debates, and that is something I think that resonates with viewers because it mirrors how they talk with friends or colleagues.

Whatever you do, whatever you say, however you commentate, you can never please everyone. There will always be somebody who doesn't appreciate your voice or manner. You have to be thick-skinned. The feedback on social media soon comes – 'Someone tell Rob Key to shut up – he talks too much', 'Get Steve Harmison on – Key hasn't got a clue what he's talking about'. I never get upset about anything I hear or read about myself on Twitter but, sadly, it is gradually becoming more and more of a platform where people have lost their sense of humour.

I take the sting out of social media by treating it as a game. Sometimes I'll go out of my way to stir things up. I was bored on the train recently coming home with the kids from a game. I put out a simple tweet that Steve Smith is a better batsman than Virat Kohli. My account went mad. People were hammering me for it. In all honesty, I don't really care who's better – I love watching Kohli and I love watching Smith. But just saying that Smith is better heated everything up to the extent even Indian news channels were getting involved. I'm thinking, 'Does anyone really care about my opinion, especially in India?' I'd imagine the only question most people in India would be asking is, 'Who is Rob Key anyway?'

I have a mate who works in the entertainment industry who kindly put something on my Twitter about how I love One Direction (I don't love One Direction) and before I knew it I was deluged with messages from what I believe are called 'Directioners'. 'What's your favourite song?' – all this kind of stuff. Insane. I couldn't even name any. Honestly.

Nowadays, a lot of my summer consists of commentating on the T20 Blast. Whereas with a Test match you let the pictures do the talking, let the game breathe, T20 is a lot more manic. You have to think on your feet, decide whether to rev it up, tone it down, have a bit of banter. It's not an easy balance to strike considering you are trying to appeal to kids, teenagers, 20-year-olds, 50-year-olds, and others who have been watching the game for decades. Like any commentary, though, the action on the pitch has to be the most important part. As Bumble always says, 'You call the game.'

Deep analysis is removed by the speed of the format, but generally I'm trying to work out what option a batsman or bowler might try next. Ian Smith helped me a lot in that respect. I have such respect for Smithy and have spoken to him a lot about commentary. To him, the skill is not only in calling the game correctly but trying, as with Warney, to predict what happens. It's not just about revealing what is happening and what is going on. As Smithy and Bumble say, a stats fest is not what the viewer wants. It's about taking a chance, explaining what's going through the batsman or bowler's mind and heart, what they might do next. If you get it wrong, so what? You just have to put your hands up and say, 'OK, well I thought they might have done it differently.' In T20 it's easier to get a sense of when something is going to happen. Two dot balls generally means an explosion is coming next, whereas in Test cricket, a very different beast, a plan might take ten overs to evolve.

I have more recently been seen on the fifteen-minute highlights package, another Sky innovation, and a time when the pressure is on. Wardy will set me up with a simple comment – 'England did well today ...', and I add a short opinion. Easy, right? But I am so desperate not to muck it up. This is right at the end of the day. Everyone is either waiting to go home or prepare for the next show. And all that depends on me not messing it up, on me making the most of this little fifteen-minute window, on my brain and tongue getting on. But I am evolving. I can now do those fifteen-minute highlights packages without messing them up. Occasionally.

As I have moved on with commentary, Hendo has always said to me to watch the senior guys, Nasser, Athers, and the rest, and that's exactly what I have done, and I have learnt so much. They are the mark. As a player, you try to copy bits of other players, the very best, and it's no different now I'm in broadcasting. It's a chapter of my life that is still unfolding, but one inextricably linked to those that came before. It's a different career path and I want to get better and better. I see how that development has happened with others around me. When we roll highlights from a decade previously, I can see how Nasser has moved on. We are all constantly trying to get better. Testing myself, seeking to develop, is what makes the job so much more fun.

My fervent hope is that when it comes to cricket, the game that has given me so much, introduced me to so many incredible people, and, occasionally, driven me just a little bit mad, there are many more words yet to add.

For better or worse, I hope 'Oi! Keysy!' is a shout I'll be hearing for a good few years to come.

Acknowledgements

Massive and heartfelt thanks to my mum and dad, Lynn and Trevor – only as a parent yourself do you truly realise the sacrifices your own parents make. Thank you; your selflessness has been incredible.

Alan Ealham – for guiding me all the way through age group cricket and into the Kent second team. There are certain people in your life whom you are lucky to meet, and he definitely counts as one of them.

Noddy Holder – the best batting coach in the world. From the moment I met him, my game and everything that went with it just got better and better.

Paul Box-Grainger – my Beckenham first team captain from when I was just 13, for looking after me and spending most Saturday nights lecturing me in the bar about captaincy, life, and cricket in general.

Kent coaches John Wright, John Inverarity, Ian Brayshaw, Jimmy Adams, Graham Ford and Paul Farbrace – thanks for, more often than not, biting your tongues.

Simon Willis – for spending more time feeding me balls on a bowling machine than anyone in history.

Freddy and Harmy – I was lucky to play sport, but what it has given me in return in friendship is worth more than anything that could ever happen out on the pitch.

John Woodhouse – thanks for listening, and your writing prowess. It has genuinely amazed me how all those hours sitting around chatting away has somehow turned into the book in front of me.

Bryan Henderson, Sky head of cricket – your relentless backing has helped me learn a new career.

More than anyone else, I would like to thank Fleur – without her, nothing would have been possible. She has seen me through more good and bad times than anyone else; the one constant throughout. And Aaliyah and Harrison, who have given me the perspective that there's more to life than chasing a ball.

Rob Key Career Statistics

Robert William Trevor Key, born East Dulwich, London, 12 May 1979

Right-hand bat; right-arm medium pace/off-break bowler

Wisden Cricketer of the Year 2004

Kent 1998–2015; cap 2001; captain 2006–15; benefit 2011

TEST MATCH CAREER RECORD

	M	I	NO	HS	Runs	Avge	100	50	Ct
2002 to 2004-05	15	26	1	221	775	31.00	1	3	11

Match list

Opponent	Venue	Date	1st Inns	2nd Inns	Res
v India	Nottingham	8-12 Aug 2002	17 B	DNB	Drawn
v India	Leeds	22-26 Aug 2002	30 Ct	34 LBW	Lost
v Australia	Adelaide	21-24 Nov 2002	1 Ct	1 Ct	Lost
v Australia	Perth	29 Nov-1 Dec 2002	47 B	23 LBW	Lost
v Australia	Melbourne	26-30 Dec 2002	0 LBW	52 Ct	Lost
v Australia	Sydney	2-6 Jan 2003	3 LBW	14 Ct	Won
v Zimbabwe	Lord's	22-24 May 2003	18 Ct	DNB	Won
v Zimbabwe	Chester-le-St	5-7 Jun 2003	4 Ct	DNB	Won
v West Indies	Lord's	22-26 Jul 2004	221 Ct	15 RO	Won
v West Indies	Birmingham	29 Jul-1 Aug 2004	29 Ct	4 Ct	Won
v West Indies	Manchester	12-16 Aug 2004	6 B	93 NO	Won
v West Indies	The Oval	19-21 Aug 2004	10 Ct	DNB	Won
v South Africa	Cape Town	2-6 Jan 2005	0 Ct	41 St	Lost
v South Africa	Johannesburg	13-17 Jan 2005	83 Ct	19 Ct	Won
v South Africa	Centurion	21-25 Jan 2005	1 Ct	9 LBW	Drawn

Double Centuries by England Batsmen v West Indies

325	A. Sandham	Kingston	3-12 Apr 1930
285*	P.B.H. May	Birmingham	30 May-4 Jun 1957
262*	D.L. Amiss	Kingston	16-21 Feb 1974
258	T.W. Graveney	Nottingham	4-9 Jul 1957
243	A.N. Cook	Birmingham	17-19 Aug 2017
226	K.P. Pietersen	Leeds	25-28 May 2007
221	**R.W.T. Key**	**Lord's**	**22-26 Jul 2004**
205*	E.H. Hendren	Port of Spain	1-6 Feb 1930
205	L. Hutton	Kingston	20 Mar-3 Apr 1954
203	D.L. Amiss	The Oval	12-17 Aug 1976
202*	L. Hutton	The Oval	12-16 Aug 1950

Double Centuries by England Batsmen at Lord's

333	G.A. Gooch	India	26-31 Jul 1990
240	W.R. Hammond	Australia	24-28 Jun 1938
226	I.J.L. Trott	Bangladesh	27-31 May 2010
221	**R.W.T. Key**	**West Indies**	**22-26 Jul 2004**
211	J.B. Hobbs	South Africa	28 Jun-1 Jul 1924
208	D.C.S. Compton	South Africa	21-25 Jun 1947
205*	J. Hardstaff	India	22-25 Jun 1946
202*	K.P. Pietersen	India	21-25 Jul 2011
200*	J.E. Root	Sri Lanka	12-16 Jun 2014

Top 10 Highest Partnerships for England at Lord's

370	W.J. Edrich/D.C.S. Compton	South Africa	21-25 Jun 1947
332	I.J.L. Trott/S.C.J. Broad	Pakistan	26-29 Aug 2010
308	G.A. Gooch/A.J. Lamb	India	26-31 Jul 1990
291†	**A.J. Strauss/R.W.T. Key**	**West Indies**	**22-26 Jul 2004**
286	K.P. Pietersen/I.R. Bell	South Africa	10-14 Jul 2008
268	J.B. Hobbs/H. Sutcliffe	South Africa	28 Jun-1 Jul 1924
255	M.E. Trescothick/M.P. Vaughan	Bangladesh	26-28 May 2005
248	L. Hutton/D.C.S. Compton	West Indies	24-27 Jun 1939
246	L.E.G. Ames/G.O.B. Allen	New Zealand	27-30 Jun 1931
245	J. Hardstaff/W.R. Hammond	New Zealand	26-29 Jun 1937

† *Record second-wicket partnership for England v West Indies.*

LIMITED-OVERS INTERNATIONAL CAREER RECORD

	M	I	NO	HS	Runs	Avge	100	50	Ct
2003 to 2004	5	5	–	19	54	10.80	–	–	–

Match list

Opponent	Venue	Date	Score	Balls	Res
v Zimbabwe	Nottingham	26 Jun 2003	11 B	37	Lost
v South Africa	The Oval	28 Jun 2003	0 Ct	1	Won
v West Indies	Leeds	1 Jul 2004	6 B	12	Won
v New Zealand	Bristol	4 Jul 2004	18 Ct	34	Lost
v West Indies	Lord's	6 Jul 2004	19 B	51	Lost

Rob Key also played one IT20 match, v Netherlands at Lord's on 5 June 2009, scoring 10*.

FIRST-CLASS CAREER RECORD

Debut v Middlesex, at Canterbury, on 17-21 April 1998, scoring 15.

Final game v Glamorgan, at Cardiff, on 9-12 September 2015, scoring 94 and 158.

	M	I	NO	HS	Runs	Avge	100	50	Ct
Kent 1998	13	23	-	115	612	26.60	2	1	11
Eng A in SA/Zim 1998-99	3	5	-	25	52	10.40	-	-	4
Kent 1999	19	33	2	125	836	26.96	1	5	18
Kent & Select XI 2000	17	29	1	83	584	20.85	-	5	4
Kent 2001	18	28	-	132	1,281	45.75	4	7	7
Kent, MCC & Eng 2002	17	31	1	160	1,255	41.83	3	6	12
Eng in Aus 2002-03	6	12	2	174*	443	44.30	1	2	3
ECB Acad in SL 2002-03	3	6	-	115	272	45.33	2	-	-
Kent & Eng 2003	14	22	2	140	754	37.70	2	1	13
Kent, MCC & Eng 2004	16	27	3	221	1,896	79.00	9	3	8
Eng in SA 2004-05	3	6	-	83	153	25.50	-	1	2
Kent 2005	15	27	1	189	1,556	59.84	4	8	8
Kent & Eng A 2006	16	29	3	136*	956	36.76	2	3	10
Kent 2007	15	25	3	182	1,250	56.81	5	4	4
Kent & Eng L 2008	16	27	3	178*	918	38.25	2	4	5
Eng L in NZ 2008-09	2	4	1	90	198	66.00	-	2	2
Kent, MCC & Eng L 2009	17	28	4	270*	1,209	50.37	4	3	15
Kent 2010	16	28	2	261	814	31.30	2	1	1
Kent 2011	12	24	2	162	895	40.68	2	5	11
Kent 2012	15	24	3	119	797	37.95	1	5	7
Kent 2013	17	28	3	180	1,169	46.76	5	3	3
Kent 2014	16	27	1	126	561	21.57	1	2	5
Kent 2015	13	24	-	158	958	39.91	2	5	1
Kent	266	459	31	270*	17,391	40.63	49	68	132
MCC	3	3	-	77	95	31.66	-	1	1

	M	I	NO	HS	Runs	Avge	100	50	Ct
ECB Academy	3	6	-	115	272	45.33	2	-	-
England A	5	9	1	136	277	34.62	1	1	6
England Lions	4	8	2	90	285	47.50	-	2	2
First-Class Cos Select	1	2	-	22	22	11.00	-	-	-
England †	17	30	3	221	1077	39.88	2	4	13
Total	299	517	37	270*	19,419	40.45	54	76	154

† *Total includes two matches that were not Tests.*

First-Class Centuries

Match	Venue	Date	Score	Balls
Kent v Durham	Canterbury	21-23 May 1998	101	189
Kent v Nottinghamshire	Canterbury	17-20 Jun 1998	115	235
Kent v Somerset	Taunton	18-21 Aug 1999	125	307
Kent v Surrey	The Oval	20-23 Apr 2001	101	199
Kent v Pakistanis	Canterbury	12-14 May 2001	119	194
Kent v Essex	Southend	18-20 Jul 2001	123	293
Kent v Lancashire	Manchester	12-15 Sep 2001	132	195
Kent v Hampshire	Canterbury	19-22 Apr 2002	160	179
Kent v Yorkshire	Canterbury	15-18 May 2002	114	156
Kent v Leicestershire	Leicester	24-27 Jul 2002	127	217
England XI v Australia A	Hobart	15-17 Nov 2002	174*	386
ECB Acad v BCCSL Acad	Colombo, NCC	24-27 Feb 2003	115	116
ECB Acad v Sri Lanka A	Dambulla	8-11 Mar 2003	105	158
Kent v Cambridge UCCE	Cambridge	18-20 Apr 2003	129	155
Kent v Nottinghamshire	Maidstone	9-11 Jul 2003	140	239
Kent v Gloucestershire	Bristol	16-19 Apr 2004	118*	171
Kent v New Zealanders	Canterbury	13-16 May 2004	114	130
Kent v New Zealanders	Canterbury	13-16 May 2004	117*	143
Kent v Northamptonshire	Northampton	19-22 May 2004	173	255
Kent v Surrey	The Oval	25-28 May 2004	199	358
Kent v Lancashire	Tunbridge W	2-5 Jun 2004	180	327
England v West Indies	**Lord's**	**22-26 Jul 2004**	**221**	**288**
Kent v Northamptonshire	Canterbury	3-6 Sep 2004	131	158
Kent v Middlesex	Canterbury	16-18 Sep 2004	131	157
Kent v Gloucestershire	Bristol	27-30 Apr 2005	164	322
Kent v Surrey	Tunbridge W	25-28 May 2005	112	262
Kent v Surrey †	Tunbridge W	25-28 May 2005	189	285
Kent v Middlesex	Canterbury	24-27 Aug 2005	142	214
England A v Pakistanis	Canterbury	6-9 Jul 2006	136	269
Kent v Hampshire	Canterbury	2-5 Aug 2006	136*	312
Kent v Durham	Chester-le-St	9-12 May 2007	169	279

Match	Venue	Date	Score	Balls
Kent v Hampshire	Canterbury	23-26 May 2007	120	221
Kent v Warwickshire	Birmingham	14-17 Aug 2007	153	268
Kent v Worcestershire	Canterbury	21-24 Aug 2007	125	149
Kent v Lancashire	Canterbury	28-31 Aug 2007	182	332
Kent v New Zealanders	Canterbury	28-30 Apr 2008	178*	260
Kent v Yorkshire	Canterbury	11-14 Jul 2008	157	267
Kent v Surrey	The Oval	10-13 Jul 2009	123	193
Kent v Glamorgan	Cardiff	15-18 Jul 2009	270*	339
Kent v Derbyshire	Canterbury	31 Jul-3 Aug 2009	110	144
Kent v Derbyshire	Derby	2-5 Sep 2009	141*	247
Kent v Loughborough MCCU	Canterbury	10-12 Apr 2010	140	144
Kent v Durham	Canterbury	17-20 May 2010	261	270
Kent v Surrey	The Oval	10-13 Jul 2011	162	289
Kent v Surrey ‡	Canterbury	10-12 Aug 2011	110*	202
Kent v Hampshire	Southampton	27-30 Jul 2012	119	235
Kent v Leicestershire	Leicester	17-20 Apr 2013	104*	199
Kent v Leicestershire	Tunbridge W	29 May-1 Jun 2013	106	188
Kent v Hampshire	Canterbury	15-18 Jul 2013	180	285
Kent v Northamptonshire	Northampton	17-20 Sep 2013	101	149
Kent v Lancashire	Canterbury	24-27 Sep 2013	134	162
Kent v Surrey	Canterbury	4-7 May 2014	126	206
Kent v Lancashire	Canterbury	1-4 Sep 2015	113	201
Kent v Glamorgan	Cardiff	9-12 Sep 2015	158	255

† *Sharing in Kent record third-wicket stand of 323 with M.van Jaarsveld.*
‡ *Carried bat throughout the innings.*

He scored a century against every county barring Sussex, against whom his top score was 84 (Hove, 21-23 September 2005), one of only two half-centuries against them in 24 innings.

Most First-Class Centuries for Kent

122	F.E. Woolley	1906-38
78	L.E.G. Ames	1926-51
73	H.T.W. Hardinge	1902-33
58	M.C. Cowdrey	1950-76
55	A.E. Fagg	1932-57
53	J. Seymour	1902-26
49	**R.W.T. Key**	**1998-2015**
48	M.R. Benson	1980-95
42	N.R. Taylor	1979-95
39	B.W. Luckhurst	1958-85

He captained Kent in 121 first-class matches.

He took three first-class wickets in his career, dismissing David Willey (v Northamptonshire, Canterbury, 21-24 April 2009) and taking a career-best 2-31, dismissing Peter Trego and Ben Phillips (v Somerset, Canterbury, 3-6 August 2010). In 622 senior games, they were his only wickets.

LIST-A CAREER RECORD

Debut, Kent v South Africans, at Canterbury, on 19 May 1998, scoring 54.

Final game, Kent v Warwickshire, at Birmingham, on 4 September 2014, scoring 23.

	M	I	NO	HS	Runs	Avge	100	50	Ct
Kent 1998	16	13	–	62	342	26.30	–	4	1
Eng A in Zim 1998-99	2	2	–	26	40	20.00	–	–	–
Kent 1999	12	12	3	76*	462	51.33	–	4	2
Kent 2000	5	5	–	16	41	8.20	–	–	–
Kent 2001	18	16	2	59	386	27.57	–	3	3
Kent 2002	23	23	1	114	846	38.45	1	7	4
Eng in Aus 2002-03	1	1	–	11	11	11.00	–	–	–
ECB Acad in SL 2002-03	2	2	–	46	68	34.00	–	–	1
Kent & Eng 2003	18	18	1	68	451	26.52	–	1	4
Kent & Eng 2004	14	14	1	61*	265	20.38	–	1	1
Kent 2005	13	13	1	67	279	23.25	–	2	2
Kent 2006	16	15	1	89	447	31.92	–	4	3
Kent 2007	16	15	1	108	695	49.64	3	2	8
Kent & Eng L 2008	17	17	1	120*	594	37.12	1	4	5
Eng L in NZ 2008-09	2	2	–	44	65	32.50	–	–	–
Kent 2009	9	9	–	27	123	13.66	–	–	3
Kent 2010	10	10	1	87	352	39.11	–	2	1
Kent 2011	5	5	–	59	126	25.20	–	1	1
Kent 2012	11	11	3	101	283	35.37	1	–	2
Kent 2013	11	11	1	144*	505	50.50	2	2	2
Kent 2014	4	4	–	47	88	22.00	–	–	1
Kent	212	205	17	144*	6,180	32.87	8	36	42
England A	2	2	–	26	40	20.00	–	–	–
England Lions	3	3	–	51	116	38.66	–	1	1
ECB Academy	2	2	–	46	68	34.00	–	–	1
England †	6	6	–	19	65	10.83	–	–	–
Total	225	218	17	144*	6,469	32.18	8	37	44

† Total includes one match that was not an international fixture.

List-A Centuries

Match	Venue	Date	Score	Balls
Kent v Nottinghamshire	Nottingham	16 Jun 2002	114	98
Kent v Surrey	The Oval	22 Apr 2007	108	108
Kent v Derbyshire	Derby	29 Jul 2007	104	100
Kent v Glamorgan	Cardiff	7 Sep 2007	107*	91
Kent v Essex	Canterbury	13 Sep 2008	120*	117
Kent v Yorkshire	Canterbury	22 Aug 2012	101	109
Kent v Netherlands	Tunbridge W	27 May 2013	144*	121
Kent v Worcestershire	Worcester	11 Aug 2013	112	91

Most List-A Runs for Kent

7,814	M.R. Benson	1980-95
7,432	T.R. Ward	1988-99
6,797	C.J. Tavaré	1974-88
6,602	N.R. Taylor	1981-95
6,518	C.S. Cowdrey	1976-91
6,180	**R.W.T. Key**	**1998-2014**
5,993	M.V. Fleming	1988-2002
5,666	G.W. Johnson	1969-85
5,665	M.J. Walker	1994-2008
5,554	Asif Iqbal	1968-82

He captained Kent in 87 List-A matches.

He did not bowl in any List-A match.

Kent won the Norwich Union League in 2001.

TWENTY20 CAREER RECORD

Debut, Kent v Surrey, at The Oval, on 9 July 2004, scoring 66* in 38 balls.

Final game, Kent v Surrey, at Canterbury, on 25 July 2014, scoring 14.

	M	I	NO	HS	Runs	Avge	100	50	Ct
Kent 2004	3	3	1	66*	114	57.00	-	1	-
Kent 2005	6	6	1	15*	59	11.80	-	-	2
Kent 2006	7	7	1	41*	89	14.83	-	-	2
Kent 2007	6	6	2	68*	282	70.50	-	4	-
Kent 2008	13	13	-	52	345	26.53	-	1	5
Eng L in NZ 2008-09	1	1	-	12	12	12.00	-	-	-
Kent & Eng 2009	10	10	3	58*	212	30.28	-	1	2
Kent 2010	12	12	1	98*	277	25.18	-	1	4
Kent 2011	15	15	-	75	269	17.93	-	1	3
Kent 2012	8	8	1	51*	116	16.57	-	1	5
Kent 2013	5	5	-	26	80	16.00	-	-	-
Kent 2014	12	12	1	89*	384	34.90	-	3	2
Kent	96	96	10	98*	2,217	25.77	-	13	24
England Lions	1	1	-	12	12	12.00	-	-	-
England	1	1	1	10*	10	-	-	-	1
Total	98	98	11	98*	2,239	25.73	-	13	25

Twenty20 Half-Centuries

Match	Venue	Date	Score	Balls
Kent v Surrey	The Oval	9 Jul 2004	66*	38
Kent v Hampshire	Southampton	22 Jun 2007	59	53
Kent v Sussex	Canterbury	26 Jun 2007	62	46
Kent v Nottinghamshire	Nottingham	17-18 Jul 2007	54	43
Kent v Sussex	Birmingham	4 Aug 2007	68*	54
Kent v Middlesex	Southampton	26 Jul 2008	52	30
Kent v Hampshire	Tunbridge W	22 Jun 2009	58*	52
Kent v Sussex	Hove	27 Jun 2010	98*	55
Kent v Essex	Canterbury	1 Jul 2011	75	52
Kent v Surrey	Beckenham	17 Jun 2012	51*	46
Kent v Hampshire	Southampton	5 Jun 2014	89*	63
Kent v Essex	Canterbury	11 Jun 2014	62	40
Kent v Somerset	Canterbury	18 Jul 2014	72	42

1,000 Twenty20 Runs for Kent

3,358	J.L. Denly	2004–
3,128	D.I. Stevens	2005–
2,282	S.A. Northeast	2010-17
2,224	D.J. Bell-Drummond	2011–
2,217	**R.W.T. Key**	**2004-14**
1,826	S.W. Billings	2011–
1,601	A.J. Blake	2010–
1,585	M. van Jaarsveld	2005-11
1,128	Azhar Mahmood	2008-12

Kent won the Twenty20 Cup final in 2007, beating Gloucestershire by four wickets in the final on 4 August at Edgbaston, with Rob Key scoring 18.

He captained Kent in 82 Twenty20 matches.

He did not bowl in any Twenty20 matches.

All figures correct to the start of the 2020 season.